O c e a n

NORTH

AMERICA

ALEUTIAN TRENCH
4210 FATH.

KURILE TR.
5679 FATH.

JAPAN
TRENCH
5740 FATHOMS

RYUKYU
TR.

BONIN TR.
4760 FATH.

MINDANAO
TR.
5740 FATH.

MARIANAS TR. (36,056 FT.)
6,009 FATH.

P a c i f i c

MIDDLE AMERICA
TRENCH

CAYMAN TR.
4000 FATH.

EQUATOR

NEW BRITAIN TR.
5140 FATH.

O c e a n

SUNDA TR.
4510 FATH.

AUSTRALIA

TONGA TR.
5814 FATH.

PERU-CHILE
TR. 4170 FATH.

KERMADEC TR.
5907 FATH.

BYRD TR.
4700 FATH.

CONTINENTAL SHELF
100 FATHOMS

1000 FATHOMS
2000 FATHOMS
3000 FATHOMS
4000 FATHOMS AND OVER

Lenz

FRONTIERS OF THE SEA

FRONTIERS OF THE SEA

THE STORY OF
OCEANOGRAPHIC EXPLORATION

BY ROBERT C. COWEN

REVISED EDITION

INTRODUCTION BY ROGER R. REVELLE

DRAWINGS BY MARY S. COWEN

GARDEN CITY, NEW YORK

DOUBLEDAY & COMPANY, INC.

1969

TO ANNA AND MARY COWEN

PREFACE TO REVISED EDITION

In the decade since I wrote the preface to the first edition, much has happened to change the contents of this book. Yet the statement of that preface remains valid. Developments reported in the revision only sharpen the challenge it outlines.

Now men live for days, even weeks, dozens of fathoms beneath the sea and astronauts do look at earth from the moon and see a water world. Oceanographers and businessmen are assessing the ocean's mineral wealth for more extensive exploitation. Biologists and food technologists seek to develop the sea's food potential to the point of meeting most, if not all, of mankind's hunger for additional protein. In short, over the past decade, men have turned from daydreaming about marine riches to finding better ways to enjoy them. Over the next decade, practical uses for this fast-growing knowledge should burgeon.

At last, man has ceased to look upon the sea with awe and a sense of alienation. He is moving to take full possession of his water world. This new spirit of "conquest" has invigorated oceanography and made necessary this extensive revision.

ROBERT C. COWEN

Concord, Mass.
January 1, 1969

PREFACE

Earth is a water world.

If you could look back at our planet from the moon, through the obscuring haze of the atmosphere, its most striking characteristic would be the dark cast of the oceans. The continents and islands on which so much human history has been lived account for less than a third of the planet's surface. Indeed, half of that surface is under 10,000 feet or more of water.

The sea, spreading as an irregular but unbroken envelope, dominates our world. It regulates the weather. It is the ultimate source of all our water. It provides a habitat for plants and animals far greater in area and volume than the life zone of the land, so that marine organisms can be thought of as the most broadly representative life forms of the earth. Moreover, billions of years in the past the sea is believed to have been the birthplace of all terrestrial life. Yet in spite of their importance, we have scarcely begun to learn about our oceans. Oceanography is a relatively young science. Its efforts so far have raised more questions than they have answered. But it is a fast-growing science that today is tackling problems of importance to all mankind.

Can men look to the seas to meet their ever-growing needs for food and minerals? Can they learn to farm the waters as they do the land and take advantage of the teeming oceans? Can they extract the mineral wealth that lies in dilute form at every seacoast? And, in another vein, can men use the sea as a vast dump to solve the problem of what to do with the radioactive wastes that may become the greatest liability of the atomic age? These are the kinds of questions that now are helping to shape the research concerned with the sea. They are not strictly "scientific" questions, although it will take a good deal of basic scientific research to answer them. They have a practical flavor that is foreign to the pure search for knowledge for its own sake that has characterized oceanographic work until recent times. After millennia of neglect, the oceans are beginning to command the attention of land-based men as something more than a hunting ground for fishermen or a highway for ships. The fact that such questions have begun to share a place in the thinking of ocean scientists along with the traditional questions of the biology, chemistry, and physics of the sea indicates that, in terms of its broad perspective, oceanography is emerging from the academies and institutes and the restricted circles of its maritime applications. It is tackling problems of immediate and long-range significance for men everywhere. Its emergence is the theme of this book.

It has been impossible to cover comprehensively so large a subject. Some aspects of it are treated in detail. Other aspects which might be judged equally important are mentioned only briefly if they are referred to at all. However, it is hoped that in balance and emphasis this book will give the reader a layman's understanding of this important field of scientific exploration and a background against which to evaluate the new developments it generates.

I should like to express thanks individually to each one of the many specialists who gave generously of their time and knowledge to guide a reporter through the complexities of their fields, but the list is too long to be included here. However, I should like to thank, at least collectively, the directors and staffs of the Scripps Institution of Oceanography at La Jolla, California, and of the Woods Hole Oceanographic Institution in Massachusetts. I am especially grateful to Dr. Harold Edgerton of the Massachusetts Institute of Technology and the National Geographic Society for permission to reproduce a selection of his striking deep-sea photographs, and to Dr. Robert R. Guillard of the Woods Hole Oceanographic Institution for permitting reproduction of several of his beautiful electron microscope photographs of diatoms. Grateful acknowledgment is owed as well to the U. S. Navy and to R. G. Munns, William S. von Arx, and Claude Rönne, all of Woods Hole Oceanographic Institution, for other photographs used in this book. I also wish to thank the Board of Trustees and manager of The Christian Science Publishing Society for permission to make use of material that has appeared in *The Christian Science Monitor*. Finally, there are two others who deserve special mention—Erwin D. Canham and Saville R. Davis, who are, respectively, the editor and managing editor of *The Christian Science Monitor*. I shall always be grateful for the example they have set as journalists and for the encouragement they have given me as a science writer.

ROBERT C. COWEN

Concord, Mass.
October 1, 1959

ACKNOWLEDGMENTS

The author and Doubleday & Co., Inc., are grateful to the following authors, magazines, and publishers for permission to use material contained in this book:

A Century of Darwin, edited by S. A. Barnett. Cambridge, Mass.: Harvard University Press, Copyright 1958 by William Heinemann, Ltd. Used with permission of the publishers.

The Earth and its Atmosphere, edited by D. R. Bates, Basic Books, Inc., Publishers. Used with permission of the publishers.

The Galathea Deep Sea Expedition, edited by Anton F. Bruun. Used with permission of Allen and Unwin, Ltd., and The Macmillan Company.

"To the Depths of the Sea by Bathyscaphe," by Jacques-Yves Cousteau, *National Geographic Magazine,* July 1954. Used with permission of *National Geographic Magazine.*

Larval Forms, by Walter Garstang, Introduction by Sir Alister Hardy. Special acknowledgment is made to Sir Alister Hardy for permission to use extracts from the Introduction.

The Open Sea, by Sir Alister Hardy. Used with permission of William Collins and Sons, Ltd., London, and Houghton Mifflin Company, Inc., Boston.

Founders of Oceanography and Their Work, by Sir William Herdman. Used with permission of Edward Arnold Publishers, Ltd.

Earth, Sky and Sea, by Auguste Piccard. Used with permission of Oxford University Press, Inc.

Climatic Change: Evidence, Causes, and Effects, edited by Harlow Shapley. Cambridge, Mass.: Harvard University Press, Copyright 1953, by The President and Fellows of Harvard College. Reprinted by permission of the publishers.

The Earth Beneath the Sea, by Francis P. Shepard. Used with permission of The Johns Hopkins Press.

The Search Beneath the Sea, by J. L. B. Smith. Used with permission of Henry Holt and Company, Inc., and Longmans, Green and Co., Ltd., the British publishers of the book (under the title of *Old Four Legs*).

"*The Circulation of the Abyss,*" by Henry Stommel, *Scientific American,* July 1958. Used with permission of *Scientific American.*

The Planets: their Origin and Development, by Harold C. Urey. Copyright 1952 by Yale University Press, New Haven. Used with permission of the publishers.

Living Resources of the Sea, by Lionel A. Walford. Copyright 1958 by The Ronald Press Company. Used with permission of the publishers.

CONTENTS

FRONTIERS OF THE SEA

INTRODUCTION

BY ROGER R. REVELLE

*Director, Center for Population Studies, Harvard
College, School of Public Health
Formerly, Director, Scripps Institution of Oceanography*

It is an ironic fact that we are learning to leave this planet just when we are beginning to think about it as a whole, as our planetary home. With our Sputniks and Explorers, our deep-space probes and Project Mercuries, we shall soon soar beyond all horizons. But men were never as aware as they are today that their survival depends on careful husbanding of every resource of Earth. This realization has led to a great surge of interest in the largest and least-known feature of the Earth's surface, the ocean. Mr. Cowen's book, with its clear exposition of what we know and what we hope to find out about the ocean, is thus completely timely.

Men like ourselves have lived on Earth for perhaps five hundred thousand years, yet through all but a tiny fraction of that time our ancestors might have been bacteria proliferating on the skin of an orange, for all they knew about their world. Only within the last few centuries have men had sufficient understanding to be able to think of the Earth as a whole, as a sphere unsupported in space, isolated and complete in itself, yet held in its appointed place by describable though invisible forces. This sphere did not always exist and will someday die; it has changed and will change continuously throughout its lifetime—in short, it has a long history that is part of the universe's history. Only within the last few decades have we developed the tools to decipher that history.

This is not to say that our remote ancestors did not ask meaningful questions about the earth. They were hunters and farmers; to survive they had to be good observers. More important, they were men; they could not help being filled with wonder at the world of wonders they saw about them.

Consider, for example, Chapter 38 of the Book of Job. The unknown poet who wrote this chapter imagined the Lord appearing out of a whirlwind to give Job an oral examination about the Earth. Some of the oceanographic and meteorological questions He asked were these:

"Hast thou entered into the springs of the sea, or hast thou walked in search of the depth?

"Who shut up the sea with doors? . . . saying 'Hitherto shalt thou come but no further; and here shall thy proud waves be stayed?'

"Hath the rain a father? . . . and Out of whose womb came the ice?

"Canst thou lift up they voice to the clouds, that abundance of waters may cover thee?

"Who can number the clouds in wisdoms, or who can pour out the bottles of heaven?"

These are difficult questions. No wonder Job failed to answer them, for we can give only partial answers today. We don't yet know from whence the ocean waters sprang, although we have searched for some of the depths. We know why the sea's proud waves do not cover the earth—the waters are enclosed in deep basins, underlain by heavy rock, above which the comparatively light rocks of the continents float like giant rafts. But no man knows how the continental rafts rose from the seas or why areas that were once dry land are now deeply covered by the ocean.

We know the ocean is the parent of the rain and the ice, in the sense that all the water falling on the land was originally sucked up by evaporation from the surface of the sea. With our Earth satellites we are beginning to count all the clouds of the air. But we are far from being able to ensure abundant rainfall when we need it, for we cannot as yet pour out the bottles of heaven. Our hopes for such weather control rest on gaining more understanding than we now possess about the great interlinked heat engines of the sea and the air.

The questions asked by the unknown poet were natural ones in a semi-desert country bordering the sea. They must have been asked many times by the watchful shepherds and the keen-eyed merchants of Israel. Today we know that to answer them we must formulate and answer more wide-ranging questions—questions about the ocean and the atmosphere as a whole, how they interact under the sun and with the solid Earth. These questions are the subject of this book. With skill and insight Mr. Cowen has shown how far we have come in answering them, how the questions are related to each other, and what we still need to know. It remains to say something about the basic objectives of oceanography, and why men become oceanographers.

As men's knowledge has increased, their attitudes have changed. The ends of the Earth were once a terrifying distance away. Now it is fashionable to speak of the Earth as a small planet chained to a second-rate star, an insignificant cinder circling through the splendid Galaxy. By an inverted humility, we are thus enabled to feel superior to our ancestors, who thought of the Earth as the center of all things, and of the stars as a kind of indirect lighting arranged in musical spheres above their heads. This is all very well, provided we keep in mind two things.

First, although our planet is small, it is inconceivably old; its age, in fact, appears to be a very respectable fraction of the age of the Galaxy. Because the Earth is so old, its history must reflect much of the history of the Galaxy. The records of that history still exist. They are locked in the rocks laid down in ancient seas, in the mud and rocks under the present ocean, in the chemical composition of the waters and the air, and in the bodies of living plants and animals. One of the prime objectives of oceanography is to learn to read these historical records.

Second, life as we know it is nearly impossible except on a little, old planet like our Earth, revolving around a star like our Sun. If the Sun were much bigger, it would have existed for such a short time that life could not have evolved on any of its planets; if the Earth were much bigger, its gravitational force would be too great for creatures like ourselves. But the most important biological characteristic of our planet is the presence on its surface of liquid water in large quantities, for water is the pre-eminent substance of our kind of life. It is hard to think of life beginning except in the sea, and we know that most of the evolution of living things took place there.

No other planet of our solar system has an ocean, with the possible exception of cloud-covered Venus, and planets with oceans may be few and far between in our Galaxy. Thus the old idea of the Earth as the mother of life has gained new meaning in recent years; we now believe the ocean was the placental fluid which nourished and protected Earth's children. Consequently a second objective of oceanography is to discover the many ways in which the existence of oceans on the Earth has affected the nature of living things.

Why should we study the ocean? There are several so-called practical reasons: to learn how to increase our use of marine resources; to be able to use the ocean more effectively in defending this great island, the North American continent; hopefully to learn how to fit our earthly environment more closely to men's needs through controlling climate, which depends on both the ocean and the atmosphere. But it seems to me that the really practical reason was given by the poet of the Book of Job. Not the questions but the admonitions of the poet's dialogue are important to us today, for they state the most profound justification for studying our Earth, and indeed for all scientific work. The Voice out of the whirlwind said: "Gird up now thy loins like a man, for I will demand of thee and answer thou Me. Declare, if thou hast understanding." Man is challenged by the voice within him, the voice out of the whirlwind of consciousness, to seek and to know all he can. Knowledge of the air and the sea and the solid Earth, and of our fellow creatures who share this planet, increases our ability to use the Earth wisely and well. But the challenge out of the whirlwind is not this; it is to gain understanding simply for its own sake, because we are that one among God's creatures who is capable of understanding.

However, oceanographers are not such a serious-minded lot that they keep asking themselves why they are doing their job. The spiritual ancestor of most of them was Ulysses. He was called the Wanderer, because he was the first to venture into the River Ocean, out of the salt and fishy Sea-between-the-Land, the wine-dark Mediterranean. Perhaps he disliked administration, hated farming, and was bored by Penelope. In any case, Ulysses managed to spend a great deal of time away from home. He never stated his reasons very clearly, but he still lives in the hearts of oceanographers, the scientists who go to sea:

> There lies the port; the vessel puffs her sail:
> There gloom the dark, broad seas. My mariners . . .
> That ever with a frolic welcome took
> The thunder and the sunshine . . . Come, my friends . . .
> Push off, and sitting well in order smite
> The sounding furrows; for my purpose holds
> To sail beyond the sunset, and the baths
> Of all the western stars . . .
> Some work of noble note, may yet be done . . .

ONE

EXPLORING THE HINTERLAND

There are two ways you might look at the oceans.

On a planetary scale, they are the thinnest of liquid films, irregularly wetting the global surface. Their average depth of 2.4 miles is an insignificant fraction of the earth's 3957-mile average radius. Together, continents and ocean basins form a surface relatively smoother than a polished billiard ball, albeit a slippery billiard ball since there is over twice as much water as land.

But on a human scale, the oceans are incredibly vast. Their 139,400,000 square miles of surface cover a volume of water so great that if the earth had an absolutely level crust the sea would form an envelope over 8800 feet deep. These waters, in turn, cover a bottom scenery more rugged and grander than anything the land can boast. Mountain ranges tower above their surroundings, sometimes to heights greater than those reached by land elevations, while the deepest ocean trenches could swallow Mount Everest with several thousand feet to spare.

Here is the great hinterland of humanity, a virgin territory as challenging and more promising of economic reward than the forbidding regions of outer space. Men are becoming aware of its potential at a time when their technical powers and scientific capabilities are becoming equal to its challenge. They are becoming aware of it at a time when the pressing needs of mankind for food and materials have given them a mandate to take up this challenge, to learn to know and begin to exploit the 70.8 per cent of our planet's surface that lies in and under the seas.

The effort to learn is what specialists call the science of oceanography. The exploitation, on a small scale today and a bigger scale tomorrow, is the province of a number of technical fields. Its

prospects shine with the promise of a virtually inexhaustible supply of minerals and metals, and of a significant increase in the
world's food supply. But since first things must come first, more
basic knowledge about the oceans has to be gained in many
cases before exploitation can begin. The immediate task is to get
to know our oceans better.

Actually, oceanographers already know a good deal about the
oceans. After a century of modern oceanographic research they
are able to chart the major surface currents. They have measured
the general physical characteristics of the world's water. They can
map the ocean basins in broad outline and tell something of the
history of the earth itself from the accumulated sediments on
the bottom. And they have learned many things about life in the
seas, although biological surprises continually appear.

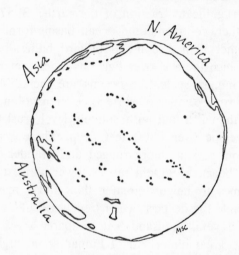

FIG. 1 : The water hemisphere of the Pacific illustrates the
prominence of the earth's oceans.

There is also much that the scientists don't know. A report
from the National Academy of Sciences in the United States, which
surveyed the needs and problems facing oceanographers in 1959,
outlined some of the research questions to be answered. Prepared
by a special committee on oceanography headed by Dr. Harrison
Brown of the California Institute of Technology, it summarized
some of these questions in language that remains valid today:

The seas present a challenge to man which in magnitude approaches
that of space . . . We know less about many regions of the oceans today

than we know about the lunar surface. Yet we have learned enough to know that major features of the ocean floor—35,000 foot deep trenches; 2000 mile long fracture zones; flat-topped undersea mountains; broad ocean-long ridges; abyssal plains as flat as a calm sea—are uniquely different from anything either on the surface of the moon or the land surfaces of the earth. How and when were these features formed and why are they so different? An answer to these questions is essential if we are to decipher the history of our planet and its sister planets. Part of the answer lies in the records of ancient history locked in deep-sea sediments; part will come from an intensive study of the rocks under the ocean. These studies, combined with studies of the waters and the living creatures of the sea, will also tell us much about the origin and evolution of life on earth.

During the last few years . . . great subsurface ocean currents—rivers in the depths of the sea one thousand times greater in flow than the Mississippi—have been discovered using newly developed current-measuring techniques. We suspect that others exist and we need to know where the waters come from and where they go.

On the subject of weather and climate, the report explained that climate is influenced by the oceans in profound but as yet unknown ways. If scientists are ever to understand the mechanism of the weather, to predict or control its action, they must first understand the role played by the oceans.

Considering possible exploitation of ocean food resources, the report noted that "on the practical side, the problems to be solved concerning the oceans are at least as urgent as those of space. How many fish are in the sea? No man knows, nor do we know what determines the numbers of fishes in different regions, the quantities of plant and animal material on which they feed, or what could be done to increase these numbers. We must learn these things if we are to help solve the increasingly acute problems of providing animal-protein food for the growing numbers of underfed people in the world. Given more study, man can economically harvest considerably more food from the seas than is now possible."

Here, then, is the challenge of the ocean hinterland. It is both a challenge to know and a challenge to put the knowledge gained to practical use. Oceanographers have learned much during the decades in which they have studied the sea. But today's knowledge has only begotten larger questions.

Birth of a Science

Modern oceanography can be said to have begun about a hundred years ago. However, men have been interested in the sea for millennia and there was a scattering of scientific ocean studies before the mid-nineteenth century. Aristotle, for example, was the first, and an expert, marine biologist. He made remarkable observations of many marine animals, both anatomically and in their natural habitats.

Blessed with brilliant sunshine and clear Mediterranean waters, the ancient Greek philosopher-scientist spent hours peering over the side of a boat, studying marine life in relatively shallow depths. His perceptive observations were translated into detailed descriptions of the habits and life cycles of marine creatures. He also recognized important distinctions between animal groups which enabled him to classify them in a hierarchical system of categories, some of which are considered valid today. He correctly separated vertebrates from invertebrates. He also was the first to note that dolphins, porpoises, and whales are mammals rather than some sort of fish, as was generally believed.

Aristotle, who took all knowledge as his province, tried to arrange what he saw into a universal scheme. Many of his generalizations have since proved to be erroneous. Nevertheless, he based his biological thinking on objective study. As applied to marine biology, this meant extensive field observations and careful dissections. If these procedures had been followed since the fourth century B.C., marine biology would be immeasurably more advanced than it is today. Aristotle founded a school and influenced many thinkers in his own and subsequent periods. But his scientific methods died with him, and there was no significant progress in marine biology for over two thousand years.

With the advent of open-ocean sailing voyages, navigators began to take an interest in the physical side of oceanography, at least as far as major ocean currents were concerned, although the old sailing records produced little that could be called scientific studies of currents. Benjamin Franklin, however, was able to draw up a tolerable chart of the Gulf Stream, based partly on reports of Yankee sailing captains, which he eventually published in the *Transactions of the American Philosophical Society* in 1786. He

also made his own observations of water temperatures on several
Atlantic crossings by picking up buckets of surface water and
measuring their contents. This technique he then recommended
to sailing captains as a guide to when they entered or left the
relatively warm waters of the Gulf Stream. The British explorer
Captain James Cook also gathered scattered oceanographic information during his three celebrated voyages of exploration which
occupied the latter part of his life (1768–79) and included cir-
cumnavigation of the Pacific.

In spite of such early sporadic interest, oceanography as an
organized research effort is a young science. It grew up in the
latter part of the nineteenth century partly because of the rapid
spread of science in general and partly because the basic sciences
that lie behind it—physics, chemistry, geology, biology—and the
technology of research had reached a point where scientific exploration of the deep oceans became possible.

One of the pioneers who helped turn men's curiosity about the
sea into a science was Matthew Fontaine Maury (1806–73), an
American naval officer of notable vision and perseverance.
Maury's interests were those of a practical sailor. But his intensive
study of currents helped lay the foundation for the modern science
of physical oceanography. Before Maury, men sailed without accurate knowledge of currents, winds, or storm patterns. When his
lifework was finished, charts of major currents, prevailing winds,
and storm tracks were part of every navigator's equipment.

Maury early set himself an ambitious program. The rigors and
uncertainties of life at sea, often with only a sailor's instincts to
guide him, made him acutely aware of the potential value of
charts showing the average direction and strength of winds and
currents. He once described his goal as "nothing less than to blaze
way through the winds of the sea by which the navigator may
find the best paths at all seasons."

His first book—New Theoretical and Practical Treatise on Navigation, published in 1836—was received with a degree of interest
at the time. Then in 1839 Maury began extracting from ships'
logs the data on winds, currents, temperatures, and the like, that
were to be the raw material for his principal lifework. His ap-
pointment in 1842 as superintendent of the Navy's Depot of Charts
and Instruments, including the Naval Observatory, gave him the
opportunity to collect information on the ocean-spanning scale he

needed. He began at once to search the files of old logbooks now at his disposal for data pertinent to the charts he envisioned. Five years later he published his first chart of winds and currents.

The oceans are vast and the data at Maury's personal disposal were limited. He overcame these difficulties by enlisting the aid of navigators the world over. They apparently were glad to co-operate, for Maury's charts were cutting their sailing times drastically. The average voyage between London and San Francisco, for example, was shortened by 180 days.

By 1851, log abstracts from a thousand ships had poured into Maury's office. These and subsequent reports enabled him to draw up charts on many aspects of marine climatology, including a guide to the principal whaling grounds, and to write the world's first text book of oceanographic physics—*Physical Geography of the Sea,* published in 1855. The American Navy still pays tribute to this pioneering work in the monthly "Pilot Charts" of the Hydrographic Office that carry the legend: "Founded upon the researches made by Matthew Fontaine Maury, while serving as a Lieutenant in the U. S. Navy."

Maury's work led directly to one of the first international scientific conferences. It met at Brussels in 1853 to consider setting up a uniform marine weather observing system. Maury played a leading role in the conference and would have thrown it open to consider land as well as ocean weather observing if others had not wanted to restrict it to the sea. Nevertheless, he is credited with inspiring the establishment of the official meteorological offices in both Great Britian and Germany. Because of the demonstrated value of Maury's charts and partly as a result of this conference, other maritime nations began establishing hydrological services, which often co-operated with one another and with Maury in charting the seas. Thus Maury was something of a pioneer in stimulating international co-operation in ocean research as well as the first to chart the great currents.

Maury was essentially a climatologist, a statistician who extracted an average picture of what went on in and above the oceans from the mass of spot reports sent in from ships' logbooks. He was not a scientist, in that his chief aim was to aid navigation rather than to build a fundamental understanding of the sea. His contribution lay in the practical realm, demonstrating how a jumble of observations taken at widely scattered times and places could be analyzed to give a meaningful picture of average conditions in the oceans.

Meanwhile, in Britain, that other great branch of ocean science, marine biology, was being shaped in its modern form by a Manxman named Edward Forbes (1815–54). In a real sense, Forbes was the nineteenth-century heir of Aristotle in this field. He lived in the heyday of the field naturalists and collectors, some of whom were turning to the shallow waters of the sea for their specimens. While these naturalists often were amateurs, Forbes was a lifelong professional scientist and teacher who, like Aristotle before him, saw his subject in large perspective and was widely recognized as the intellectual leader in his field.

He made extensive surveys himself and encouraged others to take up this line of research. In analyzing biological collections, he made full use of the geological knowledge of the day, relating the succession of fossils in rock strata to living marine plants and animals and tracing the effect of the past history of land and sea on the present distribution of these organisms.

Among other things, he pointed out that the shape of the sea bottom is an important environmental factor. Ridges and other obstacles, for example, can isolate adjacent but quite different animal populations from each other. He also noted that the chemistry and physics of the sea—the concentrations and interactions of nutrients and minerals held in the water and the play of currents—were important influences in the lives of marine animals. By urging investigation of such factors, he encouraged the development of other phases of ocean science in addition to his own, although he may not himself have realized he was helping to open up such a wide-ranging research field.

By the 1850s the universities of Scotland, where Forbes had been educated at Edinburgh, had produced a school of marine biologists that was familiar with and had written monographs on all important groups of marine organisms. Forbes was the leader of that school. He was also a contemporary of such famous marine naturalists as the Norwegian Michael Sars and the Frenchman Henri Milne-Edwards. He shares with them the distinction of developing the handling techniques that stimulated wide use of the naturalist's dredge and thus greatly facilitated the collection of bottom-dwelling creatures. The dredge is a coarse netting bag on a rectangular frame that is dragged along the sea bottom and

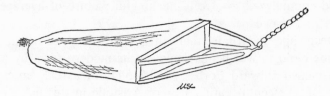

FIG. 2 : Nineteenth-century naturalist's dredge.

willy-nilly picks up hapless animals in it path. It can be handled easily by one or two men and was first introduced in the mid-eighteenth century by the Italian zoologists Marsigli and Donati. But it did not find wide use until effective techniques for handling it, especially in relatively deep water, had been worked out.

Forbes's contribution to oceanography, for which he is considered to be the founder of modern marine biology and for which he is remembered above his predecessors and contemporaries, lay as much in the inspiration he gave as in his own sizable output of research. That inspiration now is recognized as one of the main driving forces that got the budding science of oceanography going.

One of his biographers describes him as "a genial and lively genius, with a free and independent spirit that roamed over a wide range in quest of knowledge and occupation." He adds that "Forbes was certainly the most brilliant and inspiring naturalist of his day—a day when it was still possible to make original contributions to knowledge in several departments of nature." An indication of the breadth of Forbes's talents is seen in the fact that he held with distinction the posts of professor of botany at King's College in London (1842); paleontologist to the Geological Survey (1844); and finally professor of natural history at Edinburgh (1854). The first two posts, moreover, were held simultaneously for a time.

Besides his brilliance as a naturalist, Forbes had a sparkling sense of humor and a dash of literary talent which he combined with scholarship in a way that raised his scientific writing several cuts above the drab style of a laboratory report. His first important large work, entitled *British Starfishes* and published in 1840 at the age of twenty-six, is a classic illustration. Take, for example, the following description of his struggles with a disconcertingly self-destructive starfish aptly named *Luidia fragilissima* (page 138):

The first time I ever took one of these I succeeded in getting it into the boat entire. Never having seen one before, and quite unconscious of its suicidal powers, I spread it out on a rowing bench, the better to admire its form and colors. On attempting to remove it for preservation, to my horror and disappointment I found only an assemblage of rejected members. My conservative endeavors were all neutralized by its destructive exertions, and it is now badly represented in my cabinet by an armless disk and a diskless arm. Next time I went to dredge on the same spot, determined not to be cheated out of a specimen in such a way a second time, I brought with me a bucket of cold fresh water, to which article Starfishes have a great antipathy. As I expected, a Luidia came up in the dredge, a most gorgeous specimen. As it does not generally break up before it is raised above the surface of the sea, cautiously and anxiously I sunk my bucket to a level with the dredge's mouth, and proceeded in the most gentle manner to introduce Luidia to the purer element. Whether the cold air was too much for him, or the sight of the bucket too terrific, I know not, but in a moment he proceeded to dissolve his corporation, and at every mesh of the dredge his fragments were seen escaping. In despair I grasped at the largest, and brought up the extremity of an arm with its terminating eye, the spinous eyelid of which opened and closed with something exceedingly like a wink of derision.

Although Forbes is justly honored for his many positive contributions, the history of science will never forget his celebrated and erroneous theory of the azoic zone. In this, he set a hypothetical depth limit on marine life, which sea animals themselves quite regularly ignore. As doubts about the theory grew, they stimulated deep dredging activities that opened a new phase of oceanographic research.

The theory sprang from Forbes's researches in the Mediterranean. In 1841 he sailed as naturalist on H.M. Surveying Ship *Beacon*. The principal mission was hydrographical surveying in the eastern Mediterranean. But as far as Forbes was concerned, it was his first opportunity to study sea life away from Britain and he made the most of it, collecting and studying marine organisms in the same waters Aristotle once had explored.

He dredged the Aegean bottom more deeply than anyone before, to a limit of 1380 feet. To his own surprise, he brought up living starfishes and other invertebrates from 1200 feet, in those days an astonishing depth at which to find living animals. He noted that shellfish from the deeper hauls were types hitherto known only as fossils. He was the first biologist to see them alive.

As a result of his eastern Mediterranean studies Forbes distinguished eight major zones of depth, each characterized by a particular array of organisms. He further suggested the then plausible theory that marine life would fade out with increasing depth. Plants, which depend on sunlight, would disappear first, then the animals which feed on the plants and on each other. Below 1800 feet, he speculated, there would be no animal life. He assigned all waters deeper than that to what he called the "azoic zone."

Forbes's theory reflected prevailing scientific opinion at the time. But disturbing evidence to the contrary was not long in coming. In 1860 a cable broke in the Mediterranean at a depth of 7200 feet. When it was hauled up for repairs, a deep-sea coral was found firmly attached at the place where the break had occurred. Mollusks, worms, and other sessile animals—animals that lead sedentary lives firmly anchored to some kind of base—were adhering to parts of the cable that had lain at shallower but still unexpectedly great depths.

Prior to this, animals had been found in abundance as deep as 2400 feet during the 1839–43 Antarctic expedition of H.M.S. *Erebus* and *Terror* under command of Sir James Ross. There is an even earlier instance on record in which a single deep-sea animal was found. During Sir John Ross's expedition to Baffin Bay in 1818, a starfish-like animal came up entangled around a sounding line from a depth of 4800 feet. Also, in the decades of 1850–70, Michael Sars and his son George Ossian Sars were dredging organisms from depths as great as 2700 feet. But skeptics either overlooked or discounted such dredge hauls partly on the grounds that the animals might have been caught in intermediate waters above the azoic zone as the dredge was brought back to the surface. The sessile animals that had grown in place at depths below 1800 feet on a cable could not be so easily dismissed.

For a while some biologists clung to the prevailing azoic concept. As one of Forbes's students (C. Wyville Thomson, of whom more in a moment) subsequently wrote, "It was almost as difficult to believe that creatures comparable with those of which we have experience in the upper world could live at the bottom of the sea, as that they could live in a vacuum or in the fire." Water pressure in the sea increases at a rate of about .442 pounds per square inch per foot of depth, or nearly one and a third tons per square inch for every thousand fathoms (6000 feet) of depth. It seemed incredible that life could exist in the crushing pressures and cold blackness of great depths. But we ourselves live under an atmospheric pressure of about 15 pounds per square inch and take no notice of it because the pressure is equal within and without our bodies. Likewise, delicate deep-sea animals, whose tissues are permeated by fluids under pressure equal to that of the surrounding water, can easily withstand pressures of tons per square inch in the abyss. It was gradually realized that, while Forbes had believed his Mediterranean observations were sufficient to support his azoic theory, he had based his reasoning on exceptional conditions that did not correspond to those of the major oceans or, for that matter, to other parts of the Mediterranean.

One of the younger biologists whose imagination was fired by the new discoveries was Charles Wyville Thomson (1830–82), later Sir Wyville, a student of Forbes who was destined to lead the most celebrated oceanographic expedition in history, the voyage of the *Challenger*. Like Forbes, Thomson brought a broad knowledge of the sciences to his study of marine life. Also like Forbes, he ended his career in the natural history chair at Edinburgh. It was he more than any other scientist who proved the azoic theory wrong, and it was he, through his leadership of the *Challenger* expedition, who brought Forbes's oceanographic pioneering to fruition as a full-fledged science.

Inspired by the catches being made in relatively deep water by George and Michael Sars, Thomson was eager to begin deep-sea dredging himself. Through the help of friends and the good offices of the Royal Society, the British Admiralty was persuaded to furnish the means for several research cruises. For two months in the fall of 1868, Thomson and his colleague, Dr. W. B. Carpenter, had the use of a small gunboat, H.M.S. *Lightning*. Another gunboat, H.M.S. *Porcupine,* was placed at their disposal in 1869 and 1870. These various cruises explored deep waters from the Faeroe Islands to south of Gibraltar. One of the results was the first general textbook on oceanography, Thomson's *The Depths of the Sea,* which drew heavily on his cruise researches and was published in 1872.

Thomson describes the *Lightning* as "a cranky little vessel . . . which had the somewhat doubtful title to respect of being perhaps the very oldest paddle-steamer in Her Majesty's Navy." But although Thomson and his shipmates "had not good times in the

Lightning," they were able to dredge animals from as deep as 3600 feet. With the *Porcupine,* a more comfortable and sea-worthy ship, they hauled specimens from depths of nearly three miles.

The dredging showed abundant life at all the depths they probed. Some of the creatures brought up seemed closely related to extinct forms of remote geological periods. Thomson was especially pleased with the remarkable discovery of a flexible sea urchin, a living "fossil" whose kind had been known only from remains in chalk formations. His description of this discovery in his book conveys something of the excitement such finds were causing in his day:

> As the dredge was coming in, we got a glimpse from time to time of a large scarlet urchin in the bag . . . as it was blowing fresh and there was some little difficulty in getting the dredge capsized, we gave little heed to what seemed to be an inevitable necessity—that it should be crushed to pieces. We were somewhat surprised, therefore, when it rolled out of the bag uninjured; and our surprise increased, and was certainly in my case mingled with a certain amount of nervousness, when it settled down quietly in the form of a round cake, and began to pant—a line of conduct, to say the least of it, very unusual in its rigid, undemonstrative order. Yet there it was with all the ordinary characters of a sea-urchin . . . and curious undulations were passing through its perfectly flexible leather-like test. I had to summon up some resolution before taking the weird little monster in my hand, and congratulating myself on the most interesting addition to my favorite family which had been made for many a day.

The dredge hauls from the deep settled the question of whether or not life could exist in the abyss. But they only whetted the scientists' curiosity. Moreover, the rise of transoceanic telegraphy had aroused a practical interest in sea-bottom conditions that might affect the cables. Because of this, a certain amount of abyssal exploring had been done by several countries, including Great Britain and the United States. But the results were indifferent and only served to underscore the lack of general oceanographic knowledge. The time was ripe for a thorough-going scientific exploration of the sea.

Professor W. B. Carpenter, who had successfully interceded on behalf of oceanographic research in the past, wrote to the Admiralty urging dispatch of an expedition around the world. The successes of the *Lightning* and *Porcupine* spoke for themselves and the request was granted, provided the Royal Society concurred and drew up a feasible plan for the voyage. The Royal

Society at once appointed a special committee which wrote out a comprehensive program for the project. In due course a navy ship, the H.M.S. *Challenger,* was made available to the scientists and the expedition was soon under way. It marked the beginning of oceanography as an integrated science.

It has been said that those who objected to spending government funds for such a purpose were mollified by being shown that the expedition would cost little more than keeping the ship in commission. But the fortunes of the voyage gave the government a better bargain than even this cost estimate implied. During the subsequent study of rock samples collected by the expedition, a naval commander sent some rock samples from Christmas Island to John Murray, a naturalist on board the *Challenger,* who had been collecting rocks as part of his coral-reef studies. Murray saw that this particular rock had come from a rich phosphate deposit. He persuaded the government to annex the island and obtained a concession to mine the deposits. The British Government subsequently received far more money in royalties and taxes from Murray's company than the entire cost of the *Challenger*'s explorations.

The Great Voyage

On December 7, 1872, H.M.S. *Challenger,* a full-rigged spardecked corvette of 2306 tons with auxiliary steam power and a penchant for rolling like a barrel (46° one way and 52° the other),

FIG. 3 : H.M.S. *Challenger.*

sailed out of the mouth of the Thames. From then until May 24, 1876, she sailed around the globe, logging 68,890 nautical miles in the major oceans and gathering data and biological specimens from waters of all depths and at almost all latitudes. The end product was a vast collection of marine organisms such as the world had never seen and fifty fat quarto volumes of new knowledge, some of which are still useful as reference works today.

The three-and-a-half-year voyage of the *Challenger* still holds the record as the longest continuous scientific expedition. It also has been unsurpassed in the scope and intensity of its oceanographic probing. Wyville Thomson headed the *Challenger*'s civilian scientific staff, while Captain George S. Nares commanded the ship and the navy crew. Nares was transferred halfway through the voyage, with Captain Frank Thomson taking his place.

Wyville Thomson had been appointed professor of natural history at Edinburgh in 1870. When he recruited his small scientific staff, he included two others from the university—the naturalist John Murray, later Sir John, who eventually saw the *Challenger* results through long years of analysis to final publication, and the chemist J. Y. Buchanan. The rest of the staff included three other naturalists, H. N. Moseley, Dr. Rudolf von Willemoes-Suhm, who died during the voyage, and J. J. Wild, who, among other duties, acted as Thomson's secretary and helped illustrate some of the expedition's publications.

As a naval vessel, the *Challenger* usually mounted eighteen 68-pounders. All but two of these guns were removed, and the main deck was set aside entirely for scientific work. There were two compact laboratories, one for biological work and one for chemistry, a small but select reference library, and cramped private rooms for each of the civilian scientists.

Equipment for the voyage was the best that nineteenth-century technology could provide. In addition to a well-stocked chartroom and ample navigational equipment, the ship carried an assortment of hydrographic, magnetic, and meteorological instruments. There were water-sampling bottles adapted specially for deep-sea work, dredges and trawls for catching specimens on the bottom and at intermediate depths, and miles of sounding line and heavier rope for handling the dredges.

Lord Kelvin had contributed a system for taking depth soundings with wire, which he thought would be easier to handle than

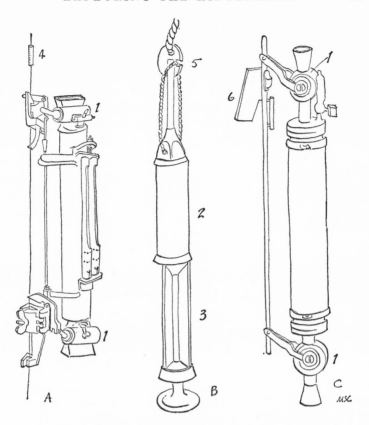

FIG. 4 : Water-sampling bottles: A—modern Nansen bottle with thermometers; B and C—*Challenger* bottles. A bottle is sent down open, allowing water to flow through it freely until it is closed at sampling depth. In A, a "messenger" weight (4) slides down the wire releasing the top of the bottle, which then turns upside down, pivoting about the lower fastening and closing valves (1). In B, the cylindrical sheath (2) slides down over the chambered shank (3), trapping water within the compartments. In C, valves (1) are closed at the desired depth by stopping the descent of the instrument and pulling it up slightly. The resistance of the water against the plate (6) forces the valves closed. A similar arrangement (not shown) releases the rope (5) in B to drop the cylindrical sheath.

the customary rope. But the wire snarled so badly, all the official *Challenger* soundings were made with fine hemp rope. To make a sounding, a 200-pound lead weight was dropped over the side on the end of a line that lay coiled on a ten-foot-diameter drum. The

FIG. 5 : Route of the *Challenger* expedition.

MSC

weight of the lead was enough to unwind the rope. But by the time it hit bottom it had carried down so much rope that the line kept unwinding of its own weight. The only way to tell when the lead hit bottom was to time the rope, which was marked in hundred-fathom lengths, with a stop watch and estimate when the speed of the running line slackened off. The whole operation—to make one sounding and wind in the line—took several hours. How amazingly easy, by contrast, are modern techniques of echo sounding, in which a sound pulse sent out by a ship returns an echo from the bottom to give an immediate and continuous measurement of depth.

The *Challenger* technically was the first steamship to cross the Antarctic Circle. But as a practical matter she generally traveled under sail and reserved her 1234-horsepower steam engine for holding a position on station and for running the winches that hauled in the deep sounding and dredging lines. It is doubtful that the expedition would have been possible without steam power; much of the deep sampling equipment was too heavy to handle by hand. Moreover, it would have been virtually impossible to make a sailing ship stay put long enough to occupy what oceanographers call a "station." This means occupying a spot in the ocean whose latitude and longitude are carefully calculated and remaining there as stationary as possible while various measurements and samplings are taken.

The *Challenger* made 362 such stations in all. At each of them the exact depth was determined, a bottom sample weighing anywhere from an ounce to a pound was brought up, water samples were taken near the bottom, and the temperature of the bottom was measured with a registering thermometer. At many of the stations, bottom animals were also dredged up, water samples and temperatures taken at various points between the surface and the bottom, and animals were sometimes taken at intermediate depths with tow nets.

All in all, the *Challenger* team was given everything needed to do its job, and its mission was an unqualified success. When the expedition left Sheerness at the mouth of the Thames, knowledge of the deep sea was almost a total blank. When it returned home and all the subsequent reports were published, the ocean was still a largely unknown wilderness, but its gross measurements had at last been taken. New and often bizarre-looking animals were found by the hundreds. Naturalists eventually identified 4717 new species and 715 new genera from the specimens brought back. All of these were related to known contemporary forms, however, and scientists and laymen alike were somewhat disappointed that the *Challenger* had dredged up no "living fossils."

The expedition also disposed of a rather grotesque scientific myth. Careful examination of samples from some of the early deep-sea dredgings uncovered a gray gelatinous material that many biologists thought to be the remains of some kind of living protoplasmic slime. Ernst Haeckel, the great German zoologist, and the English naturalist Thomas Huxley named the "creature" Bathybius. It was generally supposed to cover much if not all of the sea floor, providing food for more highly organized animals. In *The Depths of the Sea,* Thomson described this material as "capable of a certain amount of movement, and there can be no doubt that it manifests the phenomena of a very simple form of life." The *Challenger* dredgings brought up bits of Bathybius too. But Buchanan was skeptical. He noted that, when the strong alcohol used to pickle specimens was mixed with sea water, sulphate of lime was precipitated as a slimy deposit. His analyses soon proved that this was what the biologists had supposed to be the remains of protoplasm. "Bathybius," Huxley later observed, "has not fulfilled the promise of its youth."

Yet Bathybius may "live" again. Modern chemists find amino acids, protein-like substances, and other organic materials in Buchanan's calcium sulphate blobs. Dr. Ross F. Nigrelli of the New York Aquarium suggests that basic chemical-building blocks of life may be intimately bound to inorganic compounds in the bottom mud.

The expedition had a strong interest in biology, but it did not neglect other aspects of the sea. Its small team of scientists, most of whom were naturalists, made many physical, chemical, and geological observations. Thus when the *Challenger* data were analyzed there were so many deep soundings that the main contours of the ocean basins were well established. The deepest spot sounded was 26,850 feet in the vicinity of the Marianas Islands in the North Pacific. This region still holds the record for depth. During the International Geophysical Year, the Soviet ship *Vitiaz* plumbed the deepest spot yet found—36,056 feet in the Marianas Trench.

Moscow Radio has reported that a subsequent sounding by the *Vitiaz* in this trench reached 36,173 feet.

The *Challenger* data also marked out major current systems and water-temperature patterns. Some of the latter are so persistent that there are areas where measurements taken today give the same temperature readings at the same locations as those found by the *Challenger*. The data also highlighted the cold, bottom temperatures that prevail throughout most of the oceans—temperatures everywhere close to the freezing point.

In one sense, the work of the *Challenger* expedition was just beginning when the gallant ship reached home at Spithead in 1876. Some preliminary reports had been prepared during the voyage, but the bulk of the analytical work and writing lay ahead. Fortunately the small scientific team did not have to bear the whole burden. A "Challenger Office" was established at Edinburgh. Wyville Thomson was appointed director of the Challenger Commission and charged with seeing to the distribution of the data and collections and the publishing of results. For the next two decades, until the last volume was published and the Challenger Office closed down, the Scottish capital was the mecca of marine biologists and the leading center of oceanographic research.

Thomson and Murray asked specialists in several countries to share in examining the findings and preparing the *Challenger* reports. Thus the fifty volumes eventually published include the work of the most distinguished naturalists of the day. When Thomson was no longer able to carry on, Murray succeeded him and saw the work of publication to a successful conclusion. He even paid some of the costs out of his own pocket. In the end, the *Challenger* reports stood as a solid foundation for the science of oceanography.

After the return of the *Challenger*, two small subsidiary expeditions were undertaken to the Faeroe Channel north of Scotland. These had their roots in the old investigations of the *Lightning* and *Porcupine*. On those cruises Thomson and others had noticed that the Faeroe Channel was divided by temperature into two distinct regions—one relatively cold, the other warm. In comparing these early temperature observations with those taken in the same area by the *Challenger*, there seemed to be a sizable and unsuspected submarine ridge rising to within 1200 to 1800 feet of the surface. In the summer of 1880, John Murray conducted the

"Knight-Errant" expedition under Thomson's direction to investigate this. He made four traverses over the area, which revealed a ridge rising to within 1800 feet of the surface. It ran from the northwest of Scotland to the southern end of the Faeroe fishing bank.

Encouraged by this, Murray conducted a second expedition in H.M.S. *Triton* in the summer of 1882. He found distinctly different arrays of animals on either side of the ridge, which was named posthumously for Thomson. There were Arctic animals on the north side, and Atlantic animals to the south. The Wyville Thomson Ridge rising between the two groups was an insurmountable barrier to fishes and bottom animals that could not withstand the change of water conditions and pressure they would have to endure in rising high enough to pass over it. Here was a remarkable phenomenon whose discovery capped the explorations of the *Challenger* scientists, and it was found in their own Scottish waters.

The Glorious Amateurs

The success of the *Challenger* set off a spate of national oceanographic expeditions from a number of other countries throughout the remaining quarter of the nineteenth century. These were important in further extending man's scant knowledge of the oceans, but their chief importance was in supplementing in one way or another the fundamental discoveries of the British explorations, and there is no need to detail them here. There are, however, two post-*Challenger* oceanographers who deserve special mention. Each of them explored the seas as an avocation, yet each in his contribution to the field outshines many of the professional marine scientists of the day. One was Alexander Agassiz (1835–1910), a wealthy Swiss-born American mining engineer and son of the famous naturalist Professor Louis Agassiz of Harvard. The other was His Serene Highness Prince Albert Honoré Charles (1848–1922), sovereign ruler of Monaco from 1889 to 1922.

Unlike his father, who reputedly was unable to manage practical money matters, the younger Agassiz was a successful businessman. He was educated as a mining engineer and early in his career he and his brother-in-law, Quincy Shaw, took over control of the then unsuccessful Calumet and Hecla copper mines on Lake Superior. Under Agassiz' management the company prospered. He made a considerable personal fortune and remained president of the company throughout his life.

But Agassiz' first love was scientific exploration of the sea, and his financial success gave him the means to pursue this end. He made a number of cruises in United States Coast Survey ships, principally the U.S.S. *Blake* and *Albatross,* as well as in chartered vessels. As in the case of his father, the United States Government seemed happy to co-operate in the marine research. The elder Agassiz had made several marine biological expeditions that resulted in important collections for the Museum of Comparative Zoology which he founded at Harvard and for which a special building was erected. But Alexander was the oceanographer of the family. All told, he traveled over 100,000 miles in tropical seas, notably in the Caribbean, the Indian Ocean, and the tropical Pacific. And for many years after his work was finished, it was accurate to say that his expeditions had mapped more lines across deep-sea basins and made more deep soundings than had all other scientific expeditions combined.

Agassiz' skill as an engineer enabled him to make a number of contributions to the purely practical business of collecting specimens and taking data at sea. For example, sounding wire, which was tried out experimentally on the *Challenger,* soon came into general use in one form or another. But the use of rope for hauling dredges and other heavy apparatus remained the bane of deep-sea research. The ropes were cumbersome to handle and susceptible to rot. Agassiz replaced hemp with steel cable and devised mechanisms to facilitate handling it.

The *Challenger* had employed a system of huge rubber bands that stretched from three to seventeen feet to absorb sudden tensions or slacking in the rope. Agassiz invented mechanical systems that did the job more satisfactorily and made it easier to bring apparatus aboard. If he had never done anything else, he would be remembered by oceanographers for doing away with the old system of rope and rubber. He also improved on some of the sampling devices then in use. He helped design a new type of double-edged bottom trawl that would work whatever way it happened to hit bottom. And he invented a tow net that could be lowered to any desired depth, then opened and towed and closed again before being hauled back up. This helped eliminate the uncertainty about the depth at which a net's contents had been caught, an uncertainty which had plagued marine biologists for years.

After his father's death in 1873, Agassiz took over direction of the museum at Harvard. He gave it devoted service throughout his life and spent something like $1.5 million of his own money for endowment purposes and various operating costs. But he remained primarily a seagoing oceanographer. His voyages took place mainly from 1877 to 1905 and embraced all phases of oceanography. Among other things, he made extensive studies of Pacific bottom deposits, of submarine topography and marine life in the Caribbean, and visited every important coral reef, atoll, and island. In fact, he devoted the last thirty years of his life to coral-reef problems and became a leading expert on the subject.

As a result of his explorations in West Indian waters, Agassiz noticed that Caribbean deep-water animals seemed to be more closely related to those of the Gulf of Panama than to those of the deep Atlantic. He then reasoned that the Caribbean Sea had once been directly connected with the Pacific Ocean and had since been cut off by the uplifting that made the Isthmus of Panama. Later investigations by geologists have supported Agassiz' conclusion.

He also made a close study of the Gulf Stream. This enabled him to relate the distribution of plankton—tiny plants and animals that drift in the surface waters—to the flow of currents. These planktonic organisms are the primary food supply of the sea. The microscopic plants are akin to grass and other land vegetation that form the basic food supply for animals. Tiny planktonic animals that feed on the ocean plants are the grazers of the sea. They convert the vegetable material into flesh that is in turn eaten by other animals. Thus the abundance of marine life in the surface waters is obviously related to the abundance of plankton. Agassiz showed that the occurrence of bottom-dwelling animals, which in one way or another feed on material drifting down from upper waters, was directly related to the distribution of this surface plankton too.

Sir John Murray summed up Agassiz' contribution to science by saying, "If we can say that we now know the physical and biological conditions of the great ocean basins in their broad general outlines—and I believe we can do so—the present state of our knowledge is due to the combined work and observations of a great many men belonging to many nationalities, but most probably more to the work and inspiration of Alexander Agassiz than to any other single man."

Prince Albert, descendant of the ancient family of Grimaldi and hereditary ruler of Monaco, had a far different background from Agassiz, the millionaire son of an impecunious scholar. Yet he shared Agassiz' passion for exploring the sea and, like him, had ample independent means to finance his avocation.

In his youth the prince had served as a lieutenant in the Spanish Navy. He was an accomplished navigator and quite competent to command his own ship. Thus he was a double rarity among oceanographers, for he owned his research vessels and served as both captain and chief scientist. It is a striking coincidence that the modern oceanographic successor of Prince Albert is another such sailor-scientist—Captain Jacques-Yves Cousteau, the present director of the Oceanographic Museum at Monaco. Cousteau is also a naval officer turned oceanographer. He has not had a royal fortune to work with, but he has managed to own and command his own ship—the *Calypso*. His contributions to oceanography have already been substantial. His invention of the Aqualung and his work with research submarines and underwater living have helped open a new era in oceanography. Like the prince before him, he is an energetic scientific leader in a period when oceanography is in the midst of vigorous growth.

Prince Albert carried out his numerous expeditions in a succession of yachts. Starting with the 200-ton schooner *Hirondelle* and ending with the 1420-ton, 240-foot steamship *Princesse Alice II* acquired in 1898, each was fully equipped for deep-sea research and was larger than its predecessor. The prince's companions on his cruises often included such scientists as Baron Jules de Guerne, onetime president of the Zoological Society of France; Dr. Jules Renard, later director of the museum Albert established at Monaco; J. Y. Buchanan, who had sailed with the *Challenger;* and the British Antarctic explorer, Dr. W. S. Bruce.

Like Agassiz, Prince Albert had a practical skill at engineering which helped him improve the apparatus and techniques of ocean research. Among his inventions were huge baited traps, new types of nets and trawls for use at various depths, and a system of underwater electric lights to attract fish and other animals.

His most famous innovation was the mass use of drifting floats to track major currents in the Atlantic, beginning around 1885.

At first he used bottles or wooden blocks. These were later replaced by copper floats adjusted to drift just below the surface and out of the direct influence of wind. Each float contained instructions in nine languages asking the finder to fill in certain information and return it to Monaco.

In all, he released some 2000 floats. Enough of these were returned to enable him to draw up a fairly comprehensive chart of the Atlantic surface circulation. He became the leading authority on this subject and, after World War I, was able to give navigators valuable advice on where leftover mines were likely to have drifted.

The prince engaged in all phases of ocean research. Over the years he contributed much useful data on water conditions and bottom topography in the Atlantic and Mediterranean. But his most sensational investigations concerned the giant squid. Here, certainly, is the king of the invertebrates, the only one of them able to give the great-toothed sperm whale a stiff fight even though the latter feeds upon it. In fact, these huge mollusks seem to be part of the regular diet of this whale, the "cachalot," which averages 60 feet in length. That is why the best place to find a giant squid has been the cachalot's stomach.

The giant squid are among the most powerful animals in the sea. They are strong swimmers, probably living in deep intermediate water, neither close to the bottom nor near the surface. Their great muscular arms, thick as those of a man, are covered with powerful suckers. No one knows how big these animals can become. By actual measurement they can at least grow larger than the basking and whale sharks, the largest of the fishes. Measurements reconstructed from fragments of one squid indicate that its main body was 4.6 feet in diameter and 24 feet long, with an over-all length, including outstretched arms, of 66 feet. It probably weighed about 42½ tons.

One can imagine the prince's astonishment when he first saw the remains of such a beast in 1895. He and Buchanan had been taking oceanographic data near the Azores when a native whaling crew killed a sperm whale nearby. The whale charged the Monegasque yacht and expired as it passed under the keel. When it floated to the surface on the other side of the ship, it gave up fragments of its last meal. They were parts of giant squid, in good enough condition for zoological studies to confirm the existence of a hitherto unknown species of deep-sea monster.

The prince returned home from the Azores and equipped his yacht for whale fishing. The squid were too big and fast to be taken by net, but if he could catch the whale that caught the squid he might be able to get some good specimens. He hired a Scottish whaler named Wedderburn, and the two of them organized a number of highly successful whale hunts. At one point the beautiful beach at Monaco was virtually turned into a whaling station to prepare specimens for the museum, but in this way the prince learned a good deal about the occurrence and structure of both whales and giant squid.

Although the existence of giant squid has been known for centuries, relatively little is known about the natural history of these animals. However, the giant mollusks may have been encountered at sea without being recognized. Their powerful arms may have occasionally been seen above the surface, giving rise to at least some of the stories of sea serpents. Perhaps, also, these squid are brought to the surface by whales before being eaten, which would account for stories of fierce battles between cachalot and squid that have figured in sailors' yarns. Whales have been found with wounds and scars apparently caused by huge arms and suckers and indicating a violent struggle. The prince caught one specimen with sucker marks around its lips, showing that its prey had resisted to the last.

In 1882, Professor A. E. Verrill published an appendix to the 1879 "Report of the United States Commission of Fish and Fisheries" in which he summed up the knowledge of giant squid based largely on studies in the Newfoundland area by an amateur naturalist, the Reverend Moses Harvey. During the 1860s, in an unusual occurrence, fishermen spotted several dozen giant squid off Newfoundland, some of which they caught. Otherwise, most of the information on these mysterious monsters is based on the researches of Prince Albert of Monaco.

Before he died, the prince gave oceanography an enduring legacy in the form of two endowed institutions—an institute for marine studies at the Sorbonne in Paris and the famous museum at Monaco. The establishment at Paris started as a lecture series in 1903. Three years later Prince Albert gave the university a building to be devoted to teaching oceanography and three endowed chairs—one in physical oceanography, one in biological oceanography, and one in the physiology of marine life. Four years later, in 1910, he dedicated the Oceanographic Museum.

There is a legend that Hercules once came upon the ancient port that lay between the rock of Monaco and the present site of Monte Carlo. The harbor is still called the "Port of Hercules." Struck by its beauty, he overcame the savage natives, took possession of the rock, and dedicated it to the advancement of knowledge, naming it after his own title of Monoechos. This is the rock on which the prince built his museum. It is an imposing structure, built into the cliff on the ocean side of the rock and rising steeply from the sea. It has been a modern fulfillment of Hercules' legendary purpose.

Growth and Challenge

By the turn of the century, oceanography was firmly established as a vigorous, albeit slowly growing science. Many countries had at least a small group of researchers interested in the sea, and the numerous government, university, and private institutions active in the field today were beginning to spring up in various places. There are too many to list here, but the Stazione Zoologica at Naples must be mentioned. Founded by Dr. Anton Dohrn, a wealthy German biologist, the year the *Challenger* sailed, it has been the progenitor and, to some extent, the prototype of the many marine biological laboratories that have been established since then.

Even while the marine naturalists of Dohrn's and Thomson's day were excitedly dredging up strange animals, the need for something more than simply collecting and classifying had become apparent. Dohrn saw this need, and the station at Naples supplied the answer. In this and subsequent seaside laboratories the biologist can study many sea creatures at leisure as they live and grow in tanks. He can study development and behavior and to some extent conduct experiments. Also, he has full facilities to run all types of analyses he may care to make. These things are impossible at sea or with preserved specimens, which usually lose all hint of having once been living creatures by the time they reach shore.

The station at Naples was and is an international enterprise. Dohrn contributed generously from his own funds and saw that the institution was successfully established as a permanent under-taking. He fostered and directed its growth and activities for three decades.

A number of countries have shared in its support. Dohrn had help from both the German and the Italian governments in founding the station, and soon other countries were participating in a unique system of annual subsidy. The station provides a num-ber of working places, called "tables," although they may in fact be rooms or segregated parts of rooms. A government or an in-stitution may rent one or more of these tables annually and assign it to a scientist of its own choosing. Such visiting scientists have to bring some equipment of their own, but the institution pro-vides many facilities—for example, assistants, an ample aquarium, chemical facilities, a library, and a permanent scientific staff. It is an international institute for advanced marine studies that remains unique even today.

But while research centers proliferated, oceanography as a sci-ence grew slowly after its portentous nineteenth-century beginning. There were three interlocking reasons for this—lack of money, lack of manpower, and lack of a technology that could cope with the immense task of probing the seas. Except for an Agassiz or a Monegasque prince, oceanographers have been chronically poor, while sea research has always been expensive. Physics flourished during the first half of this century partly because physicists could produce significant results on a shoestring; it is only since World War II that their research tools have become behemoths that only governments can afford. The oceanographer's tools have always been in that category. However simple his instruments might be, he has had to use them from a ship. While ships, usually govern-ment owned, were made available from time to time, massive government support for research didn't start until after World War II. Even then, oceanography was far down the list for aid. For example, during the International Geophysical Year (IGY, July 1, 1957 to Dec. 31, 1958) when oceanographers were unusually active, the United States Government was budgeting less than $35 million a year for ocean research. It was as generous as most other governments in this regard. Because of the lack of oppor-tunity in a financially underfed science and because of the hard life at sea, few first-rate scientists chose oceanography for their field. Dr. Roger Revelle, former director of the University of

California's Scripps Institution of Oceanography at La Jolla, defines an oceanographer as "a sailor who uses big words." That's a hard kind of sailor to find. Scientists who could stand the rigors of life at sea in the ships generally available before the 1960s were rare.

Today the situation is changing rapidly. Oceanography is again growing vigorously. In the United States, research funds have increased nearly tenfold in the years since publication of the Brown report (1959). In the United States, and elsewhere, new opportunities are opening for oceanographers and they have been matched by the appearance of a fleet of new research ships on which the old hardships have been lessened. At the same time, a technological revolution is providing research tools to overcome the third factor that has held back oceanography—the sheer magnitude of its subject matter and the inability of former research tools to cope with it. Oceanography is not so much a science as it is the application of other sciences—physics, chemistry, biology, mathematics, geology—in trying to understand the oceans. These sciences need data to work with and the collection of that data is an awesome task.

In *Challenger* days and for several decades thereafter, the immediate problem was to try to determine the gross characteristics of the seas and what lived in them. The scattered soundings, samplings, and dredgings then taken were adequate to delimit the ocean basins and the major characteristics of their waters, to give rough indications of what was on the bottom and a broad look at what lived in the seas. But even this strained the technology of the times. Once it had been accomplished, further significant progress could be made only by extensive detailed studies which were difficult, expensive, and sometimes physically impossible.

Maury's charts and those worked up by the early oceanographers showed average current and water conditions over broad areas. But to find out what really is going on in the sea, later oceanographers needed closer networks of observations. Moreover, these observations needed to be taken repeatedly so that sequences of charts could be compared and changes in currents and water characteristics followed over time. But this kind of surveying has seemed an overwhelming job, for it requires a number of ships working together or a very intensive effort by one ship in a limited area. The German ship *Meteor* conducted such a survey in the South Atlantic during a cruise in 1925–27. This remained the only one of its kind until the IGY, when one of the important projects was the reoccupation of the old *Meteor* stations so that new measurements could be compared with those taken earlier.

Another source of difficulty is the fact that water, often miles of it, overlies many things oceanographers want to study. To map the ocean bottom, they needed many more soundings than it was possible to take with a weighted line dropped from a ship. To study submarine geology, they needed to poke and probe extensively into the bottom and to examine rocks in many places. But the best they could do for a long time was to send down a dredge and hope it would snag a meaningful sample. Then too, marine biologists learned a good deal by studying specimens and watching such animals as could be housed in aquaria. But they all realized they would never really understand plant and animal life in the sea until they could study it in its own environment, and that, for the most part, seemed impossible.

Thus the technology of research was a severe handicap to oceanographers. Until recently this technology had changed little from that of the late nineteenth century. There were modifications in water-sampling bottles, dredges, winches, tow nets, and the like, which made them easier to handle, but no fundamental advance. There were, however, a few notable exceptions to this.

During the 1920s, for example, the Scandinavian meteorologists, V. Bjerknes, B. Helland-Hansen, and J. W. Sandström developed mathematical theories that, applied to the sea, enabled oceanographers to translate data on water temperatures and salinities into the speed and direction of currents, allowing them for the first time to trace water movements beneath the surface. They still could not observe deep currents directly, which remained a great disadvantage, but something of the nature of such currents now could be inferred from the kind of water-sampling observations oceanographers could make.

The development of the depth-ranging echo sounder in the 1920s was another major advance. It was a forerunner of the electronic age, whose technology is beginning to make many of the oceanographer's old obstacles look surmountable. The principle of echo sounding is simple. It consists of measuring the time it takes a sound "ping" to reach the bottom and echo back. Since the speed of sound through water is known, the distance to the bottom can be determined. Corrections have to be made for varying temperature conditions which affect the transmission of sound through water, but these have been reduced to a simple routine.

The general idea of using sound for depth measurement was first suggested by the French physicist Arago in 1807, but little serious work was done along this line until the early 1900s, when a number of people in Germany, France, and the United States began evolving practical echo sounders. The first series of echo-sounder depth measurements at sea was made in 1920 by the Centre d'Etudes of Toulon. Three years later the survey ship U.S.S. *Guide* of the United States Coast and Geodetic Survey was fitted with an echo-sounding depth probe. From that time on, the echo sounder was gradually developed into a precision instrument that today can plumb any ocean depth with an accuracy of about three feet.

One of the most useful improvements was made during World War II, when instruments were developed that converted the echo-sounder readings into a continuous record that traced out the profile of the bottom over which the ship passed. Before this, the instruments merely gave numerical depth figures and the profile had to be drawn manually from plotted charts of these individual depth measurements.

The biggest limitation of echo sounding is the spread of the sound beam. If this were a narrow pencil, one could trace out the bottom in precise detail. But the sound spreads out in a cone, so that there is always an area of uncertainty in making a detailed chart of the bottom. This is particularly disturbing in probing deep trenches or close to underwater cliffs. The sound cone sometimes echoes off the cliff face or canyon wall, giving a false reading. Nevertheless, even allowing for this inaccuracy, echo sounding has removed one of the historic frustrations of oceanography.

Echo-sounding records sometimes showed a weak second reflection coming from the harder bottom underlying loose sediments. This phenomenon was put to work in the Sonoprobe, which uses low-frequency sound to penetrate as much as 200 to 300 feet of sediment. Developed primarily by the Magnolia Petroleum Company, the Sonoprobe uses the difference in the speed of sound through water-saturated sediments and through sea water. It gives a kind of "X-ray" picture showing the outlines of

soft muds and sediments and of the underlying rocky "skeleton."
Today sonar (sound ranging) has been refined to the point where
it can distinguish fine structure in shallow-water sediment layers
with a resolution of two feet. It can map a strip of bottom
roughly half a mile wide on one pass of the ship, picking out
features as small as a few feet across.

Another sonic technique that has enabled marine geologists to
probe what they cannot see is deep-sea seismology. Explosions of
dynamite or TNT in the ocean generate sound waves that penetrate deeply into the crust of the earth. The speed of sound varies
in layers of different density. This causes sound waves to be reflected and refracted and to arrive back at the surface at different
times and places. By studying the arrival times and patterns of
these returning sound waves, geologists can determine something
of the nature of the crustal layers through which the sound waves

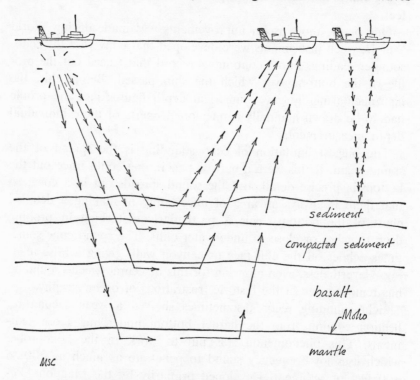

sediment

compacted sediment

basalt

Moho

mantle

MSC

FIG. 6 : Probing with sound. On the left, sound waves from
a small underwater explosion are refracted by the different
layers of sediment and crust. Right, pulses from an echo
sounder give depth to top of sediments.

have passed. This technique has long been used on land for oil prospecting. It was first used for probing beneath the ocean bottom on research ships from Woods Hole Oceanographic Institution at Woods Hole, Massachusetts, by Dr. Maurice Ewing, now director of Lamont Geological Observatory, in conjunction with Drs. Allyn C. Vine and J. Lamar Worzel of Lamont and Dr. George P. Woollard of the University of Wisconsin.

World War II interrupted this work, but it was taken up again and extensively developed as soon as peace came by Ewing, by Dr. Russell W. Raitt at Scripps, and by a group at Cambridge University in England under Sir Edward C. Bullard. At first, explosives and seismographs were placed on the sea bottom, but this was found to be unnecessary. As now used, the technique requires two boats working as a team. One of them shoots off explosions of known intensity, while the other picks up the sound waves through electronic hydrophones.

Except for a few advanced techniques such as echo sounding and seismic probing, however, the main data-collecting methods of the oceanographer had until recently changed little since the days of the *Challenger*. They were largely refinements of the time-honored method of throwing over a bucket and seeing what it brought up. In a sense, these older systems have been merely extensions of human arms and hands. Men float on the sea surface and reach down, so to speak, to touch and grasp what they can. The sounding lead and line were just a deep-sea version of the arm-and-stick method for measuring the depth of a pond. The dredges, bottom samplers, tow nets, and water-sampling bottles can be thought of as a grandiose system of grabbing what one can put one's hands on in blindly groping about the sea.

Considered in this perspective, the newer instruments and methods are the beginning of a revolution. The swift flight of a sound pulse has replaced the fish-and-feel method of measuring depth. Hauling up water samples for analysis is giving way to instruments that measure temperature, pressure, salinity, and oxygen content directly at any depth. They relay their data by electric cable or sound beam to surface ships. Computers on land, and increasingly on board the research ships themselves, are analyzing masses of data. In a few minutes or days, they do analyses that once kept an oceanographer busy for weeks or years, if he could do a comparable analytical job at all. Soon, many of the measure-

ments will be taken automatically without the need for oceanographers or ships. The instruments can be strung from buoys
anchored in deep water. Data thus gathered can be recorded on
board for periodic recovery. It can be radioed to shore or re-
layed via a data-collecting satellite. Networks of such buoys will
enable oceanographers to keep continuous track of currents and
water conditions over large areas of the sea. Eventually, they will
enable men to keep ocean and weather conditions under sur-
veillance throughout the world.

Meanwhile, the old limitation of groping blindly from the surface is being overcome by underwater photography and television
and by the growth of a fleet of research submarines. These submarines are the heirs of the famed bathyscaphes in which men
have reached the deepest parts of the sea. The bathyscaphe is a
kind of underwater "balloon." (See pages 289–294.) Its descent
and ascent are regulated by siphoning off small amounts of gasoline and dropping ballast. Invented by Auguste Piccard, one of
the famous twins who soared miles above the earth in some of the
first stratospheric balloons, the bathyscaphe at this writing is still
the only craft in which men can reach the deepest parts of the sea.
But it has been supplemented by a host of more maneuverable
subs that operate at moderate depths, generally of several thousand feet. These will soon be joined by deeper diving craft. The
United States Navy is sponsoring development of research subs that
will operate down to 20,000 feet. That will bring most of the
ocean floor within their reach.

In shallow water, men themselves are able to carry out research
directly. The freedom of SCUBA diving (SCUBA for self-contained underwater breathing apparatus) is being augmented by
the technique of "man-in-the-sea." In experiments and in some
commercial operations, men are living for days or weeks under
the pressure of a given depth. They have underwater houses in
which to rest when not working in the water. The atmosphere in
these houses is kept at the pressure of the working depth. Useful
work, such as clearing away debris from a toppled oil rig, is already being done down to 200-foot depths by such aquanauts.
Men have lived for two days at the pressure of 650 feet in an
experiment carried out by Ocean Systems, Inc. The United States
Navy's Man-in-the-Sea program aims to have a manned station at
a depth of 600 feet or greater during the 1970s. The ability to

live and work at such a depth for extended periods of time will bring virtually all of the mineral-rich shelves that border the continents within the range of direct human exploration. These shelves are marked by the 100-fathom line on the endpaper map. (See also pages 61–64.)

Thus the exploration of the sea is at a critical juncture in its evolution as a science. Long-standing research limitations are being overcome at a time when government and commercial interest in the field is increasing. The day is over when ocean research meant essentially voyages of exploration by single ships. For one thing, the international research begun during the IGY has continued. An international committee called SCOR (Special Committee on Oceanic Research) has continued to organize multinational expeditions. Practical considerations are also entering into oceanographers' planning. There is rising pressure for them to take up specific research to enable men better to exploit the food and mineral resources of the sea.

In releasing a report of its Panel on Oceanography in the summer of 1966, the Science Advisory Committee of the President of the United States (PSAC) recognized that a new era is opening in oceanography. "Until recently," the panel said, "oceanographic observations could be characterized as being exploratory in nature. Expeditions were undertaken, usually with a single ship, to survey unknown regions or to observe special phenomena discovered on an earlier expedition." The panel added, "It appears to us that it is now appropriate to end an era in which the main emphasis . . . has been on exploration." It noted that "there are many clearly identifiable problems. Although there remains a need for special ocean surveys, we need no longer give special emphasis to them. The broad outlines of the subject are clear. What is needed is a much greater emphasis on . . . [specific] problem areas. . . ."

These "problem areas" cover wide-ranging research questions such as those raised by the Brown committee and outlined on page 8. They include such basic unknowns as the food chains of the sea and the weather and climate of the deep oceans. These are the kinds of questions that modern oceanography now can begin to answer, the unknowns it is now equipped to explore in detail. However, this research no longer will be carried out largely for the sake of knowledge, the quest that has sparked ocean exploration for so many decades in the past. Men now are looking

to oceanography to give them the know-how to exploit the vast
resources of the sea. The PSAC panel reflected this aspiration in
recommending that, for the United States, the President set the
ultimate goal of the country's oceanography program as the "effective use of the sea by man for all purposes currently considered
for the terrestrial environment: commerce, industry, recreation,
and settlement; as well as for knowledge and understanding."

The science of the sea is in a period of growth and activity as
ebullient as that which followed the explorations of the *Challenger*.
Much of today's oceanographic knowledge is rapidly being outmoded by a flood of new information. Thus the following chapters
are as much a prelude to the future as they are a summary of
accomplishment.

TWO

BEGINNINGS

Where have the oceans come from? How old are their waters? When and how did life arise in the ancient seas? These are fundamental questions of oceanography that have yet to receive definitive answers. They are inseparable from the larger question of the creation of the earth itself.

Up to a few hundred years ago, Christian cosmologists thought this perplexing problem of beginnings had been solved once and for all by the Biblical account of creation, which many scientists and clergymen alike accepted literally. By studying such things as the ages of post-Adamic generations listed in the Bible, a seventeenth-century Irish clergyman, Archbishop James Ussher, fixed the epoch of creation at just 4004 years B.C. His computations were popular around 1650, but subsequent scientific analysis and discovery have freed geology from this kind of dogmatic dating. Yet even today one can't talk about the origin and age of earth and its oceans without taking part of the story on faith. The Nobel Prize-winning chemist Dr. Harold C. Urey of the University of California notes wryly, that when it comes to cosmic origins "even scientists have a marked tendency to call for miracles whenever some phase of the subject moves outside their own specialities." Because no one was there to see, this may always be the case. On the other hand, science has learned enough to have something meaningful to say on the subject of creation even though its competing theories are constantly in flux.

To trace the genealogy of the sea, oceanographers have joined with chemists, geologists, and astrophysicists in trying to reconstruct the birth and early history of our planet from processes and phenomena that can be observed today. For one thing, they have found that Archbishop Ussher hit very wide of the mark. The ancient Hindus came closer in compiling their sacred book, the Manusmitri, which received its final form in the second century B.C. The mystical cosmology spelled out there fixes the earth's age at just under two billion years, a figure that is at least of the right order of magnitude. At this writing, scientists put the earth's age at somewhere between five and six billion years, which is close to the age of the sun itself. How do they know? As Dr. Urey points out, there is a bit of miracle-working mixed with the computations, but here is one way to estimate it.

The "Atomic Clock"

From estimates of the extent to which the sun's initial charge of nuclear fuel (hydrogen) has been used up and from comparison with stars in its astronomical neighborhood, the sun is thought to be about six billion years old. This age may be in error by a factor of ten and almost certainly will be revised as more is learned about stellar processes. Nevertheless, as today's best-informed guess, it puts an upper limit on estimates of the earth's age, for it is inconceivable that the planets formed before the sun. A lower age limit can be set simply by reading some accurate "atomic clocks" that have been running throughout geological time. These are the natural radioactive elements, such as uranium, thorium, rubidium, or potassium, that lie fixed in ancient rocks and decay at a known rate into other non-radioactive elements. Let's take uranium for example.

Natural uranium comes in two slightly different varieties. Chemically, these are indistinguishable. But one weighs 238 atomic weight units and the other weighs only 235. For comparison, hydrogen has an atomic weight of 1. Atoms of the same element that have different weights are called "isotopes" of that element. The uranium isotopes are called U-238 and U-235, respectively, and there is 139 times as much of the former in a sample of natural uranium as there is of the latter. Each type of uranium decays radioactively into a particular isotope of lead. This means that a given uranium atom emits radiation and simultaneously initiates a nuclear process that turns it into an atom of lead. However, there is no chemical affinity between uranium and lead. Thus, if several per cent of lead is found in a uranium mineral, it is generally assumed that the lead is the decay product of the uranium. By measuring accurately the ratios between the amounts of the various lead isotopes and the amounts of the uranium isotopes that produce them, it is possible to tell how much uranium was present when any given sample was formed. Then, since uranium turns into lead at a known fixed rate, the sample's age can be estimated. Half of any given amount of U-235, for example, decays into lead-207 in 8.8 hundred million years. This is called the "half life" of U-235 and is a fundamental constant in determining the age of uranium-bearing rocks. Of course this technique will work only if the uranium and the lead it produces have kept together and intact in the sample and if there has been no contamination from other sources of lead. Fortunately the relationships between all of the isotopes involved are understood well enough to guard against errors of this sort.

Before they learned how to read the "atomic clocks," geologists dated rocks by their structures and the fossils they contained. These gave rough results at best. But by studying the order of succession of fossils found in the different layers of stratified rocks and by comparing observations from many parts of the world, geologists worked out a relative time scale for the past 600 million years. They split these years into three main divisions called "eras," which encompassed major phases of biological evolution. They named them the Paleozoic, Mesozoic, and Cenozoic eras in that order, the latter being the present era. The eras, in turn, were subdivided into "periods." The earliest period, which began some 600 million years ago, is called the Cambrian, while the current period, covering the past 3.0–3.5 million years, is called the Quaternary. Some of the periods are further subdivided into "epochs."

While these methods gave an idea of the relative timetable, they couldn't fix absolute ages or date rocks older than the Cambrian. Prior to that period, the fossil record is dim. The "atomic clock" has removed much of this uncertainty. It has fixed the geological eras, periods, and epochs more accurately than ever before. It has dated the oldest-known crustal rocks at three to three and a half billion years. These formations include carbon-rich rocks and cherts formed from ancient sediments and metamorphic rocks such as quartzite as well as igneous granites. Usually, it is the igneous rocks that are dated. The sedimentary rocks

FIGURE 7. GEOLOGICAL TIME SCALE

Era	Period	Epoch		Age in millions of years	Principal Events
CENOZOIC	QUATERNARY	Recent		0.01	Crustal folding, volcanoes.
		Pleistocene		(10,000 years) 3.0-3.5	Glacial epoch with four ice ages separated by warm periods, fluctuating sea levels. Rise of man.
	TERTIARY	Pliocene		13	Crustal folding, volcanoes.
		Miocene		25	Sea invades many lowland areas. Plants and animals evolve rapidly, mammals become dominant. Prehumans appear.
		Oligocene		36	
		Eocene		58	
		Paleocene		63	
MESOZOIC	CRETACEOUS			135	Crustal folding. Small mammals.
	JURASSIC			181	Pacific border folding. Marine reptiles, first birds, dinosaurs.
	TRIASSIC			230	Volcanoes. First mammals.
PALEOZOIC	PERMIAN			280	Crustal folding, continental uplift, volcanoes. Glacial epoch beginning in the Carboniferous with several ice ages separated by warm periods, glaciers in equatorial belt, extremes of cold and aridity. Rapid biological evolution.
	CARBON-IFEROUS	Pennsylvanian		345	Warm humid climate; swamp forests and coal formation, ferns and mosses. Amphibians, first insects.
		Mississippian			
	DEVONIAN			405	Mountains uplifted (some never again submerged). Fishes are dominant.

may be considerably older since the igneous material invaded them some time after their formation. The oldest sedimentary rocks known at this writing are in the so-called Fig Tree sediments of South Africa. Believed to be over 3.2 billion years old, they contain equally ancient fossil microbes.

Era	Period	Age in millions of years	Principal Events
PALEOZOIC	SILURIAN	425	Crustal folding, volcanoes. Seas invade widespread low areas. Warm, locally arid climate. Coral reefs widespread, first land life.
PALEOZOIC	ORDOVICIAN	500	Seas spread widely over low continents, mountains uplifted. Shelled invertebrates, trilobites, first fishes appear.
PALEOZOIC	CAMBRIAN (Beginning of era is somewhat uncertain.)	600	Seas advance and withdraw, at one time covering much of North America. Abundant fossils of marine life. Eocambrian glacial epoch.
PRE-CAMBRIAN		3000	Earliest known rocks and mountains. Several glacial epochs. Faint traces of seaweeds and invertebrate animals. Fossil microbes in rocks roughly three billion years old.
UNDECIPHERED		4500 to 5000	Solidification of mantle. Beginning of geological time.
PRIMORDIAL		6000	Sun and planets, the earth and moon form from cosmic nebula.

This is the span of the earth's history that can be read in the rocks. It sets a minimum age for the earth. But certainly our planet is older than that, for these rocks are not the first that were formed. Older crustal rocks have melted, sunk far out of sight, or been changed so that their "atomic clocks" can no longer be read.

Then too, at best, these clocks will date only the solidification of the earth, not its true beginning. This is estimated from astronomical considerations.

For example, radioactive dating of the meteorites that occasionally fall out of the sky indicates they solidified about 4.6 billion years ago. The meteorites are assumed to be either fragments of the asteroids, which are small chunks of planet material that whirl about the sun in an orbit between the orbits of Mars and Jupiter, or to be material left over from the formation of the asteroids by the breakup of a planet. In either case, it is further assumed that the earth and asteroids solidified at the same time and that their primordial material was assembled at the same time as well. Allowing time for this material to compact, melt and solidify, present calculations put the epoch of the asteroid's (and presumably the earth's) initial formation at between five and six billion years ago. This at least gives a feeling for the time scale involved.

Birth of a Planet

What happened at that dim time is any expert's guess. Perhaps it was something like this, to quote a theory popular in the last half century. Because of a collision or near collision with another star, a great fiery mass was expelled from the sun. Flying outward, it eventually settled into a planetary orbit. This "proto-earth," as we shall call it, was a seething mass of incredibly hot gas. But as it radiated its heat into the vastness of space it gradually cooled. First it became partly liquid. Then, with further cooling, the outer crust began to form. Meanwhile the materials of the protoplanet were sorting themselves out. The heavier ones moved toward the center, the lighter ones toward the outer parts. Gases, such as water vapor, collected as an atmosphere. This resulted in the layered earth we know today with its dense fluid metallic core, its semi-plastic (but extraordinarily rigid) mantle, and its outer crust.

With the solidification of the outer layers, cooling of the inner parts was slowed tremendously. Even today the core is thought to retain most of its primordial heat. But the young planet was in constant turmoil. The thin crust broke in many places, letting through fiery lavas, while overhead the face of the sun was hidden by a thick curtain of perpetual clouds. Soon after this the oceans began to form. But let's leave the story at that point and return to it later, for this is only one way it might have happened.

Some experts think that a chance encounter between our sun and a star is too unlikely to consider even on the epochal time scale of cosmic events. There have been a number of theories of the planet's origin, some of which have a long ancestry. The cataclysmic one just described was proposed early in this century by the American geologist Thomas C. Chamberlin and the astronomer Forest R. Moulton, and subsequently elaborated by the British physicists Sir James Jeans and Sir Harold Jeffreys. It was popular for fifty years and still crops up in spite of its improbability and certain highly technical objections.

In 1796 the famous French mathematician Pierre Simon de Laplace suggested that the planets evolved from material originally thrown off as a series of rings by a condensing mass that eventually became the sun. Others took this theory more seriously than did its author, who never published it in exact scientific form. It was dominant for almost a century, but it was shown to be theoretically impossible and dropped out of vogue. Prior to Laplace, in 1750, Thomas Wright in England suggested a theory, later elaborated by the famous philosopher Immanuel Kant, that sun and planets developed as centers of condensation in a cloud of cosmic dust and gas. It stirred little interest at the time.

In recent decades there has been a spate of cataclysmic theories in which the sun is either the survivor of a collision between a double star and a third star or is the surviving member of a double star whose companion exploded. The planets, of course, would form from the debris that remained. These theories, along with the related ideas of Moulton and Chamberlin, were effectively demolished by the American astronomer Lyman Spitzer, Jr. He found that the debris from a stellar collision or a wisp of material pulled out of the sun would be blown off into space almost explosively from the pressure of its own or of the sun's radiation. Under these conditions, planets would never have a chance to form. Then too, the cataclysmic theories have never been able to answer objections based on technical consideration of the motions of the sun and planets.

At this writing, an adaptation of the old Kant-Wright theory is in vogue. It was revived in 1944 by Carl von Weizsäcker in Germany and O. J. Schmidt in the Soviet Union. Since then it has been developed and expanded, especially in the United States by Urey, Spitzer, and Gerard P. Kuiper. The theory holds that it is highly likely that sun and planets condensed from the same mass of dust and gas roughly at the same time. So here, briefly, is another story of how the earth was born.

As far as stars themselves are concerned, it is generally accepted that they begin as a loose association of the cosmic dust and gas which exist in great abundance throughout the universe. Local concentrations form in a cloud of this dust and gas, which, through the pulling together of the mutual gravitational attraction between the cloud particles and the action of electromagnetic forces and perhaps even the pressures of cosmic gas and radiations, slowly contract into discrete bodies. As such a "protostar" contracts, it heats up from compression until at some point it is hot enough to kindle the thermonuclear reactions that are the source of stellar heat and light. These are akin to the thermonuclear reactions that power a hydrogen bomb. This contraction to stellar dimensions may take anywhere from a hundred thousand to tens of millions of years. Thus a star is born of a contracting dust cloud, condensing its fires from the cobwebs of the universe. So it was with our sun.

But as the protosun shrank, it left behind some of the primordial cloud as a rotating nebula. This nebula was cold to begin with. And as the developing sun shrank, the nebula radiated much of what little heat it had into space. At this time the sun itself gave only feeble light and heat in return, so that the nebula soon reached the unimaginable cold of 370° below zero Fahrenheit (minus 223° Centigrade) and perhaps even lower. Under the influence of cold and gravity, the nebula became disk-shaped, and soon local concentrations began to form within its turbulent, whirling mass. These were the protoplanets, one of which was to become the earth.

Thus, instead of a fiery mass torn out of a full-blown sun, the protoearth, according to this theory, was formed from a cloud of dust and gas in the incredible cold of interstellar space at a time when the sun itself was still dark. It had 500 times as much mass as the earth does today. Its diameter was 1800 times that of the final globe. Much of this mass was subsequently lost to space as gases escaped from the evolving planet.

At first the planetary matter condensed into fine grains which grew rapidly in size. These, in turn, began to spiral in toward the center of the protoplanet to form a nucleus. The materials involved were essentially those that make up the earth today, including a good deal of water, much of which may have been frozen. Thus the planet grew. And as the rain of matter continued, it gradually heated up from the effects of compaction, chemical reactions, and radioactivity, which was fifteen times as intense as it is today.

Slowly the protoearth began to melt. Its materials separated into the constituents of core, mantle, and eventually the outer

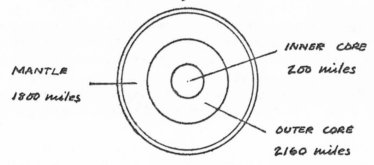

CONTINENTAL CRUST average thickness 20-25 miles
OCEANIC CRUST average thickness 3-8 miles

MANTLE
1800 miles

INNER CORE
200 miles

OUTER CORE
2160 miles

MOHOROVIČIĆ DISCONTINUITY boundary zone between crust and mantle

FIG. 8 : The earth's layered structure shown schematically in cross section.

crust. This melting and final freezing of crust and mantle took something like a billion years. Thus geological history began with solidification of the mantle 4.6 billion years ago, and the young earth was ready to receive its oceans.

Origin of the Seas and Their Basins

Until recently it was widely assumed that the great ocean basins have remained much the same throughout geological time. There have been changes at the edges as continental lands rose and sank and waters advanced into or retreated from the low-lying inland areas. And there have been some changes in the deep ocean bottom itself. But, by and large, the great basins that cover two thirds of the globe today were thought to have remained relatively unchanged. The question then was, how were they formed in the first place?

Some have thought the birth of the moon may have played a leading role in shaping such features of the earth's crust. According to this view, first advanced in 1878 by Sir George Darwin, son of the famous naturalist, the moon was torn out of the earth after the crust had begun to form but while the mantle was still fluid to some extent. Here is how it might have happened. In those distant days the sun's gravity was the major tide-producing force on earth. It pulled the viscid outer layers into enormous tidal bulges whose peaks grew progressively higher. They built up steadily until, after a few hundred years, it was more than the young planet could stand. A chunk of the earth broke off to become the moon. Held as a satellite by gravity, the moon gradually moved away from the earth and is still moving away today. The basin of the Pacific Ocean, according to this theory, is the scar left by the cataclysmic separation.

Those who hold this view point out that the mean density of the moon is similar to that of the outer layers of the earth. Also, they note that other ocean basins have a thin covering of granite, while much of the Pacific does not. Perhaps its original granite cover now is swinging through space as part of the moon's substance. The other ocean basins may have been formed at this time too. As the moon matter tore away, the new crust broke, wrinkled, and shifted, especially on the opposite side of the planet. The result was a migration of great crustal blocks to become continents and the opening of basins to receive the ocean waters.

This theory has been seriously questioned. For example, Sir Harold Jeffreys has shown it is extremely unlikely that the peaks of the solar tides could have risen more than 200 feet. This would be impressive if seen from the ground, but it would not have been enough to throw off the moon. Instead, the nebula theory of earth's origin suggests that the earth and moon formed simultaneously. Two condensation centers may have formed in the cold mass of dust and gas that became the protoplanet. The larger one became the earth and the secondary center formed the moon. Consequently, the moon is not regarded as a satellite of the earth but rather as the lesser partner of a double planet system, analogous in origin to the many double stars found throughout the Galaxy. On the other hand, the moon may have formed from its own part of the primordial cloud and then been captured by the protoearth early in its history.

As for the ocean basins, they may have formed as part of the general crust as the planet cooled. Some geophysicists think they have been shaped slowly throughout geological time as land masses slid over the earth's surface, breaking apart and moving away from each other. This process may be going on today. (See pages 100–105.) In any event, the early scene was desolate. Everywhere, there was only hot, bleak rock broken by volcanic fissures. Then as the earth continued cooling, the atmosphere is thought to have released vast quantities of water it had held as clouds and vapor. Torrential rains fell, perhaps for centuries. They began to erode the rugged landscape, beginning the long process of carrying minerals from the land into the sea. At first, the hot rocks sent the water back as steam. Then as they cooled, oceans began to form. When at last the sun shone again, earth had become a water planet ready for the great experiment in the evolution of life.

But it is questionable that the earth received the bulk of its oceans at that time. The protoplanet lost much of its mass before the earth finally took on its present shape. Most of the water it managed to keep was probably trapped chemically or physically in the subsurface rocks. For example, William Rubey of the United States Geological Survey estimates that only 5 to 10 per cent of the present oceans were formed initially, the rest of the waters having escaped from the earth's interior throughout geological time. Indeed, this is part of a dynamic new view that geologists have begun to take of the earth's atmosphere and oceans. In recent years they have begun to wonder if any of the major exterior features were formed once and for all in a single epoch.

Summarizing the present state of knowledge of the earth's crust, Dr. J. Tuzo Wilson of the University of Toronto, past president of the International Union of Geodesy and Geophysics, explained that "it seems reasonable to conclude from the many sources of information which modern geophysical science has placed at our

disposal that the atmosphere, the oceans and the crust of the earth have all been brought forth from the interior by volcanic and seismic activity during the planet's long history. Thus oceans and continents, with their vast ridges and trenches, valleys and mountains, have gradually been constructed on top of the original surface of the earth. This now forms the base of the crust. It is hidden and only known to us from the echoes of seismic waves it reflects. This view is a new one and not yet widely understood, but it seems forced upon us by our expanding knowledge. Consideration of the rate at which gases, steam and lava are poured forth by volcanoes has led to the idea that the atmosphere, oceans and rocks of the crust have all been produced by volcanicity. Studies of their composition and abundance strengthen this view. A rate not much higher than that at which volcanoes emit lava today would have sufficed to build the entire crust during [geological time]."

But whatever the origin of the oceans, it is certain that the earth has had a good deal of water for a very long time. The oceans are not only a product of earthly evolution but are a contributing factor to geological change. Time after time the restless forces beneath and within the crust have heaved up great mountain ranges. And time after time the erosive forces of wind and water have worn down these ranges, carrying great masses of land material into the sea. Some of this material has dissolved and been distributed throughout the waters to add to their hoard of minerals. Some of it has undergone chemical change or been picked up by organisms and subsequently has settled out in a different form. Some of it settled out directly. This gradual settling formed bottom sediments that, in the slow cycles of geological time, became sedimentary rocks—limestones, sandstones, shales, and the like. These were deposited over large continental areas during extensive invasions of the sea. In their turn they were often uplifted into mountains and again worn down and carried to the sea in a complex cycle. There have been some half dozen such mountain-building epochs since Cambrian times. The sea plays its role in erosion processes too, for its waves are constantly eating away at coastlines and islands. But the grandest part the ocean has ever played in the evolutionary drama has been as the womb for the rise of earthly life.

The Rise of Life

The first faint traces of life, fossil microbes, date back over three billion years. But biological evolution had been going on for a long time before that. Here again no one really knows just what took place. It is believed that the primitive oceans contained a variety of chemicals, greatly diluted and spread throughout their vast waters. Interactions between these chemicals and constituents of the primitive atmosphere were going on constantly, stimulated by radiation from the sun and perhaps by electric discharges in the atmosphere.

It is fairly certain that conditions of this kind could produce many of the organic chemicals that today are associated with living cells. For example, in 1953 Dr. S. L. Miller of the University of California, then a graduate student working with Harold Urey at the University of Chicago, ran an electric discharge through an atmosphere of methane, hydrogen, ammonia, and water vapor and produced a variety of organic compounds. These included substances called amino acids, which are the building blocks of proteins. The gases used in this experiment are thought to be among the main constituents of the primitive atmosphere.

For his own part, Urey has examined many kinds of chemical reactions he thinks could reasonably have taken place. He has concluded that if half the carbon now present on the surface of the earth had existed as soluble organic compounds in early times, and if the primitive oceans had only 10 per cent of the present amount of sea water, these oceans would have been approximately a 10 per cent solution of organic compounds. Thus the chemical turmoil of that distant age turned the ocean into a complex mixture and solution of chemicals that were favorable for the rise of a primitive form of life. It was a dilute nutritious soup that, with the advent of life, began to consume its own substance.

If life arose in this way, as is now widely believed, it may have been a long slow process of trial and error, to judge from the pace of evolution today. On the other hand, the British biochemist J. B. S. Haldane thinks that evolution may have been a good deal more rapid in that early epoch. He suggests that there may be a relatively short critical period in the early years

of a planet when life has an opportunity to evolve. The fact that it has arisen on the earth indicates that it must have evolved quickly in the beginning to take advantage of this period. He further points out that evolution proceeds by mutation. For one of today's complex organisms, mutation is usually a relatively minor inheritable change which may or may not affect its evolutionary course. But for primitive life where species were little more than living molecules, mutation could be a sudden drastic change in which molecular species superseded one another quickly and evolution could proceed at a fast pace.

Whether the process was quick or slow, in those formative times many substances must have appeared that came close to being what we would consider alive, only to disappear again in the constant chemical shifting of the primordial "brew." Indeed, if an observer could go back in time and sample the seas at different periods, he would be hard put to say just when life did appear. The line between living and nonliving has proved an impossible one for biologists to draw. Does the capacity to eat and grow, to reproduce, to organize the environment define life? Does a system have to have only one of these characteristics or all of them to be called living? Or does the criterion lie elsewhere? Viruses that are inert crystals when isolated and viable entities using the apparatus of living cells to reproduce themselves when they enter a host are an enigmatic case in point.

It is likely that a number of systems we would recognize as living appeared, struggling to keep their integrity in spite of the incessant chemical attack of their environment, competing with each other for the materials they needed to survive. At some unknown time, at least one line of these systems must have gained an advantage, however slight, that set it on the long road of biological evolution. Perhaps it was the first to evolve a means for altering hitherto unusable chemicals so that it enlarged its food supply. Perhaps it was the first to build a protective wall that would admit needed nutrients but keep out destructive compounds. Whatever its evolutionary advantage, it was the ancestor of the first living cell, the basic unit of life, which is one of the most complex chemical systems known.

A. I. Oparin, the Soviet biochemist who has long been a world leader in this field, and others have pointed out that the earliest living organisms could have developed directly from dense globules

of carbon compounds. At first these could live and grow by taking necessary chemicals out of the surrounding water. But as one or more of these nutrient substances grew scarce, only those organisms could survive that developed ways of using new materials as a food supply. This process would continue as these materials in turn became scarce. In this way very simple organisms would continually increase in complexity through the exigencies created by dwindling food supplies.

Primitive one-cell plants probably arose early in this evolutionary process. Animals could not have evolved until later, for only plants are able to perform the magical transformation of sunlight into living substance that is the basic sustenance of all earthly life. These simple plants probably got along without oxygen, as some primitive bacteria do today, since the atmosphere and ocean at that time were probably oxygen-poor. But the great adventure had started. Through the gradual processes of evolution, modifications were made as changes in the environment permitted. Oxygen began to increase as the plants released it, and oxygen-breathing organisms arose. As the plant cells proliferated, some of them modified so that they no longer used sunlight to turn inorganic materials into organic substances. They fed directly on the primitive plant cells and perhaps on each other. These were the first animals. From such shadowy beginnings, the rich proliferation of life slowly evolved throughout the periods of geological time.

A Bit of Crystal Gazing

Just as there are no cut-and-dried answers to the question of beginnings, so there is no sure forecast of the future. Nevertheless, the latest theories show an interesting trend. Instead of cataclysms, sometimes bordering on the miraculous, they envision the earth's history as a slow process of evolution guided by principles that are generally considered valid throughout the universe and wrought by forces acting over long periods of time. These principles are still valid, and many of the forces are active today. One can at least project their possible effects into the long-term future. Here is what that projection foretells.

Left to its own devices, the earth's future evolution would probably be undramatic. Over eras measured in billions of years, the heat of radioactivity would slowly diminish in the outer layers of the mantle and crust. And with the cooling of these underlying masses, the volcanism and mountain-building forces that have constantly reshaped the surface would die down. Slowly the processes of erosion would wear away the land no longer being renewed by upthrusting mountains, carrying its substance into the seas. During this period some of the atmospheric gases would escape to space, but these would be renewed by leakage from the earth's interior. Since water vapor, in particular, escapes very slowly, the earth would retain its great oceans. And as the lands eroded, these waters would slowly spread until eventually they might completely cover the planet. The time scale for this course of events would be on the order of at least ten billion years.

But the earth will not be left to its own evolutionary devices. Over the billions of years of the future, the development of the sun will again become the dominating factor in the earth's evolution even as it was at the beginning. The sun is burning up its nuclear fuel at a prodigal rate. As its hydrogen supply is used up, the sun will gradually increase in size and brightness until it becomes what astronomers call a red giant star. Then, with its fuel supply exhausted, it will collapse again to become a white dwarf star, its fires slowly cooling over an indefinitely long time.

There is reason to believe that the sun has already started down this evolutionary road. Its brightness now is some 20 to 25 per cent greater than it was when the young sun first condensed from its protostar. Its diameter also has started very slowly to increase. In another three to four billion years it will have become a red giant perhaps ten times as bright as it now is and emitting perhaps a hundred times as much radiation. But its evolution will have had serious consequences for the earth long before that point is reached.

As the solar brightness grows, the earth will heat up. Sometime around two billion years from now the oceans will begin to boil. Soon their water masses will be transformed into clouds and vapor in the atmosphere. There is no reason to think these will be lost to space. But the surface will be hot and dry. Like Venus, the earth will probably be wrapped in perpetual clouds. After another billion years or so the sun will shrink. If the earth has not been engulfed and vaporized by the expanded sun—a not unlikely event—it then will cool. The air will give up its moisture in a primordial rain and the ocean basins will again be filled. But this time the shrunken sun will be considerably dimmer. The earth will cool until its waters freeze and its lands are covered with perpetual snow.

Is this to be the end of our planet—to drift through space, the frozen companion of a dying sun? It is impossible to foretell. Certainly this is one logical result of evolutionary trends as we know them today. However, Dr. Gerard P. Kuiper of the University of Arizona, a leading theoretical astronomer, has suggested an alternative. It is possible, he says, that the frozen earth might be rejuvenated. He bases this on mathematical studies of the evolution of the entire universe.

Our stellar universe seems to be expanding. It has been expanding for a long time and will continue to do so for an indefinite time in the future. But Dr. Kuiper has worked out a mathematical theory for this expanding universe and has found that it need not go on expanding forever. There are solutions to the mathematical equations that suggest the universe someday might start contracting. If it did, it would heat up as its contraction proceeded. The earth itself might warm again as part of the general heating, its oceans melt and its continents thaw. But it would be a cataclysmic reawakening, for the universe would be on its way to a nuclear holocaust. Its contraction would progress until its temperatures could support the basic nuclear reactions that would rework its matter anew and start it again on a great creative expansion. "Nothing could be more dramatic," Dr. Kuiper observes, "than the dissolution of the earth and all that is on it in the mad rush of stars and planets during the concluding moments of the present cycle of the universe."

THREE

THE UNSEEN LANDSCAPE

Some of the earth's most spectacular scenery lies under the sea. Upthrusting mountain ranges and plunging trenches, awesome canyons and escarpments, all are hidden under hundreds and often many thousands of feet of water. If they could be viewed from the deep-sea floor, they would be found in many cases to excel the scenic grandeur of the continents. Here is a vast unseen landscape that men have scarcely begun to explore. Here, if anywhere, is the last great frontier for geographical exploration. Even the forbidding interior of Antarctica has begun to yield to the map makers under the concerted attack of the International Geophysical Year expeditions and their successors. But the ocean floor remains a challenge to man's ability to chart what he cannot see.

According to Dr. Roger Revelle, "Only about two per cent of the deep-sea floor has been even moderately accurately surveyed. As far as our understanding of the topography of the sea floor is concerned, we are now about where we were a hundred years ago in surveying the land . . ." It is easy to see why it is frequently said that men know less about many parts of ocean bottom than they do about the near face of the moon.

Men have been studying the sea bottom for the better part of a century. The first true deep-sea sounding was made in 1840 when Sir James Clark Ross plumbed a depth of almost 2000 fathoms with a weighted hemp line. Oceanographers, however, first took the measure of the sea floor during the *Challenger* expedition. These soundings gave a general idea of the outline and average depths of the major ocean basins, but they scarcely hinted the true complexity of submarine geography. For decades thereafter the ocean floor was thought to be primarily a smooth monotonous plain, its original features buried under sediments accumulated throughout geologic time.

This, after all, was the way the sea bottom appeared to be when all the oceanographer had was hemp or steel sounding lines and a few crude instruments for sampling the uppermost sediments. But with the advent of the echo sounder, oceanographers began to discover the submarine landscape. Much of this landscape remains to be explored, as Revelle's statistic illustrates. On the other hand, enough of the former blank spaces have been filled in on the charts so that one can, figuratively speaking, take at least a generalized tour of the ocean bottom. This general topography of the sea floor, as it is known today, is shown on one of the endpaper maps. Because of the small scale to which the map is drawn, only the major features can be indicated. Nevertheless, they help orient one in this unfamiliar world beneath the sea.

The Threshold

The transition from continent to ocean is rarely sudden. To the casual eye of a landsman, the sea begins at the water's edge. But to the sound beams of the oceanographer, the boundary is less distinct. Almost everywhere the land is bordered by shallow "continental shelves" where land and sea merge into one another. They are the threshold over which one must pass to enter the deep ocean.

Or, to look at them another way, the shelves geologically are part of the continents—the threshold, so to speak, above which the land rises out of the water. The 1958 Geneva Convention on the Continental Shelf, ratified at this writing by more than thirty nations, gives legal recognition to this viewpoint. It grants exclusive mineral rights on the continental shelves to the nations bordering them.

But however one looks at it, the shallow-water transition zone has in many ways been the most important part of the undersea landscape for practical human purposes. The shelves are rich in oil and minerals. This is also where the great commercial fisheries are found, such as those of the North Sea and of the Grand Banks off Newfoundland. If trawlers had to fish the abyss miles below their ships rather than the few-hundred-foot depths of the shelves and their banks, they would find it cumbersome and prohibitively expensive in gear and operating costs, even if the sparse abyssal fauna were worth hauling in.

The shelves also have long been both a hazard and an aid to navigation. Navigators must constantly be on the lookout for shoals and sand bars. At the same time, by comparing soundings with those on their charts, they can help guide themselves in their coastwise sailing. Thanks to this practical importance to navigators and fishermen, the shelves are the best-surveyed areas under the sea, at least off the coasts of maritime nations.

For the purposes of the 1958 Geneva Convention, the continental shelf was defined as the shallow-water area out to a depth of 200 meters. This is useful as a legal definition, but the shape of the shelf rarely fits the 100-fathom contour line. The shelves end in more or less distinct breaks where the bottom begins to slope more steeply, sometimes precipitously, into the abyss. This break is their natural limit. Thus by international agreement the continental shelf is defined geologically as the "zone around the continents, extending from low water line to the depth at which there is a marked increase in slope to greater depth." If the "marked increase in slope" comes in two breaks instead of one, as it often does, then the sharpest break marks the edge of the shelf, provided this break is no deeper than 300 fathoms.

However, not all of the world's continental shelves have been well enough surveyed to be delineated in this manner. Because of this, and because there would be no serious distortion for the scale with which they are drawn, the shelves are delimited on the endpaper map by the 100-fathom line.

In some places the shelves are wide, as in the North Sea area off Europe or along the Arctic coast of Asia. In other areas they are narrow or virtually nonexistent, as off the eastern tip of Florida. On the whole, to give a few general statistics, they have an average width of about 42 miles, an average depth of 180 to 210 feet, an average slope toward the sea of about 10 feet in a mile ($0°7'$), and an average depth at the outer edge of 432 feet.

These valuable undersea margins are partly a gift of the last ice age, which ended 11,000 years ago. So much water was locked up in ice that, 18,000 years ago, general sea level was from 300 to 500 feet lower than at present. Waves cut terraces in many places as new coastal areas were exposed to lowered seas. When the ice melted and the waters rose again, these were submerged. Low-lying land areas were flooded. Thus extensive shelves were formed off many coasts by submersion which was aided, in some cases, by slow sinking of the land as well. Sedimentation, river outflows, and erosional forces have further shaped many of the shelves.

Especially in glaciated areas, the shelves still show their ice-age origin. In many places, glacial rubble has been dredged up. Off northern Europe and North America, the topography of the shelf shows the same glacial scouring as the adjacent land. The fjords, in particular, are believed to have been carved by the ice. Fossil teeth and bones of ice-age mammoths and mastodons lie far from shore on the North American Atlantic shelf.

Elsewhere the shelves have a varied topography. In some places they are hilly or rolling. Occasionally they are very smooth. There are many basins, banks, sand bars, and remains of drowned river valleys, while the material covering the bottom is a veritable patchwork of muds, sediments, and rocks.

The most common sediment is sand. Some of this, the "terrigenous" sand, is land-derived. Some of it is organic, such as the "calcarcenite" sands made up of coral fragments, the shells of microscopic animals of a type called Foraminifera, and the calcium carbonate remains of other organisms. There are also the so-called "chemical" or "authigenic" sands that are deposited by chemical processes in the sea. Besides the various sands, there are muds, silts, and clays, which are respectively made up of finer and finer materials, all finer than the sands. Last, there are gravels, pebbles, cobbles, and boulders—stones ranked according to increasing size—which cover the shelf in some places.

One of the more curious and occasionally valuable features of the shelves are the salt domes, such as those found off the Gulf coast of the United States. These sometimes are associated with oil and have been used as a cheap source of high-quality salt and sulphur. These domes, which look like rounded hills, are really oval plugs of salt, sometimes over a mile in diameter, that rise up from deep underlying salt beds. They have been pushed upward by subterranean forces until they rise with vertical walls through thousands of feet of sediment. Where they have risen, these mountains of salt are surrounded by uptilted sediment beds.

Oil is often found in these beds. Being lighter than the water that is also present in the sediments, it floats up through the tilted sediments until it is blocked by the wall of salt.

By definition, the shelves end where the sea bottom begins to drop more steeply into the abyss. These more inclined areas are called the "continental slopes," and it is here that the deep sea really begins.

Descent to the Abyss

Depending on one's point of view, the continental slopes are either the edge of the ocean basins or the rising flanks of the continents. But, however one looks at them, these are the greatest slopes and escarpments on the earth. There is nothing on land to rival them. Indeed, some of them are steeper and more awesome than the famous southern face of the Himalayas.

Off the west coast of South America, for instance, the east wall of the Peru-Chile Trench combines with the adjacent slopes of the Andes to give an average vertical rise of some 42,000 feet. That is practically twice the rise of the southern Himalayan slope. The greatest height difference known on the earth is found in this same ocean area where, at one point, the crustal surface rises from an undersea depth of 25,000 feet to a mountain height of 23,000 feet. This is a vertical rise of 48,000 feet (just over nine miles) within a horizontal distance of 100 miles.

Even where the shelf is too wide for the slope in which it ends to be considered contiguous to land elevations, steep escarpments are sometimes found. Furthermore, and unlike escarpments on land, the great undersea slopes stretch for thousands of miles, surrounding entire continents. Of course they are not everywhere as steep as those off western South America. In some places they are much more gradual. In other places they are broken up into intermediate plateaus and basins so that they descend to the deep-sea floor in somewhat stepwise fashion. In a few places they are virtually nonexistent because there is no perceptible change in the slope of the shelf until it reaches the abyss. Nevertheless, as a general feature, the "continental slopes," as they are called, would afford some of the most impressive scenery on the planet if they could be viewed from the deep ocean bottom.

In general, these slopes have not been as extensively surveyed

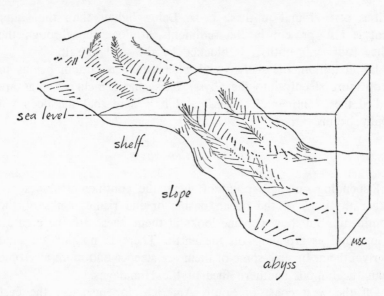

FIG. 9: The descent to the abyss.

as the shelves. The 1000-fathom line seems to be the limit of most detailed coastal exploration. On the other hand, except for the shelves, the continental slopes are the best-known features of the unseen "landscape." Again, to give a few general statistics, the inclination of the slopes ranges from about 1°20′ to 5°40′ (roughly 100 to 500 feet per mile) and more for the steepest areas. The steepest continental slopes are those of the Pacific, which average 5°20′, while the gentlest are those of the Indian Ocean at 2°55′. The Atlantic and Mediterranean slopes fall between at 3°05′, and 3°34′, respectively. Almost everywhere, these slopes end in depressions or a gentle apron known as the "continental rise" or, over local areas, as a "deep-sea fan."

Like the shelves, the slopes are often covered with a variety of sediments—about 60 per cent mud, 25 per cent sand, and a scattering of gravel, rocks, and oozes. But unlike the glacially influenced shelves, the slopes are believed to be the product of large-scale adjustments in the crust. Some geologists have suggested that the slopes are simply piles of sediment and debris built up off the end of the shelves. Others think they may be due originally to a downwarping of the crust at the edge of the sea bed or to vertical faulting, a process in which huge blocks of the crust move upward or downward. In one of the latest theories, Dr. Robert S. Dietz of the Environmental Sciences Service Administration (ESSA) Institute of Oceanography suggests the slopes are formed by a slow growth of the ocean floor which compresses and uplifts the sediments of the continental rise. (Page 102.)

Once formed, the slopes are constantly sculptured by sedimentation and erosion. They keep their steepness partly through the action of landslides and turbidity currents. These prevent the continual fall of sediments from burying the slope profile as snow blankets a winter landscape. Permeated with water, the loose sediments are easily set to sliding by slight earth movements and even by their own weight on steeper parts of the slopes.

The so-called "turbidity currents" do a similar job of sculpturing. If bottom sediments are stirred, as in an earthquake, they fill the water with a cloud of fine suspended material. This silt-laden water is a small fraction of one per cent heavier than the surrounding water. But the slight weight difference is enough to make the turbid water settle. If there is any incline at all to the bottom, it will run off as a "density" or "turbidity" current, which some experts think can become quite powerful. Certainly these currents and landslides seem able to keep the steeper parts of continental slopes relatively clean of sediments and thus help to preserve their original form.

A third factor affecting both the slopes and the shelves are the major ocean currents, which often distribute or carry away sediment. An example of this is the action of the Gulf Stream in shaping shelf and slope, as off the southeast coast of the United States. South of Cape Cod, the edge of the shelf curves ever closer to the land until, off the western tip of Florida, it virtually disappears. But beyond the shelf edge there is a plateau, the Blake Plateau, about 2400 to 3600 feet deep, which runs more or less smoothly out to sea until it terminates in a steep escarpment with inclinations of 15 degrees and more. This is roughly the area off the southeastern United States between the 1000-fathom contour line and the 100-fathom line marking the edge of the shelf as shown on the endpaper map. It is one of the geological curiosities of the continental slopes.

Dr. Henry Stetson of Woods Hole Oceanographic Institution

and a team under Dr. Maurice Ewing, director of Columbia University's Lamont Geological Observatory, and others have found that the sea bottom on the Blake Plateau is either rocky or covered by a hard material with little or no soft sediment. Furthermore, the Lamont geologists have dated rocks from the edge of the plateau and from the adjacent slope as being quite old, dating back to Cretaceous and Miocene times (see table page 46). Northward, rocks this old are deeply buried under more recent sediments, but on the Blake Plateau they lie at the surface. The plateau itself is flat enough to be considered part of the shelf if it did not lie so deep. It looks as if the top of the shelf had been sliced off with a great knife, like the frosted top layer off a cake. The reason for this curious geological feature is thought to be the flow of the Gulf Stream.

This massive current is believed to have started flowing through the Florida Strait early in the Tertiary period. Once started, the current stopped sedimentation in the Blake Plateau area except quite close to the coast. Meanwhile the sea floor slowly sank as part of the general subsidence that is known to have occurred throughout all areas off the North American coast. It once was thought that the Blake Plateau was due to downfaulting of a large crustal block or to the erosive action of the Gulf Stream. Although there may be some erosive action, the plateau and the lack of a significant shelf off southern Florida are now considered to be the result of a slow general sinking of the sea floor, which has continually been swept clean of upbuilding sediments by the Gulf Stream. As will be explained in the next chapter (pages 118–119), there is also reason to think the plateau is an ancient drowned coral reef. But however it was first formed, the fact that it has not been buried by sediment is a striking illustration of the power of an ocean current to shape major sea-bottom features even when it does nothing more violent than keep an area clean of sediments.

The continental shelves are also the location of a much-debated geologist's puzzle, the great submarine canyons that rival and often excel any the land can boast. It would seem obvious that they are simply drowned river valleys built on the scale of the Grand Canyon of the Colorado River. But no such simple explanation can account for their extent and their maintenance beneath the sea in spite of the tendency of sediments to fill them.

Canyons in the Deep

The great submarine canyons cut the continental slopes at a number of places throughout the world. Huge fans of sediment build up at their mouths. Sometimes they are located off adjacent land valleys, as in the case of the canyons off the mouth of the Hudson River in New York or the canyon off the island of Corsica, where every bay on the west coast has its continuation under the sea. But in many places the submarine canyons bear no obvious relation to the adjacent terrain.

These undersea canyons are generally too small in relation to the scale of the endpaper map to be shown there. However, if you look carefully at the east coast of North America, Long Island can be seen southwest of Cape Cod. Just south of Long Island there is an indentation in the continental shelf so narrow it appears simply as a short solid line. This is the location of the canyon off the Hudson River. Actually the canyon head is some distance from the shore, but this is difficult to show exactly on so small a map.

The canyon walls reach a maximum height of 4000 feet. Many short tributaries feed into the main valley, which runs to some 180 miles in length. This includes the inner canyon that cuts the continental slope and a shallower trench that Lamont geologists have traced across a huge deep-sea fan that extends into the western basin of the Atlantic. At its outer end the canyon system is 14,000 feet deep.

Although this canyon is unusual in that it is located off a river valley, its dimensions typify the majesty of these undersea formations. One has scarcely a hint of this from a mere listing of dimensions. But to geologists who have dived into these submarine valleys and for the extent to which they have been able to penetrate, it has been like swimming through the upper reaches of the Grand Canyon. How were these magnificent gorges created and what keeps them from filling up with sediments? There is no simple or generally accepted answer, but the forces involved link the canyons with long riverlike channels that have been discovered on the deep-ocean floor.

The first of these channels, a long winding depression tied into the mouth of the La Jolla submarine canyon, was discovered in

1948 by Dr. Henry W. Menard, Dr. Robert S. Dietz, and E. C. Buffington, who at that time were working from the United States Naval Electronics Laboratory at San Diego. Similar channels were found about the same time in the Atlantic by Bruce C. Heezen of Lamont. Since then a number of them have been found in both oceans, sometimes associated with submarine canyons on the slopes and sometimes by themselves on the abyssal floor. Menard, now with Scripps Institution, has found a puzzling twist to twelve deep-sea channels off the North American west coast which no one has yet explained. All twelve hook to the left. None hooks right or extends straight from the adjacent shelf.

The longest of the deep-sea channels, the Mid-Ocean Channel, was discovered and partially surveyed by expeditions from Lamont in 1949 and 1952. It begins off the tip of Greenland, where it may be a two-prong system with many branching tributaries, and runs for nearly 2000 miles to end in a deep basin of the west-central North Atlantic, reaching as far south as the latitude of Washington, D.C. It ranges in width from two to four miles and from 150 to 600 feet in depth.

The Bay of Bengal offers a striking example of a sea-floor channel that appears to be an extension of a submarine canyon. Analyses of echo-sounding records made in 1948 across the entrance of this bay by the Swedish research vessel *Albatross* indicate several channels in the bottom. The largest is some four miles wide and 240 feet deep. It is bordered by symmetrical levees six miles broad and rising 90 feet above the level of the surrounding bottom. This channel, which is eight times as wide and five times as deep as the Mississippi River at its southern end, is thought to run northward for some 1100 miles, where it ties into the huge submarine canyon off the Ganges River.

The echo-sounding records of these channels look very much like the profiles of big land rivers that build natural levees on their banks. On land, the levees are built when sediment-laden rivers overflow. Running fast at flood stage, the water of such rivers suddenly slows down when it spills over the banks and spreads over the countryside. Much of the heavier sediment it carried when it flowed faster is deposited along the banks, where over the years it builds up into levees. Man-made levees for flood control are often built on top of the natural ones.

Similar "levees" show up on the echo-sounding profiles of most of the deep-sea channels. In fact, this is the way these channels usually are spotted. They are only a few miles wide and a few hundred fathoms deep at most and had been overlooked in the general roughness of the deep-ocean bottom until relatively precise and continuously recording echo sounders became available to oceanographers after World War II. Since then the characteristic levees have become a kind of identification tag.

The phenomenon that gouged these channels, that could flood and build up levees on a plain already covered with several miles of water, is also involved in the origin and maintenance of the submarine canyons. In each case, marine geologists think density currents probably play a major role. In the case of the canyons, these are primarily turbidity currents. In cutting the deep-sea channels currents of water made dense by cooling and by its relatively high salt content are also thought to be involved.

Forces of Mud and Silt

In 1936 the Harvard geologist Dr. Reginald A. Daly first suggested that turbidity currents could erode the sea bottom. Few other geologists took him seriously until a Dutchman, Dr. Philip Kuenen, showed in 1951 that substantial turbidity currents could be generated in a 100-foot-long tank at Groningen University in Holland under conditions analogous to those of the sea. This lent support to the turbidity-current theory.

Meanwhile, in 1947, during a cruise of the Woods Hole Oceanographic Institution's research ship *Atlantis,* a plain over 200 miles wide was discovered in the deepest part of the western Atlantic, where the first 15-foot layer of the sediment was made up of sand and silt like that of a New England beach. Finding this material in the deep ocean where the bottom usually consists of fine oozes and clays was startling. It seemed totally out of place, with no apparent explanation for being there.

Then in 1949 the *Atlantis* again set out for the plain, this time tracing the Hudson submarine canyon westward from the edge of the continental shelf. Bottom samples showed the canyon was cut through ancient clays millions of years old. Moreover, sand, gravel, and the shells of shallow-water animals that live near shore were found along the canyon floor. All of this suggested one thing— turbidity currents. Perhaps these currents with their suspended silts and sediments could have carried shallow-water materials even to the newly discovered abyssal plain. Then came Kuenen's demonstration that the concept of such currents flowing over the ocean floor was valid. But could these currents, flowing because their turbid fluid is just a little bit heavier than the surrounding water, generate enough force to erode canyons and reach distant parts of the deep sea?

Ewing and Heezen at Lamont thought this was the case. When they looked about for evidence, the transatlantic telegraph cables gave them a clue. If turbidity currents strong enough to cut canyons actually flow down the slopes and over the abyssal floor, they reasoned, those that occurred in the northwestern Atlantic may have broken some of the cables. Looking over the records, they found circumstantial confirmation in the severe earthquake that shook the Grand Banks south of Newfoundland on November 18, 1929. Cables lying within 60 miles of the earthquake epicenter broke instantly. But for 13 hours thereafter cables on the downslope side from the epicenter continued to break one after the other in a regular sequence, starting with the ones farthest upslope and ending with one in the deep-ocean basin 300 miles from the epicenter. It looked as though some kind of massive flow had moved down the slope.

Ewing and Heezen concluded that there had been a turbidity current. From the records of the precise times of the respective cable breaks, they calculated that the speed of the current ranged from about 50 miles an hour on the steep slope to 15 miles an hour in the depths. Menard estimates top speeds of 35 to 45 miles an hour. Here was a current powerful enough to erode canyons on the continental slope and to cut channels along the deep-sea floor. The levees that border many of these latter could easily be accounted for by the same process that took place on land. As the turbidity current overflowed the channel banks it would deposit some of its load and build up the levees.

Subsequent investigation in the western North Atlantic by the Lamont group showed that the area where the deepest cable break had occurred in 1929 was covered with just the thickness of silt to be expected if a turbidity current had flowed there. In 1954 an earthquake in the Mediterranean yielded additional evidence of strong turbidity currents based on cable breaks similar to those of the Grand Banks quake.

Today, turbidity currents are a widely recognized phenomenon. Their effects have been traced over vast areas of the ocean floor. While generally that floor is rugged, large sections are quite flat. These are the abyssal plains found in all oceans. In the Atlantic, where they have been extensively studied, they cover 10 per cent of the sea bed. Although these plains have table-top flatness, echo sounding shows they too are underlain by a rugged bottom. This uneven landscape has been masked by layers of evenly deposited sediments that often contain sands and silts foreign to the deep-sea environment. It is generally believed that these sediments, called turbidites, have been carried there by turbidity currents.

Guided down the slopes by submarine canyons and by channels across the deeper sea floor, a turbidity current eventually slows down and spreads out. In so doing, it drops its sands and silts over many hundreds of square miles. They have been found hundreds of miles from shore. Sometimes the deposit of a single current is enough to carpet an entire abyssal plain. In a few cases, a plain has been gradually built up by successive turbidity currents until the sediments overflowed the ridges and hills that contain it. Then the currents moved even farther out to build yet another plain.

Whether or how much these wide-ranging currents have cut the submarine canyons is an unsettled question. Menard thinks California's Monterey canyon was carved by them. Assuming that turbidity currents there have carried a sediment load at least as great as the volume of the sedimentary fan deposited at the canyon's mouth, then these currents have transported 10,000 times the volume of rock that was eroded to make the canyon. The fast-moving, sediment-laden currents might well have cut away a mass that was one ten thousandth of their sediment load, even though that mass was solid rock. Plausible as this may be, it has not convinced geologists, generally, that the canyons are largely the work of turbidity currents.

One of these skeptical geologists is Dr. Francis Shepard of Scripps Institution. He has been unusually well located to study submarine canyons, since Scripps is close to the head of the sizable La Jolla submarine-canyon systems. Unable to accept the concept of really powerful density currents, Shepard has suggested that these canyons may be a combined product of river erosion and turbidity flows. Geologists have objected to the theory that the

canyons are drowned river valleys because many of the canyons
are not associated with land valleys and many of them extend
into quite deep water. Sea levels would have to be dropped an
unbelievable amount for rivers to have cut these canyons. Shepard
points out, however, that if the canyons are many millions of
years old, rather than geologically recent formations, river erosion
in their initial stages is no longer out of the question.

It is entirely possible that the present continental shelves and
slopes stood much higher in the early Tertiary period. At that
time they may have been above sea level and rivers could have
eroded them deeply. Then, as they sank beneath the sea, the
underwater canyons would have been preserved while the corresponding land valleys in many cases would have long since
been modified beyond recognition. What preserved the form of
the submarine canyons? What kept them relatively free of sediments through millions of years? This, Shepard suggests, has been
the action of landslides and turbidity currents.

In support of his theory he points out that almost every coast
that is inside a submarine canyon is underlain by thousands of
feet of sedimentary rock which contain evidence of having been
laid down at much higher levels than those at which they now
are found. This indicates that over a long period of time, perhaps
twenty million years, substantial sinking has occurred along such
coastal areas. He also notes that in the La Jolla submarine canyon
there has been no net fill during the more than twenty years that
Scripps oceanographers have been watching depth changes in the
canyon system. This is in spite of the rapid sand movement in the
area which is sufficient to fill the canyon head in a few years.
He attributes this to the periodic landslides known to occur in
the canyon head and to resulting turbidity currents that carry the
sediment out along the length of the canyon and deposit some of
it in basins and troughs farther out to sea.

Actually, there are several processes at work. The heads of many
submarine canyons may well have been cut by rivers in the past.
Canyon heads are kept open by slumping of sediments and by
persistent streaming of sand and pebbles down their slopes.
Masses of sediment, creeping along canyon floors, may erode like
glaciers. Abrasion by the landslides also may cut the upper canyons deeper. Farther out, turbidity currents probably keep the

canyons clean and may cause some erosion. However, no one really knows the full story of the undersea gorges.

On the other hand, it is quite probable that turbidity currents could have cut some of the shallow deep-sea channels in soft bottom sediments over long periods of time. According to Dr. Robert Dietz, however, many of these channels seem to be primarily the product of flows of cold, saline water, which would also carry some sediment and could build levees. Perhaps, he says, these channels are evidence of one of the most fundamental processes in the ocean, the formation of cold bottom water and its movement equatorward. He notes that many oceanographers now think the cold water that underlies all the major oceans is formed at very selected spots and at irregular intervals in high Arctic and Antarctic latitudes. Perhaps some of the deep-sea channels were formed in areas where the surface water, becoming cold and dense, cascades down to the abyssal floor and pours out along it, bringing Arctic cold to the depths of tropical seas.

Mountains Beneath the Sea

Like the submarine canyons, the huge channels on the deep-ocean floor are relatively too small to be shown on the end-paper map. On the other hand, the map does show the known major features of the ocean floor. With towering mountain ranges and deep trenches, it is as varied a "landscape" as anything the continents can boast. And, unlike the continents, it is not subject to erosive forces of wind, rain, and large temperature changes. Once formed, its major geological features tend to persist unless altered by forces within and below the crust itself.

Although the first accurate soundings of the deep oceans were taken by the *Challenger* expedition, a physicist named A. D. Bache had made a fair estimate of the average depth of the Pacific before the *Challenger* sailed. He did it by measuring the time it took waves generated in conjunction with earthquakes off Japan to reach the west coast of the United States. Bache fixed the time of the earthquake with the help of an early-model seismograph and detected the arrival of the waves with tide gauges. Then, using the physical principle that the speed of these waves depended directly on the depth of the water, he estimated the average depth of the Pacific to be about 2000 fathoms (12,000 feet). The *Chal-*

lenger findings confirmed his estimate as a fair average for the world's abyssal depths.

By way of comparison, the average depths as known today for the three largest oceans—the Pacific, Atlantic, and Indian—are, respectively, 2340 fathoms, 2150 fathoms, and 2180 fathoms. If one includes adjacent seas such as the Caribbean or China seas, these average depths are, respectively, 2200 fathoms, 1820 fathoms, and 2140 fathoms.

But while Bache and the *Challenger* scientists could estimate average water depths, the varied topography of the bottom remained largely unsuspected until the German ships *Meteor* and *Altair* began running lines of echo soundings across the North and South Atlantic about thirty-five years ago. From these soundings, rough charts of major bottom features were drawn up. Even then, the submarine topography could not be worked out in more than a generalized way until the continuous-recording echo sounder became available to oceanographers after the war.

The endpaper map gives only an impression of the complex relief the sea-bottom explorers have found. In the Pacific, for example, Menard estimates some 90 per cent of the ocean-basin floor to be rough and irregular. Much of the remaining 10 per cent smooth area borders continents and islands where sediments eroded from land have covered over the rough bottom. Moreover, the exceptions to this general picture are mountains and deep trenches rather than the smooth, monotonous plains that were once thought to be the rule. The Atlantic does have some sizable abyssal plains that lie in the long, wide basins flanking the mid-Atlantic Ridge. They may be partly due to sediment deposition by turbidity currents. These basins are largely between 12,000 and 18,000 feet deep, with a few deeper spots.

However, the most striking feature of the ocean floor is the mid-oceanic ridge. (See Figure 17.) Bisecting the Atlantic, it runs northward into the Arctic Ocean and southward into the Antarctic. Then it swings into the Indian Ocean where it forks into a branch running northward and another running below Australia to the Eastern Pacific. There it turns northward to disappear under Baja California, while a branch strikes southeastward toward Chile. In many places, especially in the Atlantic and Indian oceans, this vast ridge system is marked by rift valleys that notch its crest.

In the Indian Ocean, the sea-floor crack enters the Gulf of Aden where it appears to join the rift valleys of East Africa.

As a general feature, the ridge is a broad, fractured swell, usually more than 1000 miles wide and rising from under a mile to one and two miles above the adjacent ocean basins. Its crest often has mountains as rugged as the Alps. Broken and offset by fracture zones, it is recognizable as a single system over 35,000 miles long. As such, it ranks with the continents and oceans themselves as one of the three dominant features of our planet's surface. Any theory of how the earth has evolved must take it into account. Certainly it is a very active feature today. It is characterized by an abnormally high flow of heat from the earth's interior and by anomalous departures from the general pattern of the earth's magnetic field. In many places, it is an area of high earthquake activity and volcanism.

In the North and South Atlantic, where the system is known as the Mid-Atlantic Ridge, Menard has pointed out that a line drawn equidistant from the continental slopes bordering these oceans falls on top of the ridge throughout most of its length. In places the mountains of the Mid-Atlantic Ridge break the surface to form islands such as St. Paul's Rocks, Ascension, and The Azores. But, on the average, the peaks fringing the central rift lie 1000 fathoms deep. The bottom of the rift lies another 1000 fathoms deeper. This rift valley is generally 15 to 30 miles wide as measured between the crests of the bordering mountains.

In addition to the deep basins, the sea floor on either side of the Mid-Atlantic Ridge is broken by a number of transverse ridges and rises extending laterally from the central ridge or out from the bordering continents. To draw the geologists' distinction between "ridges" and "rises," the former are defined as elongated elevations with steep, irregular slopes, while the latter have smooth, gentle sides.

Bottom features such as ridges, mountains, and canyons play an important role in the general water circulation. By blocking and channeling the movement of deep water, they influence the mechanism and rate by which the oceans are stirred and overturned. As will be explained in Chapter Seven, this overturning has a significant and little-understood effect on world climate. It is also possible that some bottom water becomes trapped in deep basins. During IGY surveys in the Caribbean, samples of deep water from the enclosed basin in that sea indicate the water is a stagnant mass left over from previous ocean circulation patterns under different climatic or geological conditions. It is "fossil" water that, like the rock-bound remains of ancient animals, has been sealed off by the encircling basin and preserved.

To draw another technical line, ocean "basins" are distinguished from "trenches" in that basins are more or less broadly dimensioned depressions in the ocean floor, while trenches are long, narrow depressions with relatively steep sides. An ocean "deep" is the deepest area of a given depression when the depth exceeds 18,000 feet. With very few exceptions, the deep-ocean trenches are found in the Pacific.

Unlike the Atlantic, the Pacific has no single dominant ridge to set the pattern of its "landscape," although it does have major mountain ranges, as a glance at the endpaper map will show. The topography of the Pacific however, is nowhere near as well known as that of the Atlantic. The former embraces a hemisphere, while the latter is relatively circumscribed. It will take many more years of surveying before the whole Pacific floor has been charted in even a generalized way.

It is doubtful, though, that any more striking feature will ever be found than the deep trenches. It is in these that the greatest recorded depths of the ocean have been plumbed. Besides the *Vitiaz* deep of 36,056 feet officially reported from the Marianas Trench during the IGY (a subsequent sounding of 36,-173 feet was reported by Moscow Radio), soundings in the other trenches indicate maximum depths in the range of about 35,000 feet. It is hard to imagine a chasm so deep that seven Grand Canyons could be piled up on top of each other in it, and so long that it would stretch from New York to Kansas City. Yet this is the way Roger Revelle and Robert L. Fisher of Scripps have described a typical Pacific trench, the Tonga Trench, which Scripps' oceanographers have studied extensively.

Some of the trenches are V-shaped. Others are slightly flattened at the bottom to form more of a narrow U-shaped cross section. They ring the Pacific from Indonesia to South America and are shown on the endpaper map as narrow elongated areas of solid color. Almost everywhere these trenches are associated with mountain building, active volcanism, and earthquakes. They are one of the most geologically interesting features on the surface of the earth, and we shall hear more of them in the next chapter.

One other feature of the Pacific floor should also be mentioned, although, like the trenches, its geological history will be discussed in the following chapter. This is the peppering of individual, often isolated, undersea mountains that rise from the bottom. Many of them have rounded peaks. These are called "seamounts." Others are flattened on top and are known as "guyots" (pronounced *gee-yo,* with a hard *g* as in "get").

Seamounts are scattered through the major ocean basins. However, because of its size, the Pacific probably has the majority. Over 1400 have been found there. Menard thinks this may be only 10 per cent of the total. Although widely scattered, seamounts often form chains or groups. Many Pacific guyots have been found along three lines. There are the Emperor Seamounts running south of Kamchatka. A second line is associated with the Mid-Pacific Mountains. A third stretches between the Marshall and Marianas islands. A group of ten guyots has also been found in the Gulf of Alaska.

Built up by repeated undersea volcanic eruptions and lava flows, seamounts are easy to account for. The guyots are more puzzling. Their flat tops, beveled at the edges, appear to have been carved by waves at the surface. Yet, as will be explained later, they now lie at depths of several thousand feet, intriguing geologists with suggestions of ancient sunken islands.

Although far smaller than the Atlantic and Pacific, the Arctic and Indian oceans claim true oceanic status with average depths exceeding 12,000 feet. By this criterion, the landlocked seas could also make the claim. These are the Black, Caribbean, and Mediterranean seas and the Gulf of Mexico, whose basins are sealed even though their uppermost waters are not completely enclosed. They also have true oceanic depths, exceeding 12,000 feet over large areas. The Gulf of Mexico and the Black Sea are comparatively flat-bottomed while the other two seas have a number of ridges and basins.

Besides the mid-ocean ridge with its rifts and fractures, the Indian Ocean floor has several microcontinents. These rise from the sea bed, sometimes breaking the surface as land features such as Malagasy and the Seychelles. They are distinctly continental in contrast to the oceanic ridge. There are also several abyssal plains. The flattest areas known on earth, their relief rarely exceeds six feet.

The Arctic Ocean is studded with rugged mountains. Traveling under the ice, navigators of such submarines as *Nautilus* and *Skate* have often had to pick their way through mountains with the aid of sonar, just as pilots of small planes visually guide their aircraft through mountain passes. The ocean is bisected by the great Lomonosov Ridge. Discovered in 1948 by Soviet explorers who were stationed on drifting islands of ice, it stretches some 1100 miles between the continental shelves off Ellesmere Island,

FIG. 10 : Arctic Ocean bottom topography shown schematically: 1—Fram Deep; 2—Eurasia Deep; 3—Makarov Deep; 4—Canada Deep. Depth contours shown for 200 meters and 3000 meters; deeps range from 4000 to 5000 meters.

the northernmost part of Canada, and the Soviet Novosibirskiye
Ostrova (New Siberian Islands). Rising an average 9000 to 10,000
feet above the adjacent sea floor and with a width varying from
35 to 125 miles, this ridge dominates the Arctic submarine scenery.

Two other ridges transect the basin. One is a continuation of
the Mid-Atlantic Ridge. The other, the Alpha Ridge, was found
during the IGY by American scientists on the ice island, Station
Alpha. About 560 miles long, it parallels the Lomonosov Ridge
on the North American side. The sea bed on either side of the ridge
slopes gently until it suddenly ends in escarpments 2000 feet high.
The low Marvin Ridge runs between the Alpha and Lomonosov
ridges while a large submarine peninsula, the Chukchi Cap, lies
off northwest Alaska. With its three major ridges, the Arctic is
divided into four deep basins.

The Dustfall

One of the most characteristic features of the deep-sea floor is
the sediments. Drifting slowly down from above or spread broadly
by currents, sediments accumulate like a slow dustfall. Some of
their material has been eroded from the land. Some has drifted
down from the life-filled upper waters. There is even a small
amount that is meteoritic and has come, so to speak, from the
stars.

Many things contribute to the sediments. Rivers carry silts and
sands from the land to be spread over parts of the sea bottom
as muds. Winds bring more land debris that, gradually settling
out of the air, drifts slowly down through the water to combine
with traces of volcanic and meteoritic dusts to form the clays that
cover many of the deepest basins. A host of plants and animals,
many of them microscopic, live in the sunlit surface waters and
drop their skeletons when they grow or die. These remains drift
down to form various kinds of oozes.

As they slowly accumulate upon the bottom, the sediments,
where undisturbed, reflect the climatic and geological conditions
under which they were laid down, the deeper sediments corresponding to the earlier periods. Thus the accumulated layers of
deep-sea sediments are an ordered record of the ages. The art of
reading this record is a subject for the next chapter. Here we
are merely describing the abyssal "dustfall" itself.

The most abundant types of sediments are those already mentioned—the oozes, clays, and land-derived muds. The oozes are made up largely of skeletons of microscopic marine plants and animals. They are generally found in shallower parts of the abyss. The most abundant of these tiny animals are the order Foraminifera, of which one genus, *Globigerina,* often dominates the sediments. Foraminiferal and globigerinal oozes are found widely throughout the major oceans. On the other hand, in some equatorial oozes and especially in the Pacific, the siliceous (silica-containing) remains of tiny animals of the order Radiolaria predominate.

A third type of ooze is found extensively around Antarctica and in the Pacific northeast of Japan. Here the siliceous remains of microscopic one-celled plants called diatoms predominate. Individual diatoms are encased in little glass shells made of silica that, in some species, look exactly like tiny glass boxes. It is these that make up the diatomaceous oozes.

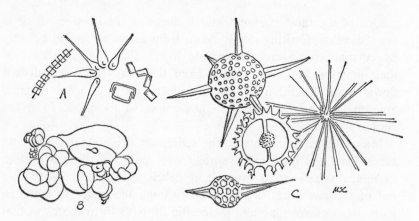

FIG. 11 : Ooze makers: A—Diatoms; B—Foraminifera: C —Radiolarians.

The various organisms named here are present in many different parts of the ocean, whether the sediments are classified after them or not. The name of a particular ooze simply indicates that one type of organism is relatively more abundant than others.

Many of the deeper parts of the ocean basins (below about 14,000 feet) are covered with a claylike sediment. This has been misnamed "red" clay because the first samples found in the South Atlantic happened to be red. But it is more often brown or buff-colored than it is red. As already mentioned, it seems to consist largely of air-borne dust and fine current-borne land debris, a little volcanic dust, and traces of meteorites.

Around the continental margins, the sediments deposited as deep-sea fans are mainly muds with large amounts of silt and interlayered with sand. The occasional appearance of sand and the remains of shallow-water animals in these fans or even on the bottom of the deep basins used to puzzle oceanographers. It now is explained as the deposit of turbidity currents.

The sediments already listed are the principal ones you would find in a standard oceanographic textbook. But so little is known about the ocean bottom that the subject is far from closed. For example, in 1959, Dr. J. Lamar Worzel, assistant director of Lamont Geological Observatory, reported discovery of a vast layer of clean white ash in the sediments of the tropical eastern Pacific. Discovered during an extended cruise of Lamont's research ship *Vema*, the ash consists of very fine-grained fragments of volcanic glass. It is similar to material that has been classed as volcanic ash in other deep-sea deposits. But unlike these other deposits where the ash is dispersed through normal sediments, Worzel's material is a layer of pure ash of great extent, according to initial reports.

So far the ash layer has been traced at least 750 miles north of the equator and about 825 miles south of it. The area is within a few hundred miles of Central and South America and in waters from less than one mile to over three miles deep. The layer ranges from an inch to a foot in thickness. In some places it lies on the surface of the sea bed, in others it is buried as deeply as 120 feet in the bottom sediments. According to Worzel, the ash probably covers a much larger area than was sampled, and was deposited in geologically recent times, perhaps within the past hundred thousand years. Also, the fact that the ash is clear and free from other sedimentary debris indicates that all of it fell within a short period, within a year or so, he says.

Until the full extent, age, and detailed nature of the ash have been determined, one can only speculate about its origin. It may have come from violent eruptions of volcanoes in the nearby Andes. Moreover, if the deposit can be correlated with those from other areas, it may turn out to be evidence of world-wide volcanism. The ash layer has been traced partly by sensitive echo sounding that picked out the echoes returned by this sub-bottom material. In a paper accompanying Worzel's report in the "Proceedings of the National Academy of Sciences," Ewing, Heezen, and David B. Ericson of Lamont noted that a re-examination of echograms taken by the *Vema* indicates similar sub-bottom echoes had been recorded in the South Atlantic and Indian oceans.

The paper noted that most of the ash fragments, called shards, "are in the form of curved, fluted or crumpled films of glass." It added that "since it is very possible that the shards of the Worzel layer were thrown to a great height in the atmosphere by an explosive eruption or eruptions, and since the shards, because of their peculiar shape, would settle more slowly in both air and water than [more] nearly equidimensional . . . particles, an ocean-wide or even global distribution of the Worzel ash is a real possibility." A rich ash layer has already been found in the Gulf of Mexico at the same depth as the Worzel layer in the Pacific. But, unlike the latter, the Gulf ash is dispersed in normal sediments, as is similar ash long known in the North Atlantic.

According to the Ewing-Heezen-Ericson paper, "Apparently we require [to account for the Worzel ash layer] either a single very large volcanic explosion, or simultaneous explosions of many volcanoes, or conceivably a cometary collision [which would have spread its debris over the planet]."

Another unusual type of sediment has given oceanographers a calendar that precisely dates the recent past. These are the varved sediments, that is, sediments stratified in virtually annual layers, first found in the Santa Barbara basin off California in 1958. Dr. John D. Isaacs of Scripps has used them to gain insight into the problem of California's "vanishing" sardines.

In most sediments, bottom-living animals work over the top few inches so much that the record of the recent past is blurred. This hasn't happened to the varved sediments. Animal remains drifting downward in the sea decay as they settle. They also tend to accumulate at some intermediate depth, say several thousand feet. This then becomes an oxygen-poor zone because decay uses up oxygen. This, Dr. Isaacs says, is the key to the varved sediments. He explains that, "If a basin where sediments build up rapidly happens to lie at the depth of this oxygen-poor zone, there will be no bottom-dwelling animals to disturb the sediments. They need oxygen to live. You then get this remarkable calendar. The sediment layers are so well defined, you can resolve the calendar into periods as narrow as five years. With most sediments, the resolution is only about 10,000 years."

The record is written in remains of many organisms. Relative abundances of organisms that like different water conditions tell of past climate. The remains also tell about fish populations. The sediments indicate that California's once-rich sardine fishery was based on a fluke.

Fish scales in the Santa Barbara varves have given an accounting of fish populations for 1000 years and more into the past. They show that, normally, the dominant fish of the area are the Pacific hake, the northern anchovy, and the Pacific sardine in that order. Dr. Isaacs notes that while "we know the sardine has been in abundance for the past 70 years, the previous abundance was 600 years ago. The anchovy has been absent for the past 20 or 30 years. It normally is more abundant than the sardine. There is an interaction between the two species. The sardine is usually in an area where its food depends to some extent on how much the anchovy lets go by in the southward-flowing California Current. It is unusual when the sardine becomes dominant." Thus, the "vanishing" of the sardine seems simply to be a return to normal conditions.

Dr. Isaacs further explains that, "From the varves, we are getting the kind of information you need to manage this fishery, perhaps to favor the more desirable species. If similar varves could be found off India, say, they would help assess the potential of new fisheries in such a food-short area." Actually, Dr. Isaacs is more interested in the prospect of tracing world-wide natural events than in fisheries management. He points out that the earthquake of 1812 seems to be reflected in two layers of the Santa Barbara varves where the record is blurred as though a layer had been shaken. If the varved sediments are world-wide in occurrence, as Dr. Isaacs thinks may be the case, then it may be possible to find out what happened around the world in a period of unusual interest such as 1812 when there were many earthquakes, unusual cold in Europe, and other anomalies.

Probably the most puzzling aspect of the deep-sea sediments, generally, is their surprising thinness. On world averages, sediment thickness in the deep basins is only 600 to 1800 feet. It thickens to 3000 feet or more near the margins. In many places there is little or no recent sediment cover. If the sediments have been accumulating throughout geological time, this implies an average build-up of only a few hundredths of an inch in 10,000 years. That's many times below the rate oceanographers have thought likely. Perhaps there have been periods in the past when sedimentation did proceed more slowly than has been imagined. Perhaps the older, deeper sediments are compacted into a hard material that has different sound-transmitting properties than the unconsolidated muds, clays, and oozes. In that case, the thinness of the sediments would be only an illusion of sonic probing. Or perhaps the ocean basins are much younger than the earth itself, so that the "dustfall" has had a relatively short time to accumulate. The history of the sediments is bound up with the geological history of the ocean basins. But this is a subject for the next chapter.

FOUR

PROBING THE DEEP-SEA FLOOR

Finding out what lies under the ocean floor is an exercise in indirection. The marine geologist is like a space traveler trying to study a planet into whose atmosphere he cannot descend and whose surface is veiled in perpetual cloud. If this planet were the earth, one can imagine how misleading a picture the explorer might get when all he had to go by were samples of ground scraped up from the surface or the profile of the land traced by radar.

With increased use of deep-diving submarines like the bathyscaphe, this blindness will gradually be overcome in studying the sea floor. But, as of this writing, when it comes to studying the deep ocean, the marine geologist is essentially as limited in his explorations as our imaginary interplanetary visitor.

Yet by extracting the maximum information from available clues, marine geologists have managed to sketch at least a generalized picture. In seismic studies they listen to the distant echoes of explosions to trace rock layers in the crust and the juncture of crust and mantle. They extend long fingers of steel into the sea bed to measure the heat flowing up from below which hints the great thermal unrest beneath the crust. They measure minute changes in the pull of gravity to find out something about the density of underlying material. And by learning to read a language far more ancient than the oldest human tongue—the signs and symbols buried in the slowly accumulated sediments—they can piece together some of the history of past epochs.

The Record of the Sediments

To penetrate a few dozen feet into the sediment-covered sea bottom is to go back millions of years in time. Wherever the sediments have been undisturbed by bottom upheavals or eroding currents, the story of past climates and geological events can be read by those who know the "language." Experts are still learning the subtler points of its grammar and enlarging their vocabulary. But they already can extract a good deal of meaning from what to a layman looks no more informative than the colored clays with which children play.

For one thing, the sediments often are neatly layered, indicating sudden changes of climate or certain geological events in the past. Sometimes distinct layers of glacial sediments are found. These are usually characterized by stones dropped by the numerous icebergs that broke off from the edge of the ice sheets. Also, the sediments are full of fossils of tiny marine plants and animals that help date the layers and tell something of past climates as well.

Take the Foraminifera, for example. This order of tiny animals has been one of the most useful for oceanographic research. They have been widely abundant for several hundred million years, and over 15,000 living and extinct species have been identified. With few exceptions they are microscopic. They generally have a calcareous shell, although in some species the shells are formed of sand grains cemented together. Some of the shells look like those of tiny snails. Others are elongated or globular, sometimes formed into little clusters of crystalline bubbles of calcium carbonate. Most of them have several communicating chambers and are perforated by many tiny holes through which the animal protrudes bits of its body as pseudopoda, or "false feet." Hence the name Foraminifera, the "hole bearers."

The shells of these animals are easy to spot in microscope studies of sediments. Some species live their lives floating and drifting near the surface as part of the plankton. Others live on the bottom even at abyssal depths. Many species also have fairly narrow temperature ranges, while extinct species often are typical of specific epochs in the past. Because of this, these curious little animals have been extraordinarily useful in dating sediment layers and in estimating the temperatures of the surface and bottom waters at the time their shells were laid down.

Before oceanographers could read the sediment record, they had to devise ways of recovering that record intact. A simple grab or dredge will suffice to find out what kind of sediment is on the bottom. But to take advantage of the time-ordered layers, oceanographers need a deep and undisturbed sample. They get it by cutting out a sediment core with a kind of hollow pipe dropped into the soft bottom material, like cutting the core out of an apple.

As with many other "firsts" in oceanography, the first deep-sea cores were taken from the *Challenger*. They were only about a foot long and scarcely penetrated the upper layers. In fact, no really long cores were taken until after World War II. Because of this inability to penetrate deeply, the pre-war interest in coring was relatively slight. The German *Meteor* expedition accounted for a good many of the cores taken in those years. Even with heavy weights attached, coring tubes could penetrate no more than a few feet with only gravity to help them punch into the sediments. At one point Charles Piggot of the National Research Council in the United States tried to improve matters by shooting the tubes into the bottom with a special kind of gun. But the method was cumbersome—being as likely to shoot a hole in the bottom of the ship as in the bottom of the sea—and the cores were only up to 10 feet long. Woods Hole oceanographers were already getting cores of that length with the less hazardous gravity corers, and the coring gun was abandoned.

The problem was finally solved during the war by what looks in retrospect like a simple and obvious invention. The inventor was Dr. Börje Kullenberg, now head of the Oceanographic Institute at Göteborg, Sweden. Kullenberg fitted a long coring tube with a piston. In practice, a tripping weight hangs below the corer as it is lowered through the water. Hitting the bottom first, this weight releases the core barrel, which then falls freely, sliding past the piston as it drops. At the same time, the piston is held stationary from the deck of the ship by stopping the winch handling the corer's cable.

The effect of the heavily weighted coring tube sliding past the stationary piston is the same as if the piston were being slowly withdrawn up the tube and "sucking" in the sediment core as it went. In this way cores of undisturbed sediments over 60 feet long are easily forced into the tube.

Kullenberg demonstrated his invention on the Swedish Deep-Sea Expedition (the *Albatross* expedition) led by Dr. Hans Pettersson in 1947–48, when over 300 long cores were taken in the

Atlantic and Pacific. Since then, use of the piston corer has spread widely, although gravity corers, punching out samples by weight alone, still are used in many cases. Thousands of long "piston" cores from the major oceans now have been taken for study and deposition in "core libraries" at oceanographic institutions. For this purpose, corers are often lined with plastic tubes which are removed with the cores and in which the cores can be stored for future study. The Soviets appear to hold the length record. Professor Lev A. Zenkevich of the Institute of Oceanology, has reported cores up to 111 feet long being taken from the *Vitiaz*. At this writing in early 1969, American oceanographers are pioneering use of a drilling ship to drill through thousands of feet of sediment into bedrock of the deep-sea floor in the Atlantic and Pacific. Called Deep-Sea Drilling Project, the effort is managed by Scripps for a consortium of leading marine-research centers. Eventually, such drilling will let oceanographers read the full sediment record and sample the underlying rock as well.

Meanwhile, oceanographers have been learning to read the sediment record with new clarity and precision. In addition to classifying characteristic fossils, they now have a chemical thermometer for reading ancient temperatures and a short-term "atomic clock" for dating fairly recent deposits.

The Oxygen Thermometer

Some of nature's most telling distinctions are the slight differences between almost identical materials. The weight difference of three parts in 238 between two isotopes of uranium, for example, is the difference between an atomic bomb and a harmless piece of metal. So it is with the oxygen in the air we breath and in the water we drink. This oxygen is made up of three isotopes—oxygen-16, oxygen-17, and oxygen-18—the lightest being by far the most abundant. Chemically these isotopes are indistinguishable. But almost imperceptible differences in their relative abundances have become a key to the past.

When water evaporates, the three isotopes of oxygen in the water molecules go off at different rates, the lightest evaporating slightly faster than the others. This leaves the water a little richer in the heavier isotopes. This suggests, among other things, that there should be a difference between the isotope ratios in the continually

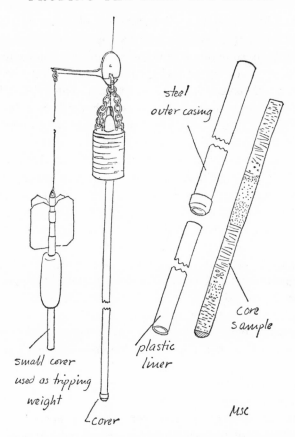

steel
outer casing

core
sample

plastic
liner

small corer
used as tripping
weight

corer

MSC

FIG. 12 : Kullenberg corer. Hitting the bottom first, the small corer releases the main coring tube. In this way (see text), sediment samples up to 70 feet and more in length have been taken. The small corer collects a comparison sample of the upper few feet of sediments, which are the part of the sample most likely to be compressed and distorted in the long core.

renewed fresh water of the land and the ratios in the sea, where evaporation has gone on for a long time. Moreover, the compounds involving carbon and oxygen, called carbonates, which make up the shells and skeletons of many aquatic animals, should reflect the oxygen isotope ratio of the water in which they were formed.

With this in mind in 1947, Dr. Harold Urey calculated oxygen-isotope uptake in the shells of marine animals and made an unexpected discovery. He hoped to find a way to tell whether ancient

carbonate deposits, such as limestones, had been laid down in
fresh water or in salt. But as often happens in research, he came
up instead with something quite unlooked for and much more
valuable to oceanographers. His study showed that the relative
concentration of oxygen isotopes in the carbonates depends partly
on the temperature of the water in which they were formed. In
his own words, "I suddenly found myself with a geological thermometer on my hands."

But at that time it was an extremely difficult thermometer to
read. For one thing, a difference of one degree Celsius in water
temperature corresponds to a difference of about two hundredths
of one per cent in the ratio of oxygen-18 to oxygen-16 in the
carbonates. The best that could be done in 1947 was to detect
a difference of one fifth of one per cent in isotope ratios. This
corresponded to a temperature range of ten degrees Celsius on
the Urey thermometer. Given the relatively stable temperatures of
the ocean, this ten degree range of error could be the difference
between glacial and temperate climates.

An important part of the subsequent development of the Urey
thermometer has been a continuing increase in the sensitivity of
mass spectrometers, the instruments used to measure isotope ratios.
By the early 1950s, the sensitivity was good enough to fix ancient
ocean temperatures to within half a degree C. This enabled Dr.
Cesare Emiliani of the University of Miami to begin temperature
analyses of some of the *Albatross* long cores, which were by then
available for study, and some of a library of 1000 cores that
had been collected by Lamont using modified Kullenberg equipment.

There now was another source of error to be contended with,
however. Urey had originally assumed that oxygen was the same
throughout the ocean. But studies at sea showed that oxygen-
isotope ratios vary from place to place. There is a difference between tropical and Arctic waters and between mid-ocean and inshore waters, where local evaporation and outpouring rivers have
a noticeable effect. This introduces a corresponding uncertainty
in readings of the oxygen thermometer, which are based on estimates of isotope ratios in ancient seas. It is hard to know how true
the thermometer reads when the ratios may reflect fresh-water
dilution or unknown but normal differences between parts of the
same ocean, differences not related to temperature.

This uncertainty is reduced by studying fossils of animals that lived in the open sea away from inshore disturbances and by careful geographical selection of cores. It may also be possible to estimate the oxygen ratios of ancient sea water from those in a compound formed at the same time as the fossils and reflecting the water's isotopic make-up. On the whole, Emiliani says that "oxygen-isotopic composition of Pleistocene, Tertiary, and even Mesozoic fossils may be reasonably interpreted in terms of temperature . . . Paleozoic fossils may not be."

Starting with cores brought up from over 10,000 feet in the equatorial Pacific, Emiliani began to develop the general climatic outline of the Cenozoic era, the great age of mammals. He looked first for long-term trends. These would most likely show up in bottom-water temperatures which are less susceptible to short-term fluctuations than surface temperatures. Formed in restricted regions of the Arctic and Antarctic, this water would follow the trends of polar climates.

For this purpose Emiliani studied the fossils of bottom-living Foraminifera. These showed that thirty-two million years ago the Pacific bottom from which the cores had come had a temperature of about 51° Fahrenheit. Twenty-two million years ago it had dropped to 44° F. When the latest series of ice ages began, it had fallen close to the present bottom temperatures prevailing in all oceans—just two or three degrees above freezing. For the past half million years it has fluctuated around an average slightly lower than the present average bottom temperature.

Thus, according to Emiliani, thirty-two million years ago, polar waters were as warm as those of temperate latitudes today. This correlates well with fossil evidence of evergreen forests on Greenland where thousands of feet of icecap now sit. The drop to near-freezing temperatures at the beginning of the Pleistocene glaciation indicates a frozen Antarctic, while the temperature fluctuations of the past five hundred thousand or so years reflect climate changes associated with the advances and retreats of the glaciers.

The next step was to pin down the chronology of the ice ages. A certain amount of chronology could be deduced from the structures of the cores themselves. But Emiliani needed a more precise frame of reference than the biological characteristics of fossils alone could provide. This is where the short-term "atomic clock" came into the story.

The method is similar to that used in dating rocks, except that in this case organic remains are involved. It was developed by Dr. Willard F. Libby when he was with the University of Chicago. The timekeeper is carbon-14, a radioactive isotope of carbon that occurs naturally in the atmosphere in known concentrations. As long as plants and animals are alive, their bodies maintain the same relative concentration of carbon-14 as found in their environment. But after they die, the carbon-14 slowly decays away at a fixed known rate. Experts use this rate to date organic remains for intervals up to about thirty-five thousand years in the past.

To help Emiliani use the carbon "clock," Hans Suess and Meyer Rubin, at the Radiocarbon Laboratory of the United States Geological Survey, undertook to analyze a number of cores from the Atlantic, the Caribbean, and the Mediterranean. This time Emiliani selected Foraminifera that lived within a few hundred feet of the surface, because the glacial record would show up most clearly in fluctuations of surface temperatures. With the help of Suess and Rubin, he found that the peak of the last ice age came about eighteen thousand years ago.

At that time, when the ice reached as far south as Chicago and Berlin, tropical ocean temperatures dropped significantly. In the Caribbean, for example, the surface temperature at 15° North Latitude was 68° to 72° Fahrenheit compared to a present-day 84° F. In the equatorial mid-Atlantic the temperature was 62° F. compared to a current surface temperature of 78° F. David Ericson of Lamont, using oxygen temperatures found by Emiliani and carbon-14 dates worked out at Lamont by Wallace Broecker and J. L. Kulp, has shown that the Atlantic and Caribbean waters warmed up significantly about eleven thousand years ago. This now is widely accepted as the probable end of the last glacial stage.

With the radiocarbon dates for the first thirty-five thousand years well established, Emiliani was then able to work out a tentative chronology for earlier parts of his cores. One way of doing this was to assume that the sediments accumulated throughout the core at the same rate they accumulated during the well-dated period. In itself, this was unreliable, because the rate of accumulation for bottom clays can vary by a factor of ten or more with different geological and climatic conditions. But by comparing his cores with others dated by other techniques, such as careful study of fossils, he cut down the margin of error.

By 1966, with the help of still other dating methods, he had a feel for long-term trends. Limited data suggest a decline in the earth's average surface temperature amounting to 5° to 10° C. over the past 150 million years. This, he said, may be due to a drop in the sun's output. Superimposed on this long-term decline, there seem to have been cycles in which temperature swung between extremes several degrees Celsius apart over periods of 20 million years.

For the Quaternary, Emiliani said glaciation may have begun only about 440,000 years ago. He thought the temperature fluctuations he has dated to that point encompass all the Pleistocene ice ages. This is a short span. Ericson, Maurice Ewing, Goesta Wollin, and others at Lamont have traced Pleistocene history through many long cores. They date its beginning about 1.5 million years ago. However, the Pleistocene is sometimes defined to include the time span identified by a group of mammals known as the Villafranchian. Many experts now think this began 3.0 to 3.5 million years ago. By this definition, the Pleistocene opened at that time with mountain building and a cooling climate with the major glaciations starting halfway into the epoch. This scheme is adopted in this book.

In 1965, the International Association for the Study of the Quaternary (INQUA) officially defined the Pleistocene as the time since a species of bottom-living Foraminifera, *Hyalinea (Anomalina) baltica,* first appeared in late Cenozoic deposits at Le Castella, Calabria in southern Italy. Until this is dated, the question of our ice epoch's beginning is open.

Beneath the Sediments

For the most part, the upper few dozen feet of sediment, such as Emiliani has been studying, is the only part of the sea bottom directly accessible to the oceanographer's instruments. All that is known about what lies below that level has been inferred from such things as seismic, gravitational, magnetic, and heat-flow studies. These are the tools that point the way for exploring by indirection.

As far as you and I are concerned, the slight variations in

gravity from place to place on the earth's surface are a geophysical refinement we can forget about. The small fractions of an ounce that are involved are of little consequence for most practical purposes. But they are a useful tool to geologists in studying masses beneath the surface that they cannot reach directly.

One way of doing this is by timing the swing of a pendulum. The time it takes for a pendulum of given length and mass to make one complete swing back and forth—the "period" of the pendulum, as it is called—depends on the local pull of gravity. This pull depends in turn on distance from the earth's center and on the mass of the underlying material. The greater the pull of gravity, the faster the pendulum swings, and vice versa. Thus careful timing of a pendulum gives a clue to the heaviness of the material under the instrument. Salt domes, for example, can be detected in this way because they have a different density than the surrounding sediments have.

The first gravity measurements at sea were made on the steamship *Fram* when it was locked in the arctic ice during Fridtjof Nansen's polar expedition of 1893–96. With the ship trapped, Nansen had a stable platform from which to work. Since it is hard to time a pendulum on a rocking ship, further gravity measurements at sea had to wait until some way was found to get a stable platform on the open ocean.

Vening Meinesz, a Dutch geologist, found such a platform in the submarine. Submerged beyond the play of wind and waves, a submarine is stable enough to work with a pendulum. Meinesz made his first gravity measurements at sea in 1923 and thereafter studied gravity in all the major oceans. But submarines are not readily available to oceanographers. As recently as the start of the IGY, only about five thousand gravity measurements had been made at sea throughout the world, and twelve hundred of them were taken by Meinesz himself before the end of World War II. These measurements had added to geologists' knowledge, but their total was insignificant compared to the vast area of the ocean. Then the invention marine geologists had been waiting for came along.

On November 22, 1957, Worzel of Lamont made the first successful measurements of gravity from a surface ship in the open ocean. He used an instrument designed by Anton Graf of Munich, Germany, which was mounted on a gyro-stabilized platform on board the navy ship U.S.S. *Compass Island,* one of the few ships on which such a platform has been installed. Unlike the pendulum whose bob responds to the slightest roll or pitch of the ship, the Graf instrument detects gravity variations by measuring slight shifts up or down in the end of a horizontal aluminum boom. The small boom is suspended and pivoted near one end by specially designed springs. These both support the boom and allow its other end to move up or down with changes in local gravity. This arrangement is much less susceptible to outside interference than a pendulum, yet is sensitive and accurate. Combined with the gyro-stabilized platform, it mastered the problems of measuring gravity at sea.

Meanwhile, Roger Revelle at Scripps and Arthur Maxwell of the Woods Hole Oceanographic Institution in the United States and Sir Edward Bullard at Cambridge University in England developed an ingenious way of measuring the heat flowing out of the ocean bottom. In particular, Revelle and Maxwell, who was formerly at Scripps, have used this technique widely in the Pacific. The instrument involved is simple. It is essentially a probe about 10 feet long and 1 to 1.6 inches in diameter which measures the temperature difference in the sediments at points near its top and bottom. At the same time, a core is taken. Back in the laboratory, the rate at which the material in the core conducts heat is measured. By using the observed temperature difference, the heat flow in the sediments can then be calculated. Thus an important geophysical effect that can't be measured directly can be determined indirectly by using the physical laws of heat conduction to interpret other characteristics that can be measured.

These various ways of probing the sea bottom have revealed a quite different structure from that underlying the continents. For one thing, the seismic studies confirmed that the earth's crust is relatively thinner under the oceans. Geologists had suspected this ever since gravity studies made during the first geodetic survey of India in 1855 indicated a thinning of the crust seaward from the subcontinent.

Because the different bottom layers are revealed by the different speeds at which sound travels through them, geologists often talk about them in terms of their characteristic speeds of sound. Thus the typical downward sequence of bottom layers as they now are known is as follows: first at the top there is a layer of sediment where the average sound velocity is 7000 feet per second; then comes a rock layer of 16,000 feet per second; then a second rock layer of 22,000 feet per second. Below this is the mantle, where sound travels at an average speed of 26,000 feet per second.

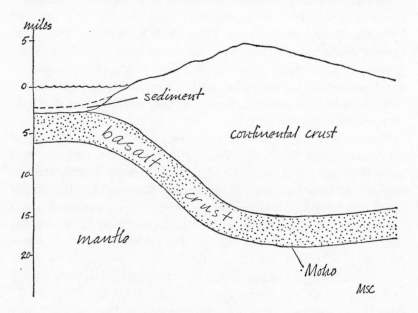

FIG. 13 : Crust beneath the land and sea.

There is a distinct break or boundary between the non-crystalline material of the mantle and the next higher rocky layer, where the speed of sound is significantly lower. This is the "Mohorovičić discontinuity," or more simply the "Moho," which separates the crust from the mantle. Beneath the continents, the Moho is 20 to 25 miles deep. But under the sea it comes within three to eight miles of the ocean floor.

Finding a thin crust under the oceans has helped geologists explain the deep basins which formerly were something of a puzzle. The relatively high sound velocity in the mantle has been taken to mean the mantle material is denser than that of the crust above. Geologists believe that the light crust literally floats on the heavier mantle. Thus, if the crust under the oceans were as thick as it is under the continents, the ocean bottom should float as high as the land. But with a thin, somewhat heavier crust, the ocean basins would be expected to float lower.

Both gravity and seismic measurements show the thin crust of the oceans is indeed heavier than that under the land. The lower layer may be a volcanic rock called basalt, while the upper layer might be some kind of sedimentary rock, such as limestone, or even a lava. In any event, the studies show that, on the whole, the ocean crust is nicely balanced against the continents, just as a relatively thin and dense block of wood floats lower in the water than a thick lighter one. Finding this "isostatic balance," as it is called, has helped tidy up the geologists' over-all picture of the crust.

On the other hand, the heat-flow data have been a surprise. Much of the heat flowing up through the continents is generated by radioactive materials which have been concentrated in the granitic continental rocks. The thinner igneous rocks of the ocean crust don't have much of this "hot" material. The heat flow there was expected to be much smaller, since it would be due mainly to the slow cooling of the earth's interior. Yet the average heat flow upward through the sea bed has been found in general to be about the same as that of the land. This hints that radioactivity

FIG. 14: Trenches of the Pacific (shaded). See endpaper map also.

under the oceans is still distributed through the mantle, where its heat causes unrest and convection even in the hard mantle material. This material is believed to be as rigid as steel yet plastic enough to flow like very cold molasses under forces that act on it for long periods of time. Although the meaning of the heat-flow data is still unclear, this interpretation fits with the other indications that much of the ocean floor lies over regions where the interior of the earth is unusually restless.

Migrating Continents

The scene of the planet's most intense earthquakes is the zone of trenches that circle the Pacific. As shown on the endpaper map, all run parallel to upthrusting island archipelagoes or nearby continental mountain ranges and are accompanied by lines of explosive volcanoes. This zone is well characterized by its geological nickname, the "ring of fire."

Many geologists think the ring of fire may be due to the same forces that underlie one of the most spectacular features of our planet, the world-girdling Mid-Oceanic Ridge. Both may be caused by convection within the mantle. Rising beneath the ridge, these currents are thought to spread outward and sink again beneath the continents. (See Figure 16.) This would explain the high heat flow and earthquakes along the ridge. The regions where the convection currents descend would also be disturbed. Trenches could be formed as the descending currents drag the crust down with them. In fact, the ocean floor itself may be formed by the lateral spread of material welling up along the Mid-Oceanic Ridge. Growing horizontally as this material moves outward, the floor may be pushing the continents apart.

The notion of drifting continents was advanced early in this century, especially by the German meteorologist Alfred Wegener. The Austrian geologist Eduard Suess had already shown that the outlines of the continents more or less fit together into a single mass like somewhat poorly fitting pieces of a jigsaw puzzle. He named his hypothetical supercontinent Gondwanaland after a province in India. Wegener and others used this basic concept to explain similarities in glaciation, fossils, and rock formations on different continents. Their various theories proposed that one, or at most two, supercontinents broke up some 200 million years

FIG. 15 : The Pacific's Ring of Fire: The band of earthquakes and volcanoes paralleling the line of the trenches.

ago. However, they couldn't explain what forces moved the continents. Most geologists found it hard to conceive of land masses
plowing through the ocean floor. They dismissed the idea as ab-
surd. But new evidence revived it.

The first encouragement came from fossil magnetism. When
rocks rich in iron oxide are formed, they are magnetized by the
earth's magnetic field. This happens readily when the rock is hot
enough. But when it cools, the magnetism is frozen in. If the
earth's field later changes strength or direction, magnetization of
the rock is unaffected. Studies by British physicist P. M. S. Blackett and others showed that the north magnetic pole had wandered
in a curve around what now is the North Pacific. The record of
the rocks on various continents agree in this. But each continent
shows the track of the pole displaced 20° to 30° to the west.
The records would harmonize if the continents themselves have
moved with respect to each other during the past 150 million
years. By the late 1950s, the magnetic studies were convincing

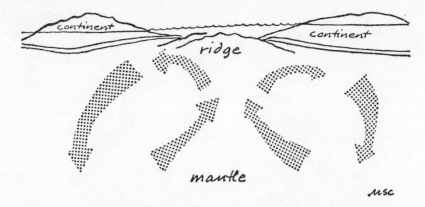

FIG. 16 : Growth of the sea bed. According to a widely accepted theory, earth's mantle is stirred deeply by slow-moving convection currents in its plastic rock. These well up beneath the Mid-Ocean Ridge. From there, they spread laterally, slowly expanding the sea bottom and push-ing continents about. The sea bed may grow outward from the ridge as much as several centimeters a year. The rock currents sink again beneath the continents to complete the convection cycle.

enough to make Wegener's idea respectable again. Since then, many marine geologists have adapted it to explain the Mid-Oceanic Ridge and the evolution of the ocean floor.

Prof. Harry H. Hess of Princeton University and Dr. Robert S. Dietz suggest that continental drift is due to convection currents in the mantle that reach to the sea bed. In their view, the sea floor may have no distinct crust. It may be formed by the lateral flow of mantle material that upwells along the Mid-Oceanic Ridge system. Moving outward, this material would tend to pull the ridge apart, as the rifts in it suggest. The outward moving ma-terial would cause the sea bed to grow and the continents to move at rates of up to a few centimeters a year. The question of how the continents move through the ocean floor doesn't arise. They move as the floor grows.

Dietz suggests that, sometimes, a continent doesn't move. Then the spreading ocean floor pushes under the continental rise the pile of sediment at the foot of the continental slope. It tilts and compresses this sediment, forcing it against the slope to form a new continental slope. In this way, the margins of the continents may be built up. It is also possible that a moving continent may overrun the sea bed. Some geologists think that North America has overrun the western Pacific floor so that part of the East Pacific Rise now runs up the Gulf of California and under the Western United States.

While a number of geologists subscribe to some form of the Hess-Dietz theory, others, such as Heezen, believe the ocean floor is growing and continents moving because of a general expansion of the earth. Heezen thinks the cleft of the Red Sea and the rift valleys of East Africa are part of the rift system of the Mid-Atlantic Ridge. He says the African rifts don't show the growth of ocean-type floor to be expected if mantle currents are involved. Yet others consider the Red Sea area a prime example of the ocean-building process. In 1966, Dr. A. S. Laughton of Britain's National Institute of Oceanography told the Second International Oceanographic Congress in Moscow that "We see in the Gulf of Aden the possibility of a young ocean being formed in the movement of Arabia away from Africa."

Meanwhile, the jigsaw puzzle game has been revived in support of continental drift. Sir Edward C. Bullard has pointed out that there is a better fit between continents using offshore contours rather than present shorelines. Using the 500-fathom line in a computer study, he was able to fit South America's bulge snugly into Africa's bight. Dietz and Walter P. Sproll of the ESSA Institute of Oceanography have made computer studies in which they fit today's land masses into two supercontinents, Laurasia and Gondwanaland, rather than Wegener's single mass, Pangaea. They think Gondwanaland was centered over what now is the Indian Ocean. About 150 million years ago, it broke apart into Africa, Antarctica, Australia, India, Madagascar, and South America. Laurasia split into Asia, Europe, and North America.

Still other scientists trace the growth of the sea floor in bands of fossil magnetism. Over the past ten million years, the earth's magnetic field has reversed itself several times. In 1963, F. J. Vine and D. H. Mathews at Cambridge University suggested that magnetic field patterns associated with the Mid-Oceanic Ridge reflect these reversals. They pointed out that, as rock wells up along the ridge and moves outward, it should be magnetized according to the earth field prevailing at the time. It would retain this magnetization when it cooled even though the earth field later changed, while newly upwelled rock would be magnetized differently. This

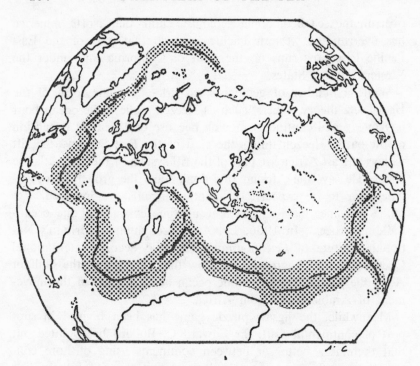

FIG. 17 : Mid-Oceanic Ridge with central rift valleys indicated.

should produce bands of magnetically distinctive rock on either
side of the ridge and running parallel to it. Studies of parts of the
Mid-Oceanic Ridge system soon tended to confirm this. In late
1966, for example, Dr. J. R. Heirzler and W. C. Pitman III of
Lamont reported a study of the Pacific-Antarctic Ridge running
between New Zealand and South America. They found magnetically distinctive zones symmetrically distributed on either side of
the ridge. This was strong evidence for a series of rock bands of
different magnetization running parallel to the ridge. Like the
growth rings of a tree, they indicate an outward growth of the
ocean floor. The Deep-Sea Drilling Project has begun to back up
such evidence. In the autumn of 1968, project scientists drilled
into the sea bed at five sites along a line from New York to
Dakar across the Mid-Atlantic Ridge. They found the sea bed to
be progressively younger as they approached the ridge. This too
implies outward growth of the floor.

Suggestive as all this is, continental drift still has its critics.

Vladimir V. Belousov, one of the world's leading geophysicists, told the 1966 Moscow conference ". . . there are very great difficulties because of the structure and development of the continents. . . . If the continents move, then the upper mantle must move too, as deep down as 700 to 1000 kilometers. From a mechanical viewpoint, it is more difficult to move both the crust and mantle than just the crust itself."

Wegener's once-despised idea has thus become the center of intensive research and debate. "Continental drift," says Dietz, "seems to be an example of an 'outrageous hypothesis' which well may turn out to be right." Meanwhile, geologists are wrestling with the question of oceanic depths as well as growth of the ocean floor. Has the sea bed risen or sunk throughout geological time? Or has it remained more or less stable vertically? The Pacific, in particular, poses these questions as oceanographers study its coral reefs and flat-topped guyots.

Sunken Islands

Marine geologists have long been familiar with seamounts which seem to be simply volcanic mounds that never reached the surface to become islands. But during World War II a young geologist from Princeton University made an intriguing discovery. He was Dr. Harry Hess, who was serving as a naval reserve officer at the time. As navigator and later commander of the transport U.S.S. *Cape Johnson,* he made many voyages in the western and central Pacific. During these voyages and in spite of the press of shipboard duties, Hess kept his interest in the ocean floor alive by studying the ship's echo-sounder records. One day he found a unique profile of a seamount. Instead of the usually rounded dome, its top had been shaved flat as if by a giant carpenter's plane.

None of the charts showed any seamounts like this. It was too big and flat to be a volcanic crater. It looked exactly like a low island whose surface had been eroded by waves. Yet it lay several hundred fathoms deep. Could this be an ancient sunken island that had once lain at the surface when the bottom stood higher or the water level lower, the first of its kind known to geological science?

Hess later found nineteen more of these flat-topped seamounts himself and unearthed a good many more in the records of the navy's Hydrographic Office. He concluded that they were indeed ancient drowned islands, which he named "guyots" after the nineteenth-century French geographer Arnold Guyot.

The next question was: When had these ancient islands been at the surface? Hess thought they were very old, dating back to the Precambrian era, over five hundred million years ago. In his view, they had been submerged by the slow rise in sea level as sediments accumulated since that time, displacing the water and bending down the crust with their weight. But according to the present consensus, the epoch of submergence was much more recent.

One of the most thorough studies of a line of guyots was made by a joint Scripps-Naval Electronics Laboratory expedition to the Mid-Pacific Mountains in 1950. The resulting monograph by Dr. Edwin L. Hamilton of N.E.L. shows that the guyots associated with this undersea range were once a chain of basalt islands that sank quite rapidly in the Cretaceous period, 60 to 125 million years ago.

Although the Mid-Pacific Mountains had been known as a line of seamounts before 1950, the Scripps-Navy expedition was the first to delineate this structurally as a great undersea ridge upon which seamounts and guyots rise as peaks. The geological history of these guyots thus is intimately connected with that of the ridge itself.

Hamilton has worked out the following hypothetical history for these mountains. At an undetermined time in the past, basalt rocks and associated material, like those of the Hawaiian Islands, were extruded from cracks in the sea bed. These formed the ridges and volcanoes of the Mid-Pacific Mountains. Eventually some of the high peaks emerged to become islands.

As the mountains grew, their weight compacted underlying sediments and bowed down the crust until isostatic equilibrium had been established. Actually, the crust under the Pacific is strong and elastic, so that the weight of structures like these growing mountains is borne partly by the crust and partly by the buoyant isostatic pressures. By the time the peaks had emerged to become islands, much of this downward adjustment had taken place, so the peaks remained above the surface for some time. That is when the waves planed off their tops and when reef corals began to grow.

Then something upset the balance, and the mountains began

to sink. They sank so quickly they reached the 50- to 85-fathom depth limit of the corals faster than the reefs could grow upward. Perhaps the weight of the mountains became too great and the whole range broke through the crust and foundered. Perhaps they sank as part of a more general subsidence of the sea floor. Whatever the cause, to quote Hamilton, "they remain today as the oldest uneroded mountains known on earth. They are fossil landforms preserved in the depths of the sea where they are disturbed only by light currents and the slow rain of . . . material from the waters above."

It is a moot question among marine geologists how much the submergence of the guyots has been due to a sinking of the crust, as suggested by Hamilton and some others, and how much it has been due to a rise in sea level by the addition of new water from deep inside the earth, as some geologists believe is happening. Either mechanism or a combination of them would give the same submergence effect. But before considering this further, let's take a look at the problem of coral reefs and atolls, for these are linked with the guyots in geological history.

Living Reefs

A coral reef is a triumph of life. Exposed to the incessant attack of waves and surf, the corals build firmest where the seas run heaviest. The eroding forces of wind-driven water, which no cliff of dead rock can withstand, have met their match in a relative of the soft-bodied sea anemones and some one-celled plants of the algae group.

Coral polyps, as individual coral animals are called, are little more than flexible bottles with a crown of food-catching tentacles. They belong to the great phylum of the Coelenterata, named from the Greek words for "hollow-boweled," and are almost literally "all stomach." Like their close relatives, the sea anemones, they live their lives quietly attached to a solid substratum, eating bits of animal food brought to them by the water. Such unenterprising animals would have been of little account geologically if they had not evolved an ability to secrete a lime skeleton that gives strength and permanence to their otherwise ephemeral bodies.

Coral reefs are essentially accumulations of these calcium carbonate skeletons. But these could not by themselves form a strong

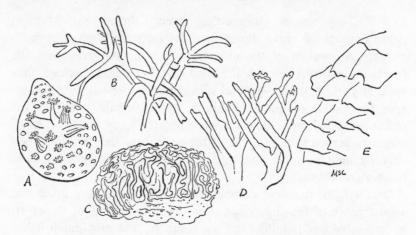

FIG. 18 : Coral colonies: A—showing individual polyps;
B—staghorn; C—brain coral; D—elkhorn; E—shingle.

enough aggregate to withstand the pounding of waves and surf.
That is where the algae, members of the Corallinaceae family,
come in. They are hardy organisms that thrive even in the zone
of breakers on the seaward edge of the reef. They secrete a hard
pink coating of lime that covers and cements the dead coral skeletons into a firm but porous limestone. Sometimes the algal deposit
accounts for half and more of the reef material. In the Indian
and Pacific oceans the algae also form a low hummocky ridge at
the very edge of the reef on the seaward side which acts as a
breakwater to protect the flat top of the reef behind. On reefs
where this protection is lacking, as in the West Indies, storm
waves cause considerable damage.

Some corals live in temperate waters and at considerable depths.
But the range of the reef builders is more restricted. They live in
harmony with a one-cell algal plant called zooxanthella, which is
embedded within them. Biologists call such an arrangement "beneficial symbiosis," a relationship in which two dissimilar organisms
live together to their mutual benefit and often could not survive
independently. In the case of the corals, the algae get food and
carbon dioxide from the animals' metabolism, while the polyps are
cleaned of waste products and may also get oxygen and perhaps
some carbohydrates in return. The exact nature of the relationship
between these organisms is hazy. But as far as active reef building

is concerned, the range of the polyps seems to be limited at least partly by the needs of the plants.

The zooxanthellae are photosynthetic; that is, they can live and grow only in waters where the sunlight can reach them. This puts a shallow depth limit on the reef corals and a premium on clear water that transmits a maximum of light. Although some live reef corals have been found as deep as 580 feet, they generally seem limited to less than 300 feet, with an optimum depth, from the viewpoint of the algae, of 12 to 15 feet. Zooxanthellae also

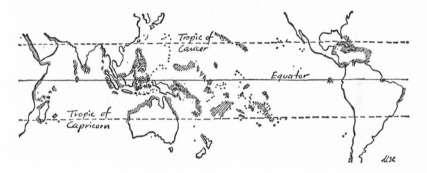

FIG. 19 : Range of the reef corals (shaded).

grow best in warm waters of normal salinity. This means a water temperature range from about 68° Fahrenheit to the low 90's, and a salinity range of about 27 to 40 parts per thousand, whereas the ocean average is about 35 parts per thousand. Thus depth or turbid waters that cut down light transmission, suffocating sediments, extremes of temperature, and fresh-water dilution are all enemies of the reef-building coral polyp and its symbiotic algae. They restrict their range to relatively clear shallow waters of the tropics.

The corals reproduce both by the budding of one individual from another and by release of free-floating larvae into the sea. When a larva comes to rest on a suitable substratum, it secretes its skeleton and begins to bud off new polyps. These are all distinct individuals. Yet groups of them remain physically tied together by a common digestive tract in colonies of marvelous complexity. Sometimes colonies grow as large as eight to ten feet in diameter, containing thousands of individuals. Some look like the branching antlers of stags or elks (the staghorn and elkhorn corals). Others form rounded masses whose grooved surfaces look like brain tissue (the brain corals), and so forth. Much of the beauty of the reefs is due to the curious structures of the coral colonies.

Reef corals will grow on any solid substratum where the water conditions are favorable. This results in a variety of reef forms. However, there are three dominant reef types—fringing, barrier, and atoll. Fringing reefs grow out directly from the coasts of many islands with scarcely a break. In some places one can wade out several miles on these shallow platforms. There is little active coral growth on top of such reefs, which often are covered with an algal crust. But corals live in holes and channels within the porous reef platform and grow profusely at its steep outer edge, where driving seas bring a continual supply of oxygen and planktonic food.

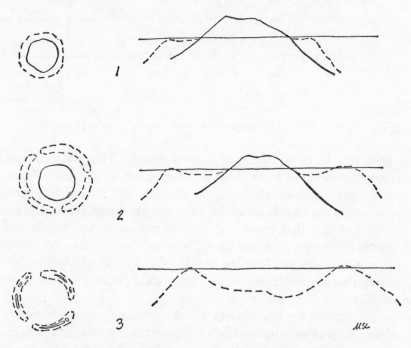

FIG. 20 : Types of coral reef: 1—fringing; 2—barrier; 3—atoll. (Vertical views left, cross-sectional views right.)

Barrier reefs are what their name implies. They are separated from the coast line and its fringing reefs by lagoon channels up to 180 feet deep, although these are occasionally cut across by out-shoots of a fringing reef. They stand literally as a barrier between land and the open sea. The most famous of these, perhaps, is the Great Barrier Reef of Australia extending for 1200 miles along the northeastern coast. It is really a series of many individual reefs that are separated by as much as 150 miles from land at the southern end.

Atolls, such as Bikini and Eniwetok, are essentially coral reefs that enclose a shallow lagoon. The word "atoll" comes from the language of the Maldive Islands, where each governmental district consists of a reef enclosing a lagoon and is called "atolu." Some atolls are ring-shaped, but more are irregular. They are the most common type of reef in mid-ocean and are found by the hundreds in tropical Pacific and Indian Ocean waters.

Crowding together in shallow surface waters, corals and algae grow profusely upward toward the sunlight, while wanderers from the main colonies may be found 200 to 300 feet deep. Wherever this upward growth reaches the surface, waves continually attack it, breaking off pieces and grinding them into fine white coral sand. Some of this collects on quieter parts of the reef and on the land. The low narrow islands that grow up on parts of atolls are built largely of this material. Some of the debris also rolls down the steep outer face of the reef and collects as a pile of "talus" of coral sediments over which the growing edge of the reef may build seaward. But the vigor of the reef builders is more than a match for the destructiveness of the sea.

It is easy to see how this living mechanism constructs fringing reefs. Wherever there is a gently sloping shore in favorable waters, the corals and algae can establish themselves and grow upward until they break the surface. Then, growing against the forces of the sea, they will build outward until the bottom falls away too deeply to support further growth. But how could these organisms that need shallow sunlit water have built up barrier reefs from the depths offshore where the bottom often drops sharply into the abyss on the seaward side of the reef? Or how could they have built up atolls that rise steeply from mid-ocean depths? These questions were uppermost in the mind of young Charles Darwin in 1835 as he prepared to sail into the Pacific from the western coast of South America during the voyage of H.M.S. *Beagle* (1831 –36).

This is the famous expedition on which Darwin served as geologist and naturalist and which, in his own words, "determined my whole career." It is the cruise during which he began collecting the evidence for, and began formulating the central points of, his theory of evolution. But he was also concerned about the problem of the coral reefs.

The subject engrossed him during the last year of the voyage. Indeed, his theory on coral-reef origins was worked out deductively before the *Beagle* left South America and before he ever saw any of the great Indo-Pacific reefs. He afterward noted in his autobiography that it was the only hypothesis he ever formulated that he did not have to change later. The theory was presented briefly before the (British) Geological Society in 1837 and in detail in his first major scientific publication, "The Structure and Distribution of Coral Reefs" (1842). Like the theory of evolution, but on a far less public scale, it was destined to spawn a scientific debate that has remained lively to the present day.

The Coral-Reef Controversy

Darwin's coral-reef theory is simple. If the limestone reefs now extend below the depth range of living coral, then the lower parts of the reefs must at one time have stood higher in the water. For two years he had been studying the evidences for slow intermittent uplifting of some land areas with concomitant erosion and deposition of sediments in low basins which gradually sank under the accumulating weight. He found many effects of these earth movements along South American shores. ". . . it was easy," he explained in his autobiography, "to replace in imagination the continued deposition of sediment by the upward growth of coral. To do this was to form my theory of the formation of barrier-reefs and atolls." Thus, he reasoned, if something caused the sea bottom to sink slowly, and the coral reefs with it, the sun-seeking reef organisms would build the reefs upward in pace with the rate of sinking. Provided the sinking was not too rapid, as Darwin believed, this seemed a simple and adequate explanation of many of the great barrier reefs and atolls.

For example, a volcanic island might rise above the sea. At first erosion and sedimentation would keep the surrounding waters turbid and clear of coral. But eventually the polyps would establish themselves as a fringing reef. Then, as the island gradually sank owing to subsidence of the sea bed, the reef would build upward.

The growth would be most active along the seaward edge because quiet waters, sedimentation, and variable temperatures would inhibit it in the shallow waters near shore. The growing outer edge would in time become a barrier reef with a lagoon between it and the sinking island. Finally the island might disappear altogether, leaving the encircling reef as a coral atoll.

This theory explained at one crack both the formation of barrier reefs and atolls and the hitherto puzzling fact that the limestone bases of some reefs were known to rise from below the depth limit of living coral. In spite of this latter fact, geologists before Darwin were inclined to explain reefs as coral growth on top of existing rock platforms. The ring-shaped atolls were said to be built on the rims of submerged volcanic craters.

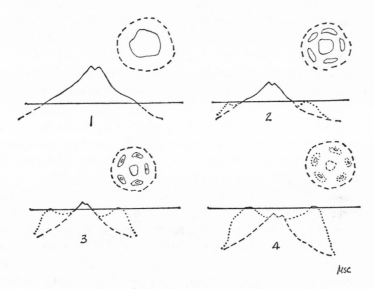

FIG. 21 : Darwin's theory of reef formation. An island rises above the sea (1). Eventually corals establish a fringing reef (2). Then, as the island slowly sinks, the corals build upward. They build most vigorously along the seaward edge, forming a barrier reef (3). At last disappearing beneath the sea, the island leaves the encircling reef as an atoll (4). (Both vertical and cross-sectional views shown.)

In presenting his subsidence theory, Darwin pointed out that corals could indeed become established on pre-existing shallow platforms and that this might account for some of the barrier-reef and atoll formations. But he discounted this explanation for the larger groups of Indo-Pacific atolls. "The idea of a lagoon island, 30 miles in diameter being based on a submarine crater of equal dimensions, has always appeared to me a monstrous hypothesis," he explained in a letter sent home in 1836.

Darwin's ideas found quick support from the American geologist Professor James Dwight Dana of Yale. He marshaled corroborating geological evidence, pointing out, among other things, that the lower reaches of river valleys on many barrier-reef-encircled islands now lie under the sea. This suggested the islands had sunk relative to sea level since the valleys were first eroded. With Dana's support, Darwin's theory was generally accepted for almost a quarter of a century. Then opposition developed.

For one thing, geologists didn't understand how the sea bed could subside. Today this would probably be explained as isostatic adjustment. As the weight of an upthrusting island and its accumulating coral overloaded the crust, the island would sink lower in the plastic mantle. It would act like a buoyant object which, when thrown into a tar pit, slowly sinks until it reaches its proper level for floating. Or perhaps a more general adjustment involving large areas of sea bed would be invoked. But in Darwin's day the theories of isostasy were not yet worked out. Alexander Agassiz, who spent many years studying coral reefs, once remarked that he had found scarcely a reef to illustrate Darwin's theory.

Then too, Sir John Murray, who had studied bottom sediments during the *Challenger* expedition, gave considerable authority to a view exactly opposite to that of Darwin. He revived the argument that the reefs grew up from pre-existing platforms, perhaps craters of extinct volcanoes. If these were not close enough to the surface to begin with, they would be built up by sediments until the reef builders could establish themselves, Murray said.

Toward the end of the nineteenth century the German geologist Albrecht Penck suggested still another possibility. The reefs, he explained, might be the result of upgrowth during the rise of sea level after the last ice age. Meanwhile it had been discovered that the lagoons inside even large atolls have shallow floors all the way across, rather than a deep moat just inside the reef with a rising bottom toward the center where the island had sunk, as one might expect from Darwin's theory. Supporters of the theory pointed out that the moats were probably filled by sediments and coral growth.

But added to Penck's suggestion, the absence of the moats was a rallying point for skeptics, among whom Professor Reginald Daly of Harvard University eventually became the chief symbol and proponent.

Daly elaborated Penck's idea into a full-blown theory of reef formation based on what he called "glacial control." As the glacial ice sheets built up, sea level dropped, the oceans cooled, and erosion from the newly exposed beaches made offshore waters turbid. These effects, said Daly, would kill existing coral reefs. Then, during the periods of low glacial sea levels, and without the protection of living reefs, small islands would be cut away to form banks, while broad sediment platforms would be built up around the larger islands. As the ice melted and the seas again rose, corals would re-establish themselves in the warming waters. New reefs would grow upward on the glacially created banks and platforms

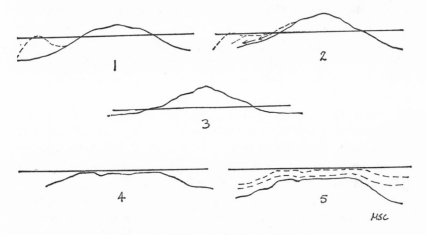

FIG. 22 : Daly's theory of reef formation. As glaciers grow and sea level drops, reefs surrounding islands (1) are killed off by exposure, cooling of the water, and by sediments eroded from newly exposed beaches (2). During low water, broad sediment platforms form around larger islands (3), which smaller islands are cut away to form banks (4). When waters rise, new reefs grow upward on the glacially created banks and platforms (5).

in pace with the rising waters, while the lower parts of river valleys cut during low water would be submerged. This implied, among other things, that all living reefs are no older than the last ice age; that is, not much more than ten thousand years old.

Here was a theory to rival that of Darwin, and for many years it held the field. It was strengthened by studies in the West Indies, where living reefs were found to be merely thin encrustations over older wave-eroded terraces. In no case did they appear to be great piles of coral skeletons extending to thousands of feet in depth and accumulated over long ages of slow subsidence.

But Daly's case had a weak point, for he insisted that glacial control could account for reefs everywhere, that subsidence had played no significant part in any living reef formation. The attacks on the Darwinian theory from this viewpoint were particularly strong in the thirty years prior to World War II. But during that same period the question was put into new perspective by an American geologist, William Morris Davis.

Davis showed that the glacial sea-level shifts had indeed had major effects on reefs along the continental margins such as those of the West Indies. Their effects, however, had been relatively slight on reefs in the deep Indo-Pacific basins. In other words, the reefs Darwin had studied and those of the West Indies which were being used to refute his theory were quite different cases. Each had to be studied and discussed in terms of its peculiar circumstances. No one theory could claim to explain all cases or exclude other theories.

One of the reasons there has been so much speculation and so little agreement on the history of coral reefs is that this is another of the problems marine geologists have to tackle by indirection. The reefs build too slowly for their growth to be watched. Geologists can only infer what happens by studying reefs in various stages of development and trying to put together a general picture. Even this kind of study has been hampered by the difficulty of finding out what lies under the surface of the reefs. It was relatively easy to discover that West Indian reefs were only thin crusts over old rock platforms. But until recently the great Indo-Pacific reefs remained an enigma. "I wish," Darwin once wrote Agassiz, "that some doubly rich millionaire would take it into his hands to have borings made in some of the Pacific and Indian atolls, and bring back cores for slicing from a depth of 500 or 600 feet."

Darwin's "millionaire" turned out to be the Royal Society, which in 1897 commissioned drillings that penetrated 1100 feet into Funafuti Atoll in the Ellice Islands. The drillers found nothing but coral. Darwinites considered this a victory for their side. But skeptics replied that the boring had actually been made through the mound of coral fragments that litter the seaward slopes of reefs and over which the living coral sometimes extends, rather than through the main reef structure itself. The same ambiguity held true for subsequent drillings made by several countries up to World War II. Then came a series of really deep drillings to prepare for the United States nuclear tests in the Pacific.

The first of these was made in Bikini Atoll in 1947. The drill reached a maximum of 2500 feet and still failed to get to the bottom of the coral. Again the Daly school insisted this was only coral talus and not the reef itself. But their insistence was broken by the second series of American drillings, this time in Eniwetok. Under the direction of Harry Ladd of the U. S. Geological Survey, a major effort was made to drill through to the underlying bedrock. Holes were bored on both sides of the atoll. The borings finally hit lava at depths of 4630 and 4222 feet, respectively, drilling through coral all the way. Careful analysis of the drill cores proved conclusively that they had gone through the reef proper. They showed an orderly sequence of coral skeletons from the Eocene to the present, an uninterrupted structure that started growing sixty million years ago. Throughout that time Eniwetok has been subsiding at a rate of two millimeters a century. Darwin had at last been vindicated, at least as far as major Indo-Pacific atolls are concerned.

But while the importance of subsidence has been confirmed, this doesn't mean that all details of Darwin's theory have been accepted even for the atolls. Shepard thinks that at least some present-day reefs, instead of growing around sinking volcanic islands, may have first become established on wave-beveled platforms and partly eroded volcanoes many millions of years ago, perhaps during the Cretaceous period. Since then, these platforms have gradually sunk, with the reef builders constantly extending the reefs upward in pace with the sinking. Where coral growth was slight or inactive, or where the sinking was too rapid for upbuilding to keep pace, these platforms have become guyots.

Also, Shepard explains, the reefs would probably have been affected by glacial changes in sea level. Atolls, for instance, may show this in the narrowness of the encircling reef. Temporary emergence during low water would have exposed the reefs to erosion by waves and to the dissolving action of rain water. With the rise again of the seas, renewed growth at the rim of the eroded reef could have produced present-day atoll formations. In this case, the shallow lagoons would be underlain by old reef material rather than by the sunken and sediment-covered tops of submerged volcanic islands.

The continental shelves of the West Indies and the southeastern coast of the United States are another interesting example of how different reef-forming processes have all played a part in the geological history of an area. The present coral formations in that area are post-glacial in origin. But Dr. Norman D. Newell, professor of geology at Columbia University and chairman and curator of the department of fossil invertebrates at the American Museum, points out that the area may also be underlain by vast fossil coral reefs similar to those of the Indo-Pacific.

Biologically, the West Indian area is isolated from other regions. But at one time it was inhabited by the same organisms that thrived in Indo-Pacific and Mediterranean waters, which interconnected at that time. Then during the Miocene epoch (thirteen to thirty million years ago), interchange of shallow-water life was restricted to the east by the rise of a land barrier at the far end of the Mediterranean and perhaps also by the deepening of the central Atlantic basin. When the Central American isthmus later arose in the Pliocene epoch, the Caribbean was cut off from the Pacific as well and became a landlocked sea.

Ever since the Caribbean first began to be isolated and as climatic and geological changes took their toll, the Atlantic reef corals have been on the decline. But Newell says there once was widespread reef building that reached a climax in late Oligocene and early Miocene times. Recent deep borings and seismic and gravity studies show that the sea floor adjacent to Florida and the Bahamas is underlain by over two and a half miles of limestone rocks similar to those laid down by the reef deposits of the Pacific. Also, the edge of the Blake Plateau farther north looks very much like the Great Barrier Reef of Australia. Its steep seaward face slopes as much as sixty degrees for thousands of feet as it drops toward the abyss. In places it is vertical, just as in many coral reefs today. Here is another possible explanation for the origin of the Blake Plateau.

Perhaps, Dr. Newell suggests, reefs were first established along an arc of volcanic islands like the Lesser Antilles. For a long time they grew steadily upward in the Darwinian manner as the sea bed slowly subsided. In time a great barrier reef was built up along the line of the present Blake Plateau. Then, as the waters cooled and became turbid from erosion of newly uplifted lands during Tertiary mountain building, coral growth began to decline.

It died out first in the north. The barrier reef was killed in the Miocene epoch. But growth continued in the Bahamian and Florida areas until the Pleistocene ice ages. Thus the sea bed of the West Indies and off the southeastern United States, according to Dr. Newell, may hide ancient reef formations as magnificent in their day as any the Pacific now boasts. Also, this area, whose minor present-day coral growths have often been cited to disprove Darwin's ideas, once underwent the same history of coral up-growth on a subsiding sea bottom that Darwin had so aptly proposed to explain the great reefs of the Pacific.

Although the complete story of the coral reefs has still to be unraveled, today the old elements of the controversy have been resolved. The theories of Darwin, Daly, Murray, and others have been incorporated to some degree in the present explanation of reef formations. But Darwin's early understanding of the role of subsidence—his grasp of this important geological phenomenon and the imaginative use of it in his coral-reef theory—was the flash of genius that has illuminated this difficult geological puzzle for over a hundred years.

Filling the Deep-Ocean Basins

The evidence for the sinking of coral reefs correlates with that of the guyots, the sunken islands, to indicate widespread subsidence of the Pacific Ocean floor. It begs the question: What caused this subsidence and how much of it may be only an illusion owing to a slow rise of sea level?

The origin of the ocean waters is a hazy subject. As explained in Chapter Two, they may have fallen as primordial rains or, in the modern view, have been released from the earth's interior. In either case, many geologists have believed that the oceans received essentially all of their water in Precambrian times. Some still hold to this view. Philip Kuenen, for example, concluded in his book *Marine Geology*, published in 1950, that the release of new water from the earth's interior, the only possible source within geological time, has been insignificant since that distant era. Others, such as William Rubey, think the water has been produced continuously throughout geological time. Roger Revelle has extended the latter theory to account for at least part of the submergence of coral reefs and guyots.

In his view, a sizable proportion of the ocean water may have been added in comparatively recent times. The increase began at the end of the Cretaceous period when, according to Revelle, great volcanic outbreaks on the sea floor brought forth large quantities of water and carbon dioxide. This may also explain why the layer of unconsolidated sediments as measured by seismic methods is so much thinner than expected. Earlier deep-sea sediments may have been buried or consolidated by extensive lava flows and other volcanic extrusions.

This probably was also the time when the foraminiferal oozes and other calcareous sediments began to accumulate in quantity. The rate at which they consumed carbon dioxide to deposit the amount of calcium carbonate that has since been laid down must have been far greater than atmospheric sources could supply. This, in turn, suggests a large amount of undersea volcanism.

As new water from the interior accumulated, the sea floor would sink under its weight and under the growing weight of the sediments. Thus, Revelle suggests, the submergence of guyots since the Cretaceous may be due mostly to a rise in sea level and only partly to a sinking of the ocean floor.

On the other hand, Rubey's own calculations of the rate at which new water has been brought forth indicate that only 3 or 4 per cent of the present ocean waters have been added since the Middle Cretaceous. This would have raised sea level by only a few hundred feet, while the guyots now lie at depths of 5000 to 6000 feet. Because of this, Hamilton and others think extensive subsidence is the most likely explanation for their submergence. Perhaps this sinking was local, occurring in areas overloaded by the growth of mountains as may have happened in the case of the Mid-Pacific Mountains. Or perhaps there was general subsidence of the sea bed or a combination of local and general sinking. No one really knows. But more than simple subsidence probably was involved. Deep borings in Pacific atolls show, in some cases, that the seamount on which the corals built had periods of re-emergence since it was first drowned. This may have been due to general subsidence being interrupted by periodic uplifting or to sea-level fluctuations or perhaps to both.

Certainly the history of the sea floor is more complex than can be accounted for by any simple theory of growth through spread of material welling up along the Mid-Oceanic Ridge. The surprising thinness of the deep-sea sediments mentioned in the preceding chapter is in accord with such a theory. If much of the sea floor is relatively young, then it would not be expected to have much sediment. But features such as seamounts, guyots, atolls, and fracture zones show the sea bed has had a complex development after it was formed.

The fracture zones are especially intriguing. Found in all oceans, they are linear disruptions of the sea floor. The topography along them is more mountainous than that of the general sea bed. They usually separate regions where the depth changes sharply. They are often marked by ridges and troughs. In fact, some of the deep-sea trenches, such as the Romanche Trench in the South Atlantic, seem to have been formed by faulting in fracture zones. In short, these zones look like great linear fractures. Some of them offset parts of the Mid-Oceanic Ridge. Others break up the sea floor outside the ridge system. In the Indian Ocean, there is a system of fracture zones outside of the ridge running more or less north-south in contrast to the general east-west tendency of fracture zones. Some of the biggest of the zones have been found in the Northeastern Pacific extending westward from North and Central America. About 60 miles wide, they run from 1600 to 3300 miles out to sea more or less along arcs of great circles. Such an arc is the shortest distance between two points along the earth's surface.

Some geologists think the fracture zones were caused by stresses put on the earth by migration of the North and South poles. There is evidence for such migration in the wanderings that Blackett and others have found for the magnetic poles. It is assumed that any major shift of the magnetic poles would be linked to a corresponding shift in the geographical poles which mark the earth's axis of rotation. Alternatively, the fracture zones may be associated with convection currents in the mantle, the same currents that may underlie the Mid-Oceanic Ridge and move continents.

The history of the ocean's floor and the origin of its waters are one of the unsolved fundamental problems of earth science. The probings of the marine geologist thus are central to the effort to understand how our planet was formed and how it has developed.

FIVE

PATTERNS OF THE WATERS

Stirred by the winds and by the tide-raising forces of sun and moon, the face of the sea is like a kaleidoscope. It presents an ever changing panorama, sometimes regular, sometimes chaotic, whose patterns often have a meaning. The booming of breakers on a western Pacific shore hints of storms that have raged thousands of miles away, perhaps in another hemisphere. Choppy waters in a channel may tell of tidal currents flowing against opposing winds or swell. The varying heights of incoming waves along a stretch of shore may reflect the character of the offshore bottom, rising higher where there are ridges and breaking with lower crests where they have passed over a submarine canyon. Even the ubiquitous tides bear the stamp of local topography.

Oceanographers have learned to read many of these patterns. They can observe the tides at any given point and, as data accumulate over the years, predict them with fair accuracy. By observing the local characteristics of offshore waters and how they behave under a variety of conditions, seaside meteorologists can include future wave conditions in their local forecasts. This latter technique was developed extensively during World War II, when it was one of the major factors in picking the exact date for the Allied D-day invasion of Europe. In fact, the invasion was postponed a day because of unfavorable wave forecasts. Thereafter, because wave conditions were so important a factor in landing men and equipment on the beaches, the wave forecasters set the pace of these landings. Today wave forecasts are invaluable for operations at sea and in building and protecting the offshore oil drillers' platforms as well as many shore installations.

But a growing ability to read the patterns of waves and tides does not imply precise scientific understanding. Oceanographers know in general what is involved. But neither tides nor waves have yet been encompassed in the kind of comprehensive mathematical theory a scientist has in mind when he speaks of "understanding."

Theory versus Reality

Actually, a mathematical theory of waves was worked out and published in 1845 by Sir George Airy. However, the waves he described are more likely to be found in a textbook than on the surface of the sea. Their crests are straight and long and run parallel to each other, while every wave is identical to the others. Only swell moving over water undisturbed by wind comes close to resembling these ideal waves. Wind-blown waves are distorted from this shape, and there is no established theory for a storm-tossed sea.

Oceanographers distinguish between the terms "sea" and "swell." When the wind is blowing up a confused variety of waves of many shapes and sizes, it is called a "sea." When the waves have run beyond the wind and have turned into a low regular undulation of the water surface, their pattern is called a "swell." It is this that most nearly approximates the long, regular, "cylindrical" waves which the Airy theory is able to handle mathematically.

Waves are described in terms of their height, wave length, and period. "Height" is the vertical distance between the high point of a wave crest and the low point of the adjacent trough. "Wave length" is the distance from one crest to the next, and "period" is the time it takes two adjacent crests to pass a fixed point, such as the end of a pier. The mathematics of wave theories are usually concerned with relationships between these and related characteristics. Even though they deal with the ideal more often than the real, such theoretical relationships have helped oceanographers understand many types of ocean waves.

One thing theory tells us is that, except where they slosh up on the shore or when their tops are blown off by the wind, waves are not moving masses of water. It is the shape that moves along, while the water stays more or less where it is. As the wave shape passes, individual water particles move up and down with it, describing a circle or an ellipse. Because of friction there is actually a little

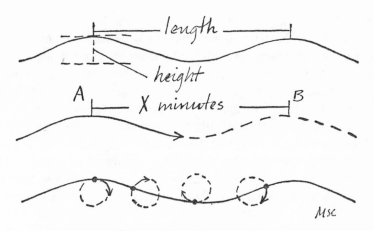

FIG. 23 : Wave elements. Wave length is the horizontal
distance from crest to crest. Height is the vertical distance
from crest to trough. Period is the time it takes a crest
to move a distance of one wave length, i.e., to move
from A to B. In a simple wave, individual water particles
(represented by dots) travel through small circles as the
wave form passes.

forward movement of the particles, like a car wheel spinning on
ice and inching slowly ahead. But in deep water the net movement is slight.

These circular motions die out quickly with increasing depth.
Heavy storm waves are felt more deeply than others. One-pound
rocks have been moved into lobster pots 180 feet deep by storms
at the mouth of the English Channel, while off western Ireland
rocks weighing several hundred pounds each reportedly have been
moved at depths of 100 feet. But, in general, wind-generated
waves do not stir the oceans deeply. This is why submarines have
smooth cruising underwater.

Sometimes the sea surface appears to be a confusion of waves
even when the winds are light. In this case, the confusion has an
underlying order. Different wave systems traveling in different directions can interact with one another to create complex patterns.
Wherever the crest of one wave more or less coincides with that of
another, they add together to build up an extra-high crest. Similarly, wave troughs and crests can cancel one another out. This
is called wave "interference." When a number of wave systems
interfere with each other, their troughs and crests come together in

an endless variety of superpositions. This interference is augmented when the wind is up, constantly generating new systems of waves and adding its patterns to the confusion of the surface. Oceanographers have progressed in their mathematical studies of ocean waves by learning to describe some of the complicated patterns in terms of simple wave systems. These latter can be added together mathematically to represent the observed pattern, while the task of analyzing the behavior of these simple waves is relatively easy. But with patterns literally as complex as the waves of the sea, one can understand why the specialists have not yet reached their goal of complete theoretical understanding.

The Pattern of the Breakers

Once a wave system has outrun the wind, it can travel for long distances without appreciable loss of energy. If it encounters new winds, the shape and heading of the waves will be altered, while a strong enough opposing wind can quickly destroy them. Under favorable conditions, however, the waves continue more or less in the direction of the original wind indefinitely. Moreover, the longer-period waves travel faster. Leaving many of the small and irregular short-period ones behind, they settle down into the rhythmic undulations of a swell.

Thus the fairly long period breakers characteristic of many windward shores may bring tidings of storms that raged thousands of miles away. Those that break on the California coast in summer, rolling in from the south with periods of eight to eighteen seconds, often originate in the winter storms of the South Pacific east of New Zealand. Across the North American continent, along the eastern shore, short choppy waves from much closer storms are the rule. In the Atlantic, with prevailing westerly winds in its stormier latitudes, the long rolling swells from mid-ocean storms break on the western shores of Europe and Africa.

When a wave leaves relatively deep water and begins "to feel the bottom," it undergoes substantial changes. Velocity and wave length decrease, while height grows. Only the period remains the same. The wave would appear to be dragging over the shoaling bottom until, stubbing its toe, so to speak, it falls over itself as a breaker. This appearance is deceptive, for a wave on water does not behave like a solid body. This is a point at which theory helps one understand what actually happens.

Waves can be thought of as carrying a certain amount of energy, originally derived from the wind and traveling with the wave system. When waves enter shallow water, the energy once carried through a fairly deep column of water is now being concentrated in water growing steadily shallower. Every pound of water has more and more energy stored in it as the wave form passes. Some of this energy makes the water of the crests hump up higher. Some of it increases the speed of the individual water particles (as opposed to the velocity of the wave form itself, which slows down). When the velocity of the water particles at the crest of a wave exceeds that of the wave itself, the wave breaks. In deep water this usually happens when the wave height gets to be about one seventh of the wave length. In shallow water it's the depth that counts. Breakage usually occurs when the ratio of wave height to depth is about 3 to 4. In other words, a 3-foot-high wave would break in about 4 feet of water, although the actual depth of breakage depends on such local factors as the character of the bottom.

With theory as a rough guide, it is easy to see why stubbing one's toe is a poor analogy for a breaking wave. The clumsy human would fall soonest where the bottom is roughest. It is exactly the opposite with waves. Waves travel farther over rough than over smooth bottoms before breaking. The rougher the bottom, the more the wave energy is dissipated by friction. This tends to decrease the amount of energy being concentrated in the water and in turn to cut down the wave height and the speed of water particles at the crest. The wave then breaks at the shallower depth appropriate for its diminished height.

Theory also shows how the pattern of waves can reflect major bottom features. Imagine a wave system coming into a straight shore line over a bottom cut by submarine canyons which are flanked by ridges. As the water grows shoaler, the waves grow higher and move more slowly over the ridges than over the valleys, where the water remains relatively deep. This gives a curving outline to the advancing wave front. At the same time, the breakers over the ridges will be built up as they approach shore, while those over the valley will be diminished. In this way, the pattern of the incoming breakers reflects the topography of the bottom.

This makes the head of a submarine canyon an ideal place for launching small boats through the breakers. A difference of ten times in breaker height is not unusual with such offshore topography. This effect was particularly noticeable in the destructive tidal waves that hit Hawaii in 1946. The waves were substantially reduced where they came in over undersea valleys, while those traveling over three ridges on the north side of Kauai Island attained the greatest heights reported.

Broadly speaking, there are two types of breakers, with individual waves showing a variety of mixtures of the two. The "plunging breaker" is by far the more dramatic. It usually occurs on coasts where the bottom rises rather steeply toward the shore. As the wave feels the bottom, its advancing face becomes steeper. Suddenly, at the moment part of this face becomes vertical, the top of the crest shoots forward as a jet. Down it falls in a graceful arc, with the rest of the crest tumbling after. And as it falls it traps a pocket of air. Then crest and air pocket plunge together into the water with a "boom" and a sudden turbulent dissipation of energy.

Where the upward slope to the beach is more gradual, the less spectacular "spilling breaker" is often seen. In this case, the incoming wave tends to keep a more symmetrical rounded crest that gradually grows up in a point until the top part begins to foam and spills down the advancing face of the wave. As the water shoals, the spilling increases and the wave crest slowly disintegrates into an advancing mass of foaming water.

These spilling breakers are the waves the surfboarders ride. Balancing their boards on the advancing wave face, they are perpetually sliding downhill. Ideally, the wave should be just on the point of breaking. Then the velocity of the water particles on the crest where the board is riding will be close to that of the wave itself. The combination of the movement of the water particles and of the board as it slides downhill through the water keeps the surfboarder moving along with the wave.

From the rider's point of view, this is a stable situation. If his board moves ahead too fast, it slows down and the wave catches up. If it starts to fall behind the wave, it moves backward toward the crest, where it is accelerated forward again. The wave face down which the board is constantly sliding is steepest at the crest, while the maximum forward speed of the water particles is also found there. Thus there is a position on the wave face to which the board will automatically return if displaced backward or forward.

This much is convenient for the rider. His skill is tested, however, by the tendency of the board to "broach to." Since the factors favoring velocity are greatest at the crest, the back end of the board tends to go faster than the front. The board keeps "trying" to swing around parallel to the wave front, and the trick of surf riding is to keep it headed toward the beach.

When an incoming wave breaks, that is not necessarily the end of it. If it hasn't yet hit the beach, the remaining wave energy may re-form into one or several new waves. These, in turn, may break and again re-form until the waves run up onto the shore. Even this may not be the end. Especially on a steep rocky shore, the back-slosh of the water as it returns seaward may still have enough energy to generate yet another wave, a "reflected wave," which can be seen heading back out to sea.

The incoming waves also bring an influx of water. This is due to the slight forward movement of the water particles as the wave form passes. At sea this doesn't amount to much. But at the shore the water piles up against the land and, having no other place to go, it runs along parallel to the shore line. This is the origin of the "longshore currents" and "rip currents" that so often take swimmers by surprise.

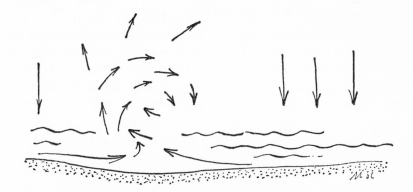

FIG. 24 : Longshore and rip currents. Water brought shoreward by waves tends to run off along the shore until it heads seaward in regions where incoming waves are weaker, sometimes creating a fast-moving current known as a rip. (View vertically downward.)

Usually the longshore currents flow more or less in the same direction as the waves, often scouring out a relatively deep trough parallel to and just outside the beach. If the waves come in from the right, the current generally runs along toward the left, and vice versa, although currents running in the opposite direction may occasionally be encountered. At some point these currents have to return their water to the sea. In the normal pattern of circulation, water flows toward and along the shore in regions of relatively high waves, with a general return flow seaward in regions where the waves are lower. Occasionally there is a second means of escape in narrow, relatively fast currents superimposed on the general pattern. These are the rip currents or, as they are often inappropriately called, the "rip tides."

Longshore currents, which develop speeds of a mile per hour or more, can be quite a challenge to the average swimmer. The rip currents, funneling the water into a narrow, turbulent flow and heading out to sea, are potentially even more dangerous. They develop speeds two or three times those of the longshore currents. Moreover, they are intermittent. Sometimes they set strongly seaward. Sometimes they die out. They can take a bather unawares, especially if he or she has wandered into a rip-current channel during one of the lull periods.

Many of the drownings attributed to the so-called "undertow" are probably due to rip currents. There is little evidence for the existence of undertow currents that physically pull a swimmer down, although near shore the rip currents do extend to the bottom, becoming surface currents farther out to sea. Swimmers becoming exhausted or frightened in a rip or caught unexpectedly by one of its sudden reversals may find themselves in difficulty. This is probably why lifeguards make many of their rescues in the rips. The easiest way to extricate yourself if caught in one of these currents is to swim across it until slack water and perhaps a shoaler bottom are found outside of the rip channel. On the other hand, for skilled surfboarders and boatmen, the rips can afford a free ride out through the breakers.

Similar currents develop on coral reefs. Water from waves and swell that occasionally top a reef runs off to sea through eroded channels. To reach these channels, it may flow for some distance along the landward side of the reef. Any one channel carries water collected from a wide area of reef and can develop a substantial current. Like a rip, this current is intermittent and can catch a wader off guard.

The longshore and rip currents are also important transporters of sediment. They help distribute and redistribute the sands of beaches and erode channels for themselves in the process. The rip channels in particular can become quite deep with steep sides, an additional hazard bathers should be wary of when jumping up and down in the surf on what is otherwise a shallow bottom.

The incoming waves and breakers that provide most of the sediment these currents carry can also cause considerable erosion. They cut back beaches or, conversely, pile up sand to build them. Of the two types of breakers, the plunging variety causes more direct erosion of the sea bed where they break. But the spilling type stirs the bottom over a wider area and may, in the long run, have a greater total effect. During high waves especially, water made muddy by erosion and carried to sea by wave-generated currents has sometimes gotten into the offshore circulation and been traced for hundreds of miles from the coast. This dynamic interplay of waves and currents, transporting sediments and tearing down or building up the beaches, is forever reshaping the shore.

Shifting Sands

A beach is never finished. It is always in the process of becoming. Built of water-borne materials, it is constantly being worked over by the waves. Much of the sand supply for the beaches comes from rivers. These bring eroded material to the sea, where waves and currents move it along the coast, depositing it in favored locations. Other sands, such as coral and shell sands, come from the sea itself, sometimes in prodigious quantities. Bulldozers have been quarrying sand on many shell beaches for years; yet the beaches remain pretty much the same. Foraminifera and other shallow-water animals living near shore produce a continuous supply of new shells which the waves bring to the beaches in abundance. On the other hand, if the bulldozers stopped operating, the beaches would go on building up until they reached what geologists call an "equilibrium profile," in which the normal pattern of waves would neither add nor take away any significant amount of material. Then the surplus shells would be moved along the coast to be deposited on another shore.

The waves are constantly working to establish such profiles of equilibrium. In each instance, these depend on the type of material deposited. You can see this if you look at the seaward slope, the "foreshore," of different beaches. Coarse sands pack together loosely. When you walk on this kind of beach your feet sink in. The loose material lets slosh from incoming waves drain through, depositing suspended material with relatively little backwash. The slope of such a beach will build up until it reaches a steepness where what backwash there is allows no more material to accumulate. Fine sand, on the other hand, packs together. Water does not sink in as readily. This enhances the backwash from waves, which more easily carries off the sand in suspension. This is why beaches of fine sand have a gentler slope than those built of coarser materials. Also, the former pack into a harder surface, so that cars can be driven on fine sand beaches but would become mired on coarse sands.

Wave patterns change and the beach profiles change with them. One good day's storm surf can completely alter the build-up of several weeks or even months. Some beaches undergo a regular seasonal cycle. During summer months the fair-weather waves bring in sand, building thick wide beaches. A beach is usually defined as extending landward to the farthest point that waves carry sand. The inner part of the beach, where it is horizontal or even slopes toward the land, is called the "berm" or "backshore."

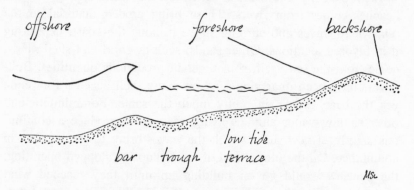

FIG. 25 : Principal elements of a beach profile. The bar and trough are formed by wave action.

During the summer this berm area may be built out several hundred feet as waves pile up sand on the foreshore.

When winter comes, heavy storm waves batter the foreshore, stirring the sand into suspension and cutting back the berm. The suspended sand is carried off by longshore currents until these find a rip which, in turn, carries the sand seaward. Sometimes the sand is deposited offshore, to be brought back again next season. Sometimes it is shifted to a nearby beach, where it remains until a change in wave pattern brings it back again. Other times it may simply be carried off, to be replaced by fresh supplies of sand moving in from another area. Occasionally a beach will go on building up over several seasons. The berm may widen so much that its inner part becomes dunes and for a while joins the land. But the waves are apt to reclaim their own at any time.

Thus beaches go through cycles of growth, denudation, and replenishment. There are short-period cycles associated with a single storm. Longer cycles, like those just described, are correlated with the seasonal patterns of waves and weather. Still others may be associated with long-term weather trends measured in years.

Because a beach is never static, it is wise to know exactly what you are getting in buying beach property. That beautiful sandy shore you saw last summer may disappear after a couple of winter storms. It is well to observe it at all seasons or, better still, to find out what has happened to it for a number of years past.

There is even greater need for caution in building breakwaters or jetties near sand beaches. These may improve anchorage facilities, but they can also destroy the beaches. The normal sand supply may pile up behind the jetty while the beach below becomes eroded and denuded. At Redondo Beach, California, for example, this effect was augmented when a jetty was built at a point where the edge of a submarine canyon caused waves to converge, enhancing their erosive attack. Before the jetty was built, sand coming in from the north had counteracted this effect. When the sand supply was cut off, the waves kept eating away at the beaches and then at the land itself, destroying valuable property.

On the other hand, by taking beach dynamics into consideration, one can have the protection of jetties and keep the beaches too. A number of harbors have been made this way along the straight Florida beaches where nature has provided no convenient anchorages. The jetties have indeed cut off the supply of quartz sand normally brought in from rivers emptying to the north. But an abundance of shell sands from offshore waters has maintained the beaches south of the jetties.

When storms and high winds drive waves against the shore, the water that shapes the beaches attacks the land itself. It chips away at rock cliffs and man-made structures with tenacity. Here is another and more violent factor that sculpts the shore.

The Force of Waves and Spray

With driving winds behind them, ocean waves become careening giants. At sea they can grow to heights of 75 feet and more. Waves over 100 feet high have been reported. But R. C. H. Russell, the British wave authority, in a comprehensive review of the subject, gives 75 feet as the highest reliable estimate. At the same time, he points out that the most damaging waves are "freak waves found in freak storms," and it is impossible to give figures for their dimensions.

Just imagine a solid wall of water rearing as high or higher than a medium-sized house! The greatest danger to ships from such a wave lies in its breaking or having its top blown off by the wind so that a mass of water crashes onto the deck. Damage to shore structures, on the other hand, is inflicted in a variety of ways. The wind-driven water sometimes picks up sand and pebbles which it uses as an abrasive to grind away at cliffs and walls. It undermines marine foundations. It tosses huge boulders like cannon balls and develops momentary pressures that even the stoutest man-made structures cannot always withstand.

Russell cites several illustrations of the force of such waves. For example, he tells how a massive breakwater at Wick, Scotland, was twice destroyed, even though, from his description, it must have been an impressive structure. It was a mass of concrete rubble tied with steel to a foundation of huge stones cemented together. It measured 26 feet by 45 feet by 21 feet thick and weighed 1350 tons. Yet in 1872 it was shifted bodily by wave action in a gale. The breakwater was rebuilt, this time weighing 2600 tons. In 1877 it was swept away again. Russell does not say what happened after that. Or take the case of Tillamook Lighthouse on the United States east coast. In one storm a 135-pound rock was thrown above the light and came down vertically through the roof. Yet the roof stood 91 feet above low water!

If waves can toss such rocks about, one can imagine what enormous forces must be involved. Russell calculates that it would have taken at least a pressure of 2440 pounds per square foot to move the Wick breakwater. He further estimates that the storm waves over 40 feet high which have been observed at Wick could develop pressures of more than 4000 pounds per square foot, quite enough to account for the damage.

The simplest kind of wave attack occurs when a more or less vertical wall is sited in deep water. In that case, incoming waves don't break against it. Instead they are reflected and interact with each other to set up a pattern called "clapotis." This is an example of the wave interference mentioned earlier in which the crests and troughs of different waves act to reinforce one another or to cancel each other out. In clapotis, the crests and troughs of reflected waves and of the incoming waves always meet in the same place, so that a stable or "standing wave" pattern is set up. Individual waves still move in, are reflected, and move back out again. But to the observer there is no horizontal movement of the crests and troughs produced by the interference. In other words, the apparent wave pattern doesn't move toward or away from the wall. It just stands where it is. In shallower water, where the bottom begins to affect the waves yet is still not shallow enough to make them break, this standing wave or clapotis pattern is modified. As in the case of the true standing wave, incoming and reflected wave crests meet in the same places, except now one can see them moving and passing through each other.

Since the waves are not breaking and hurling water against the wall, the total pressure exerted by clapotis is not especially great. The water simply moves up and down the wall, and the pressure at any point is about the same as would be exerted by still water of similar depth. On the other hand, if water gets into cracks or open joints, this constantly fluctuating pressure can pry facing stones loose. Also, the water movements set up near the bottom by the clapotis can erode and eventually undermine the structure unless special precautions are taken. Unlike traveling waves, where water particles go through a more or less circular orbit as the wave form passes, the water in the standing crests and troughs simply moves up and down. At the bottom this motion dies away,

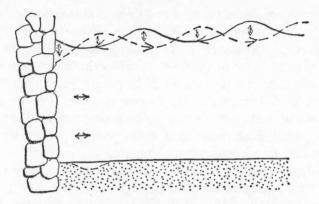

FIG. 26 : Clapotis. Individual waves move in, are reflected, and move out again. But their crests and troughs
coincide so that the over-all wave pattern stands where
it is, crests and troughs always appearing in the same
place. Water particles in the standing crests and troughs
simply move up and down (vertical two-headed arrows).
A quarter wave length away particles move horizontally
back and forth, often eroding the bottom in front of the
wall.

causing little or no erosion. But just a quarter-wave length away
from the crests and troughs, the water particles move horizontally
back and forth. This motion goes right to the bottom and can
cause substantial erosion. Thus just a quarter-wave length away
from the wall the bottom may become badly eroded.

Clapotis is a fairly simple phenomenon. It is easy to study both
theoretically and with models in laboratory tanks. Marine engineers can cope with its problems relatively well, as in the case
of structures along Mediterranean shores. Here, where the tide
range is rarely more than a foot, structures can usually be placed
in water deep enough so that waves won't break against them
even at low tide. Then the engineers' chief concern is to build
them heavy enough not to be overturned and to ensure that
erosion won't undercut the foundations.

But where structures have to take the force of breaking waves,
clapotis is a secondary problem. When a storm wave breaks, a jet
of water usually shoots out from the crest at about twice the
speed of the wave itself. The full force of a breaking wave hitting
a wall is generally equivalent to that of any other water jet traveling
at comparable speed. Moreover, if a wave breaks in a certain

way, shock pressures may develop for a few hundredths of a second. These have been estimated at over 14,000 pounds per square foot.

The highest shock pressures are generated when the breaking wave traps a pocket of air and compresses it against the wall. If the pocket is relatively thick, it will merely cushion the impact. If its thickness is much less than half its height, it will begin to exert shock pressures. These will be greatest where the pocket is thinnest. It is not known how much damage these shock pressures themselves cause, but the compressed air literally explodes, throwing water up in high-speed plumes of spray that

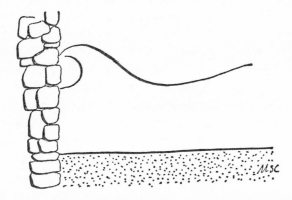

FIG. 27 : When a breaking wave traps an air pocket, compressing it against a wall or cliff face, tremendous shock pressures are often generated, causing the air literally to explode and throwing up powerful plumes of spray.

leave little doubt of their power. Pressure developed by such spray has been estimated at 16,800 pounds per square foot.

Even in the open sea where waves are not breaking against walls, entrapped gas bubbles develop enormous pressures. Storm waves tossed violently about the sea form microscopic cavities in a process called cavitation. Within a tiny fraction of a second, these cavities expand many times. Gases dissolved in the water diffuse into them. Then, within the same split second, the gas is compressed to a pressure of several thousand atmospheres with a temperature rise of several thousand degrees. Chemical reactions take place rapidly under these conditions. Their products are soon redissolved in the water as the bubbles collapse. This is called sonochemistry. A substantial part of the nitrogen that sustains life in the sea may be taken from the atmosphere by the sonochemistry of the waves.

Estimates of shock pressures cited here have been taken from Russell. They were made by a combination of observation and theoretical calculations. The theory, in turn, was based on experiments made in laboratory tanks. Thus the estimates only hint at the actual power of breaking waves and spray. Russell again cites a case that illustrates this power more graphically than numbers.

In 1864, another English wave researcher, Thomas Stevenson, described groups of huge stone blocks on the Skerry islets in the Shetlands lying well above sea level and looking as though they had been dislodged by storms. A typical group of the blocks ranged from 9½ tons down, with one 19½-tonner standing a little to one side. The blocks had been moved dozens of feet above the low-water mark and several hundred feet beyond it. There were gashes and scores in the rocks below to mark the routes by which the blocks had been dragged or pushed up from lower down on the shore where they had been broken off by breakers. Yet the tide range here is only six feet, indicating that the blocks had been moved by the force of spray. In one instance, a 5½-ton block was found 72 feet above the sea and 20 feet from a hole in the rock into which it fit exactly. It had been quarried out of solid rock by flying spray.

It is little wonder that wind-driven waves have been a powerful factor in carving the shore lines. They can attack and remove even solid rock cliffs, often creating curious shapes such as rock pinnacles standing a little way from shore or joined to it by a natural bridge. Similarly, waves can hollow out caves in the rock. Then, having eroded a cave, they may pound upward until they break through the roof. One sometimes sees spray shooting up out of apparently solid ground behind the main shore line.

On the other hand, some of the most destructive ocean waves have nothing to do with the wind. These are the misnamed "tidal waves" generated by seismic disturbances or by submarine landslides. Geologists call them "tsunamis," from the Japanese term for "large waves in harbors." They are appropriately named. Rising swiftly from the sea, they engulf even the shores of sheltered coves.

"Tidal Waves"

On April 1, 1946, a tsunami struck the Hawaiian Islands, the first of any consequence since 1877. The waves had been generated by a disturbance along the Aleutian Trench over 2000 miles away to the north. From there they had raced as a low swell at an average speed of 450 miles an hour until, feeling the rise of the sea bottom, they reared up to flood over the land. Dr. Francis Shepard was vacationing at Kawela Bay on northern Oahu at that time. The following excerpt from his eyewitness account given in his book, *The Earth beneath the Sea,* is a colorful description of what it is like to be caught off guard by one of these huge waves:

. . . we were sleeping peacefully when we were awakened by a loud hissing sound, which sounded for all the world as if dozens of locomotives were blowing off steam directly outside our house. Puzzled, we jumped up and rushed to the front window. Where there had been a beach previously, we saw nothing but boiling water, which was sweeping over the ten-foot top of the beach ridge and coming directly at the house. I rushed and grabbed my camera, forgetting such incidentals as clothes, glasses, watch and pocketbook. As I opened the door I noticed with some regret that the water was not advancing any farther but, instead, was retreating rapidly down the slope.

By that time I was conscious of the fact that we might be experiencing a tsunami. My suspicions became confirmed as the water moved swiftly seaward, and the sea level dropped a score of feet, leaving the coral reefs in front of the house exposed to view. Fish were flapping and jumping up and down where they had been stranded by the retreating waves. Quickly taking a couple of photographs, in my confusion I accidentally made a double exposure of the bare reef. Trying to show my erudition, I said to my wife, "There will be another wave, but it won't be as exciting as the one that awakened us. Too bad I couldn't get a photograph of the first one."

Was I mistaken? In a few minutes as I stood at the edge of the beach ridge in front of the house, I could see the water beginning to rise and swell up around the outer edges of the exposed reef; it built higher and higher and then came racing forward with amazing velocity. "Now," I said, "here is a good chance for a picture." I took one, but my hand was rather unsteady that time. As the water continued to advance I shot another one, fortunately a little better . . . As it piled up in front of me, I began to wonder whether this wave was really going to be smaller than the preceding one. I called to my wife to run to the back of the house for protection, but she had already started, and I followed her just in time. As I looked back I saw the water surging over the spot where I had been standing a moment before. Suddenly we heard the terrible smashing of glass at the front of the house. The refrigerator passed us on the left side moving upright out into the cane field. On the right came a wall of water sweeping toward us down the road that was our escape route from the area. We were also startled to see that there was nothing but kindling wood left of what had been the nearby house to the east. Finally, the water stopped coming on and we were left on a small island, protected by the undamaged portion of the house, which, thanks to its good construction and to the protecting ironwood trees, still withstood the blows. The water had rushed on into the cane field and spent its fury.

My confidence about the waves getting smaller was rapidly vanishing. Having noted that there was a fair interval before the second invasion (actually fifteen minutes as we found out later), we started running along the emerging beach ridge in the only direction in which we could get to the slightly elevated main road. As we ran, we found some very wet and frightened Hawaiian women standing wringing their hands and wondering what to do. With difficulty we persuaded them to come with us along the ridge to a place where there was a break in the cane field. As we hurried through this break, another huge wave came rolling in over the reef and broke with shuddering force against the small escarpment at the top of the beach. Then, rising as a monstrous wall of water, it swept on after us, flattening the cane field with a terrifying sound. We reached the comparative safety of the elevated road just ahead of the wave.

There, in a motley array of costumes, various other refugees were gathered. One couple had been cooking their breakfast when all of a sudden the first wave came in, lifted their house right off its foundation, and carried it several hundred feet into the cane field where it set it down so gently that their breakfast just kept right on cooking. Needless to say, they did not stay to enjoy the meal. Another couple had escaped with difficulty from their collapsing house.

We walked along the road until we could see nearby Kawela Bay, and from there we watched several more waves roar onto the shore. They came with a steep front like the tidal bore that I had seen move up the Bay of Fundy at Moncton, New Brunswick, and up the channels on the tide flat at Mont-Saint-Michel in Normandy. We could see various ruined houses, some of them completely demolished. One house had been thrown into a pond right on top of another. . . . Another was still floating out in the bay.

Finally, after about six waves had moved in, each one apparently getting progressively weaker, I decided I had better go back and see what I could rescue from what was left of the house where we had been living. After all, we were in scanty attire and required clothes. I had just reached the door when I became conscious that a very powerful mass of water was bearing down on the place. This time there simply was no island in back of the house during the height of the wave. I rushed to a nearby tree and climbed it as fast as possible and then hung on for dear life as I swayed back and forth under the impact of the wave. Like the others, this wave soon subsided, and the series of waves that followed were all minor in comparison.

After the excitement was over, we found half of the house still standing and began picking up our belongings. I chased all over the cane fields trying to find books and notes that had been strewn there by the angry waves. We did, finally, discover our glasses undamaged [the sand, being coral, did not produce scratches], buried deep in the sand and debris covering the floor. My waterproof wristwatch was found under the house by the owner a week later.

"Well," I thought, "you're a pretty poor oceanographer not to know that tsunamis increase in size with each new wave." As soon as possible I began to look over the literature, and I felt a little better when I could not find any information to the effect that successive waves increase in size, and yet what could be a more important point to remember? You can be sure that since then those of us who have investigated these waves in the Hawaiian Islands have stressed this danger . . .

Most of the tsunamis, like the one described by Shepard, have occurred in the Pacific, originating with seismic disturbances along the ring of trenches that circle that ocean. Usually they are associated with exceptionally severe earthquakes that shake seismographs throughout the world and give warning that one of these unusual waves may be on its way. Perhaps the disturbance causes a section of the sea floor to drop. Then as water rushes in from all sides, it humps up on the surface, causing waves to move out in all directions. Similarly, if the sea bottom is suddenly lifted, the water at the surface humps up, sending out waves. Submarine landslides may also cause some of the tsunamis.

These waves are unusually long, with lengths on the order of 100 miles between successive crests and with periods of about 15 minutes. They travel swiftly, averaging some 450 miles an hour, and cover many thousands of miles without appreciable loss of energy. In the 1946 tsunami at Hawaii, a second and even larger series of waves came in from the west 18 hours after the primary waves had arrived from the north. Shepard thinks the late arrivals had been doubly reflected, first by a submarine cliff off Japan and then from an escarpment in Oceania, to come in on what had been the sheltered side of the main island of Hawaii.

The arrival of a tsunami, especially along a steep coast, looks like an erratic and rapid rise of the tide, hence the name "tidal wave." But these waves have no more to do with the true tides than do the floods caused by high storm winds which are also called by that name. Responding to the rhythmic pulse of astronomical forces, the tides do indeed affect the oceans daily as a system of waves. However, they are quite different from the undulations of a tsunami or the wind-driven mass of a hurricane flood. Their basic characteristics are set by the sun and moon and by the shape of the ocean basins. They are a constant disturbance that writes its patterns on the waters on a truly global scale.

The Pulse of the Earth

Compared to the pull of the earth's gravity, the tide-producing forces are minuscule. They amount to only about one ten millionth of that pull at the earth's surface. Yet they leave scarcely a particle of the surface unaffected. You and I take no notice of the small fraction of an ounce increase and decrease they regularly make in our weight. But the land feels their influence and responds with crustal tides that can be detected with sensitive instruments. The atmosphere feels it, too, for meteorologists have found tides even in the heights of the stratosphere. And in the ocean the waters are affected even at abyssal depths. These pervasive forces elicit a response from land, air, and sea that geophysicists have aptly called the "pulse of the earth."

This response is greatest in the oceans, and it is the tides of the sea with which we are concerned here. These tides are rarely the same from one place to the next. Even neighboring coastal towns will often have markedly different tides in their respective harbors. No coast line is unaffected by their universal pulse. At some points this pulse may be so weak that it is masked by effects of wind and weather. Yet in other places it raises and lowers the water level as much as 60 to 70 feet. While there is no mystery as to what causes them, the interplay of factors that produce the tides characteristic of any one location is complex. Not even tidal experts can follow these factors in all their detail. Only a brief review of the major influences can be given here.

It seems paradoxical that the tide-raising forces, one of the most potent influences affecting the sea, should be the result of an almost insignificant astronomical imbalance. The earth and moon pull on each other gravitationally. At the same time they revolve about a common center. Without this revolving motion they would crash together disastrously. But the outward centrifugal force of their motion just balances the inward gravitational attraction, and earth and moon go revolving on together in their orbit about the sun. However, while the earth-moon system as a whole is in balance, individual bits of matter on the earth's surface are not.

On the hemisphere directly under the moon, the lunar attraction is slightly greater than the opposing centrifugal forces, while on the opposite side of the earth these latter forces have the edge. The result of this small imbalance is the lunar tide-producing forces.

These forces generally have both a vertical and a horizontal component. Compared to the earth's gravity, the vertical forces are negligible. As far as the tides are concerned, it is the horizontal forces that count. Facing the moon, they pull material toward the point directly under the lunar zenith. On the opposite hemisphere they pull toward the antipodal point, where the moon is at its nadir. If the earth were entirely covered by water of uniform depth, it would tend to gather in two humps, one under the moon and one on the opposite side of the earth.

As this hypothetical water-covered earth spins, it brings the various parts of its surface progressively under the tidal bulges. If there were absolutely no friction between the earth's surface and the water, these bulges would stay under the moon. If, on the other hand, there were a very large amount of friction, the bulges would tend to move with the earth. The actual situation lies somewhere between these extremes. There is enough friction for the earth to drag the bulges along a little bit. The bulges reach an equilibrium point between the forces tending to make them hump under the moon and the frictional forces tending to drag them along with the earth's rotation. This is one reason that a given spot on the surface generally passes under and beyond the moon before it has its high tide.

The tide-producing influence of the more distant sun arises in exactly the same way and is about half as strong as that of the moon. Thus at full and new moon, when sun, moon, and earth are more or less in line, the lunar and solar tidal forces add together. Then the seas literally spring up to reach the highest high- and lowest low-water levels in the appropriately named "spring tides." When sun, moon, and earth form a right angle during the first and third quarters of the moon, the solar and lunar tidal forces oppose each other, producing the "neap tides." In these, the range between high and low water is at its smallest.

Changes in the distances and relative positions of earth and moon and sun alter the tide-raising forces. The moon's orbit about the earth and that of the earth about the sun are ellipses. This

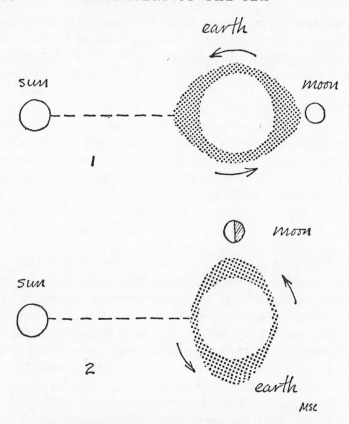

FIG. 28 : Spring and neap tides. When sun and moon are
in line, they pull together to produce the highest tides,
the spring tides (1). But when they are at right angles
to each other their tidal forces are opposed, producing
the low neap tides (2).

makes the distances between earth and moon and between earth
and sun different at different points along the respective orbits.
Also, the orientation of these orbits changes slowly, so that the
apparent path of sun and moon through the sky changes over the
centuries. The position of the moon above or below the earth's
equator produces variations in the relative heights of the two
daily high tides, in some cases, virtually eliminating one of them.
Tidal experts can calculate all these astronomical effects from the
laws of celestial mechanics. They can determine what the tide-
producing forces were at any time in the remote past or forecast
them accurately for an indefinitely long future. Yet they can predict

the actual tides only in certain carefully studied cases, for the tide-producing forces are only one factor influencing the ebb and flow of the water.

While the fictional water-covered earth helps one understand the tide-producing forces, the real tides are also shaped by geography and the dynamics of moving water. Every ocean basin, every bay, cove, or inlet has its natural mode of oscillation. If water in it is disturbed, it will slosh back and forth and up and down like disturbed water in a tub. This oscillation of the water will have a characteristic time period determined by the shape of the basin. There will also be regions where the up-and-down motion is minimal or entirely absent. These are the "nodes" about which the rest of the water oscillates. The characteristic modes of oscillation greatly modify both the ocean-wide and the local action of the tides. Friction also plays a role, especially in shallow basins, while in the open sea the Coriolis force of the earth's rotation has a considerable modifying effect. The later effect arises from the fact that, while the tides tend to advance over the ocean as waves, they also involve sizable currents running from regions of high water to regions of low water. The turning of these currents by the Coriolis force, to the right in the Northern Hemisphere and to the left in the Southern, changes the pattern of the tides in a complex manner wherever a sizable area of water is involved. [See page 153 for explanation of Coriolis force.]

Modern tidal theory takes all of these factors into account. If the shape of the ocean basins and of significant local topography were known in enough detail, it might be possible to use high-speed computers to predict the tides for any given locality on the basis of theory alone. This is an impossible task at present. On the other hand, tidal experts can work the problem the other way around. If they have enough records of past tides at any given spot, they can use tide theory to analyze the data to find the significant governing factors. Then with the aid of special tide-predicting machines, they can predict the local tides for many years ahead with a high degree of accuracy.

The interplay of the various tidal influences helps one understand some of the remarkable features of the tides. In most places the lunar influence predominates. Every day the moon rises about fifty minutes later and every day the tides are fifty minutes later too. But at some places, such as Tahiti, this correlation disappears.

At Tahiti you can almost tell time by the stage of the tides. High water regularly occurs around noon and midnight, with low water coming more or less six hours in between. The lunar cycle has disappeared and that of the sun predominates. This is probably because Tahiti is in a nodal region for oscillations set up by the moon. The waters here are free to respond to the tempo of the sun.

While sun and moon impress a basic rhythm on the tides, it is the characteristics of the tidal basins that govern their local amplitude and times of arrival. If the period of natural oscillation of a basin is very much smaller than that of the astronomical forces, then the tides tend to follow the waxing and waning of these forces. The water in such a basin, when allowed to oscillate freely, sloshes about relatively quickly, and the oscillation of the tidal forces is able to force the water mass to conform to its own tempo. But when the natural period is considerably longer than that of the tidal forces, the water responds too slowly to follow their oscillations. Then the tides tend to be small and reversed. Low water appears when the tidal forces are greatest, while the water rises highest when these forces have waned.

These are extreme cases, and the actual circumstances may fall almost anywhere in between. Thus the local tides may follow the 24-hour-50-minute daily cycle of the moon, with successive tides being about 12 hours and 25 minutes apart. But the rise of the tides may come several hours after the moon has passed through the local zenith.

The time lag between the arrival of the moon overhead and the actual onset of the next flood tide is called the local "tidal establishment." It is one of the characteristic tidal features that varies widely from place to place. At some places, as in the Gulf of Mexico, there is only one slow rise and fall of the water every 24 hours and 50 minutes.

The natural rhythm of the tidal basins also helps explain why the heights of the tides cannot be predicted from astronomical calculations alone. Again, when the natural period of oscillation is short compared to the cycle of the tidal forces, the rise and fall of the waters correlates well with what one would expect from the play of these forces. When that natural period is relatively long, it is hard to set the waters in motion and rise of the tides tends to be small. But when the natural period of the water coincides with that of the tidal forces, the two types of oscillation reinforce each other. That is when the waters mount to spectacular heights in resonance or "sympathetic" tides. On the southern side of the Bay of Fundy, New Brunswick, which is famous for having the greatest tides in the world, the tidal range is almost 70 feet. Here decreasing width and shoaling side margins accentuate the remarkable resonance tides in this elongated basin.

One of the most striking local effects occurs when the tide enters certain river estuaries. The narrowing of the channel and shoaling of the bottom sometimes change the shape of the incoming flood tide so much that the water surges upstream with a steep front. These "bores," as they are called, can be massive. One of the most famous is that of the Tsientang River in China, where the advancing face of the water reaches heights of 25 feet during spring tides. Another famous bore, called the Pororoca, rushes regularly some 200 miles up the Amazon, often making the river temporarily impassable. It is like a waterfall up to 16 feet high moving upriver at a speed of 12 knots and with a roar that can be heard for miles.

Because the ocean waters are not homogenous, the patterns of their waves and tides are not confined to their upper surface. Wherever there is a vertical change of temperature or salinity marking a boundary between different water masses, as at the thermocline, there is a "surface" for the play of waves. Thought of in this way, even the top of the ocean is an interface between two fluids of different density, air and water. Waves can also occur within water layers where there is a well-defined vertical density change.

Within the sea, these internal waves do not die out quickly with depth as do the wind-waves at the surface. They have some amplitude at all depths except at the very bottom and at the surface itself. They are much harder to observe than surface waves. It takes a rapid series of density, temperature, or salinity measurements to detect them. However, those that have been studied show great heights. In deep water, internal waves may reach heights of several hundred feet, while waves in the main thermocline are generally 20 to 50 feet high. Some such waves have been related to weather disturbances. Others seem to correlate with the tides. Still others may be caused by water flowing over an irregular bottom. For the most part, however, oceanographers know little about these waves in the deep ocean except that they appear to occur even at great depths. Among other things, they may account for the ripple marks that have been photographed on some parts of the deep-sea floor, marks that resemble those left by waves on a sandy shore.

Internal waves are also thought to account for some of the slicks often seen on the ocean surface. These are smooth, glassy patches, or streaks of relatively calm water on the rippled face of the sea. Within the slicks, rippling is suppressed by a scum of organic matter. It may come from decay of remains of marine organisms or, near shore, from the land. At wind speeds over about eight miles an hour, the patches of this film are probably formed by the water-flow patterns set up by the wind. Below this wind speed, the slicks reflect the motion of the internal waves. Water circulation associated with waves in the thermocline is generally such that slicks form over spots that are somewhere between the crest of an internal wave and the trough that follows it.

Another type of wave that is poorly understood is the so-called long wave. This is a wave with a period longer than that of ordinary wind-waves but shorter than the period of the tides. Many of these waves seem to be born of wind stress and fluctuations in air pressure. Others arise from the interplay of wind-waves and swell relatively close to shore. These ordinary waves interact in a process called beating, hence the name for the long waves they produce—surf beat. Like the tides, long waves are often related locally to the natural oscillations of a basin. Arriving at the mouth of a harbor, for example, they may excite back-and-forth water movements strong enough to snap mooring cables.

A particularly destructive type of "wave" is sometimes generated by storms. Low air pressure associated with the storm causes the sea surface to hump up slightly. Augmented by storm winds blowing across an expanse of shallow water, this sea level rise may inundate coastal regions. Like tsunamis, these storm surges are sometimes misnamed "tidal waves." And like tsunamis, they can be devastating when they finally hit land. Such surges may last several hours and be followed by recurrences after the storm has passed if they excite oscillations in a basin. They are marked by a slow rise of water and then a sharper rise that may reach ten or more feet above normal high tide. Surges are often identified by noting the rise of water above that predicted for the tide. In the shallow, enclosed basin of the North Sea, particularly bad surges are generated by storms that move southwestward at certain speeds. They form surges that race anticlockwise around the sea at the speed of the normal wave of the tide. The great surge that flooded British East Anglia in 1953 raised the average level of the entire North Sea by some two feet for about two hours. Meteorologists have set up a fairly effective forecasting and warning system for the North Sea area. It is as badly needed there as is the tsunami-warning network of the North Pacific.

Tsunami warning is an international venture. It goes into action as soon as an earthquake that might produce a tsunami is detected. Reports from wave observers at locations around the North Pacific are sent to data centers where they are processed to see whether or not a tsunami is on its way. The system is constantly being improved. Computer programs for data processing and forecasting tsunami impact on coast lines are steadily made more effective. New wave detectors, such as unmanned buoys, are being developed. These should fill in one of the biggest blank spots in the tsunami reporting system, the vast expanses of open ocean where, at this writing, no observatories were located.

Indeed, reasonably accurate and repeated observations in the open sea are needed to understand many aspects of the ocean's wave patterns. Without them, oceanographers still do not know just how storm winds generate waves or how tides affect the earth. British geophysicist Sir Harold Jeffreys once calculated that about half the energy of tides is dissipated daily by the friction of tidal currents against the bottoms of shallow seas. The Bering Sea is an especially large energy sink. This tidal friction should gradually slow the earth's rotation. In fact, studies of the daily-growth rings of ancient corals indicate that there were more than 400 days in the year some 400 million years ago. However, neither the tidal friction nor the true course of the tides can be accurately assessed until oceanographers know the full range of the tides in the open sea.

At this writing, a few such measurements had been made off San Diego and in the North Sea. The International Oceanographic Commission of the United Nations has endorsed a world survey of deep-sea tides. This involves placing 300 tide gauges on the sea bed as a first step. Also, with the continuing development of faster computers, tide theorists should soon be able to compute the tides using mathematical models that take account of the real shape of the ocean floor. Meanwhile, oceanographers must live with the uncomfortable knowledge that some of the most commonplace features of the ocean—the waves and tides with which practical seafarers long ago learned to cope—have an inherent complexity that so far has put them beyond full scientific comprehension.

PLATE 1: Lowering deep-sea camera. *R. G. Munns, Woods Hole Oceanographic Institution.*

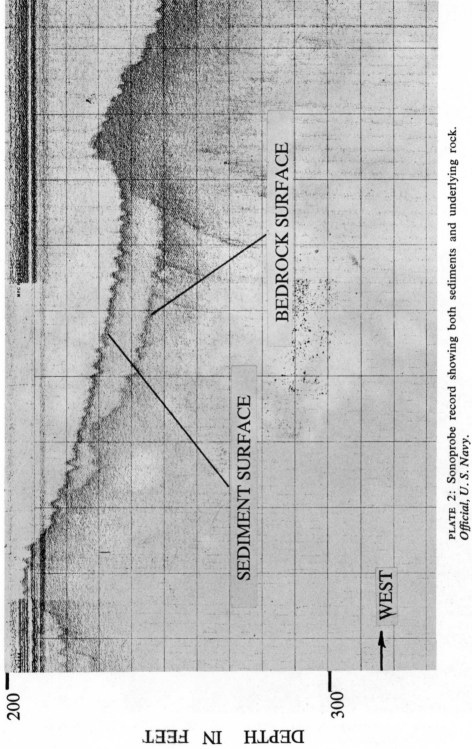

PLATE 2: Sonoprobe record showing both sediments and underlying rock. *Official, U. S. Navy.*

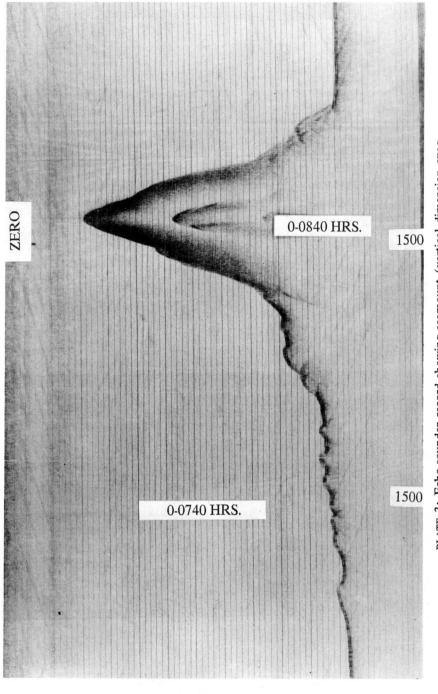

ZERO

0-0840 HRS.

1500

0-0740 HRS.

1500

PLATE 3: Echo-sounder record showing seamount (vertical dimension exaggerated). *Woods Hole Oceanographic Institution.*

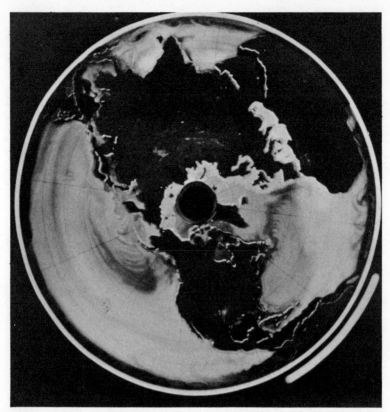

PLATE 4: Cooled at the center (pole) and heated at the rim (equator), rotating cylindrical tanks of liquid simulate circulation patterns of the sea. Wooden blocks carved to appropriate shapes represent major land masses. Colored liquid in water mimics currents. *William S. von Arx, Woods Hole Oceanographic Institution.*

PLATE 5: Wave approaching beach at La Jolla, California shows classic form of a breaker as it begins to "feel" the bottom. *Robert C. Cowen.*

PLATE 6: Famed Outermost House on Cape Cod overlooks Nauset Marsh. Such inshore waters will be prime sites for fish farms of the future. *Robert C. Cowen.*

PLATE 7, A & B: Man invades the deep. Above, research submarine *Deepstar*. Below, North American Aviation's submarine *Beaver* and aquanauts from sea-bottom house service an oil rig. (*Above, artist's conception from Westinghouse Electric Corp.; below, artist's conception from North American Aviation, Inc.*)

PLATE 8: The bathyscaphe *Trieste* as she appeared shortly before carrying men to the deepest part of the sea, diving 35,800 feet into the Marianas Trench on January 23, 1960. *Official, U. S. Navy.*

PLATE 9: This sculptured cliff face illustrates the erosive power of waves and spray. *Robert C. & Mary S. Cowen.*

PLATE 10 & PLATE 11: The rockweed "forest" (above) and some of its denizens (below). This is one of the shore's most populous habitats. *Robert C. & Mary S. Cowen.*

PLATE 12 & PLATE 13: Shore creatures must endure pounding surf and des-iccating exposure. Above, mussels on rocks; on facing page, barnacles on a cliff face. *Robert C. & Mary S. Cowen.*

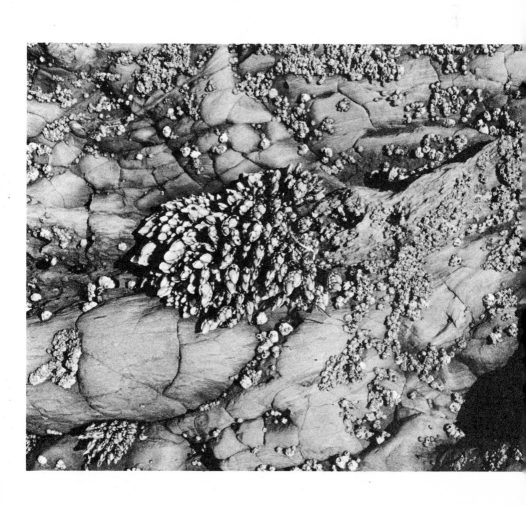

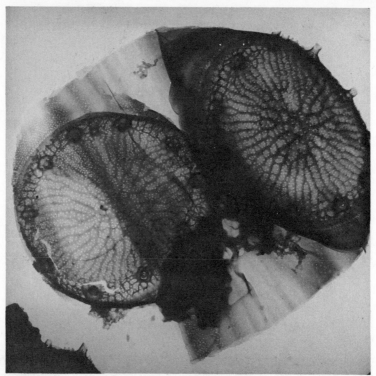

PLATE 14 & PLATE 15: Diatoms as seen through an electron microscope. Above, unknown species of *Detonula*, slightly crushed; below, *Skeletonema costatum*, valves of two individuals joined by spines. *Microphotos from R. R. Guillard, Woods Hole Oceanographic Institution.*

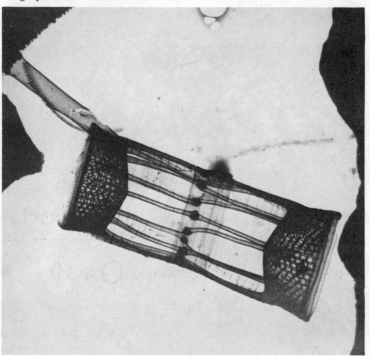

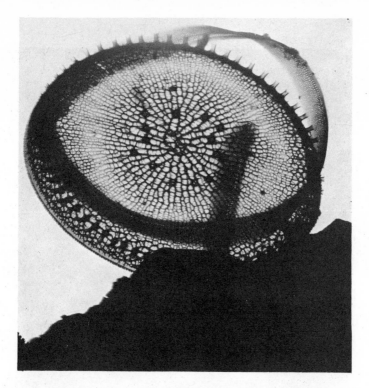

PLATE 16 & PLATE 17: Two unknown species of *Thalassiosira*. Both photos show a valve and connecting band. Magnifications range from about 5000 to 9000 times for these and previous two plates.

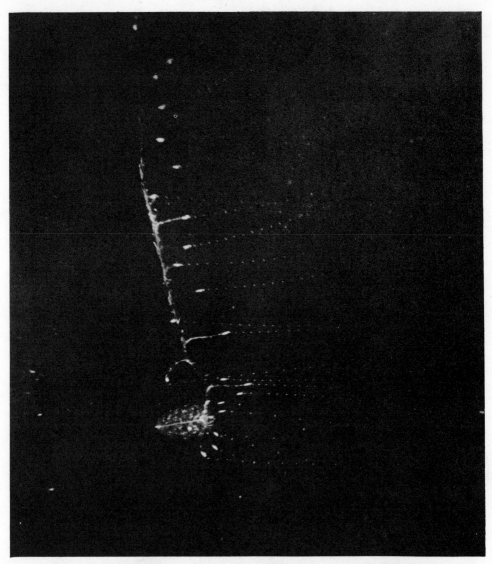

PLATE 18: Siphonophore photographed 2000 feet down off Pilo, Greece. *Photograph by Harold E. Edgerton, courtesy National Geographic Magazine, © National Geographic Society.*

PLATE 19: Life thrives 25,000 feet down in Romanche Trench. Note animals circled. *Photograph by Harold E. Edgerton, courtesy National Geographic Magazine,* © *National Geographic Society.*

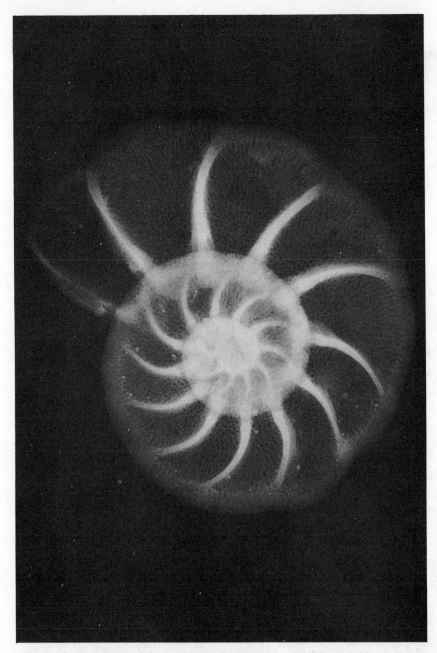

PLATE 20: X-rays reveal the intricate structure of a coiled Foraminifer shell the size of a grain of sand. The animal that inhabited this fossilized shell probably lived 60 to 90 million years ago. It was of the species *Placenticeras whitfieldi*. *Eastman Kodak Company.*

THE RESTLESS WATERS

Seven tenths of our planet's surface is never at rest. Quite apart from the phenomena of tides and waves, the interlocking water masses of the oceans are forever on the move. Sometimes they are in a hurry, as when the Gulf Stream pours past Miami like a millrace. Sometimes they barely creep along, as in the case of the cold bottom currents that may take decades, even centuries, to complete their journey. But somehow, over no one knows how long a time, any given droplet of sea water will find its way to almost every part of the sea's domain.

This constant movement of the waters, this restless stirring which we classify as great current systems, is one of the most characteristic features of the sea. It mixes the oceans so thoroughly that, in spite of the local salinity variations that continually develop, the general composition of their dissolved salts is everywhere the same. It helps even out the unequal distribution of the sun's heating and regulates the weather. It creates vertical upwelling currents that bring nutrient minerals from the depths. These fertilize rich plant growths in many areas, which in turn are the mainstay of the world's great fisheries.

Because the ocean circulation is so basic, it is one of the first things oceanographers must understand to build a comprehensive science of the seas. Yet they have scarcely begun to unravel its puzzle. Relevant observations with an acceptable degree of accuracy have been made only within the past half century. Even then most of them have been so scattered that it has been difficult to draw comprehensive pictures of the currents. The many fine current charts that have been made are really only averages based on data often taken years apart. They don't begin to show what happens day by day, or even month by month, in the oceans.

Think what a fix the weatherman would be in if he had only charts of monthly average winds to guide his forecasting!

Fortunately the meteorologist can draw up maps several times a day which show in some detail just how the atmosphere is behaving. Oceanographers need something equivalent to these "synoptic charts" of the weatherman if they are ever to understand the oceans. Since the ocean is more stable than the atmosphere, however, data for a large area taken over several weeks or months are quite useful. But until recently even this kind of survey was little more than an oceanographer's dream. Ship time is expensive and the ocean is immense. The German ship *Meteor* made a comprehensive survey of the South Atlantic during 1925–27 that long remained a lonely example of the rest of the oceanographic world.

The International Geophysical Year changed all that. Twenty-five of the thirty-seven nations that shared the oceanographic phase of IGY put eighty research ships to sea in a co-ordinated effort that gave oceanographers the broad, integrated surveys they had needed. Some of them teamed up to make a comprehensive hydrographic survey of the entire Atlantic, while others cruised the Indian Ocean and made broad sweeps over the half hemisphere of water we call the Pacific. The knowledge they gained marked the start of a revolution in this part of ocean science. Some startling discoveries were made, such as that of a current system in the Pacific as sizable as the Gulf Stream. But the most important gain was the mass of data covering vast water areas which oceanographers could only study piecemeal before.

The success of the IGY set a precedent for international co-operation that has characterized oceanographic research ever since that time. The International Indian Ocean Expedition (1959–65), for example, has made the Indian Ocean one of the best known of the seven seas. Thus, a wide basic knowledge of ocean currents is being built up. The over-all pattern of these currents is outlined on one of the endpaper maps. It is an interwoven flow that embraces the world in its web.

Pattern of the Currents

If there were no other factor influencing the oceans, solar heating near the equator and cooling toward the poles, plus the ever-

present force of gravity, would be enough to start the waters
circulating. However, the unequal heating sets the atmosphere
to moving as well. The wind systems this creates interact so strongly
with the oceans that the winds are the major driving force of the
surface currents. This vast heat-driven mechanism of wind and
water is guided by two all-pervading forces—gravity and the
earth's rotational spinning. They grip every tiny parcel of air or
water individually, yet they control the courses of the wind and
current masses.

The action of gravity is simply the familiar tendency of heavier
water to sink and lighter water to rise. You see it every time you
boil water in a saucepan and set up convection currents. The action
of the earth's rotation is more subtle. If a missile were fired from
either pole to hit a point on the equator, it would have to be
aimed some distance ahead of the target in the direction of the
earth's spin. Otherwise it would miss the mark, because while
the missile was in flight the equatorial target would have rotated
out of its path. To an observer on the ground it would have
looked as if the missile had curved in its path, as though some
invisible force had continuously made it shift course. Scientists
call this fictitious force the "Coriolis force." It influences every
object moving freely over the earth's surface. Of course it really
isn't a force at all. It is simply the effect of the planet's turning
beneath the objects while they move along. In the Northern Hemisphere it seems to turn them toward the right relative to the
surface, and in the Southern Hemisphere toward the left. It is the
second guiding influence of winds and currents. Its effect on the
currents is to make them flow somewhat to the right of the wind
in the Northern Hemisphere and to the left in the Southern Hemisphere. Actually the water starts to move in the direction of the
wind but is immediately turned toward one side by the Coriolis
force, the degree of turning depending on several factors, including latitude and frictional resistance in the water.

The combined result of winds and these guiding forces is an
interconnected system of clockwise- and counterclockwise-flowing
currents. Oceanographers call these swirling systems "gyres." You
find them in all of the major oceans, current merging into current, weaving their arabesques between equatorial and polar seas.

In tropical latitudes, the main driving force of these oceanic
rivers is the Trade Winds. Blowing with a force often between

30 and 40 miles an hour, these are the steadiest winds on earth. They blow northwestward and southwestward, respectively, in the Northern and Southern hemispheres right around the planet, forcing the waters into the strong westward-flowing North and South Equatorial currents. These are the currents that old-time navigators used to ride. More recently the South Equatorial Current in the Pacific carried Thor Heyerdahl and his raft *Kon-Tiki* on their epic adventure.

In the Atlantic, these currents are diverted by the land mass of the Americas and blocked by the slender Isthmus of Panama. Driven against this western barrier, the waters pile up so that the sea surface slopes upward to the west about three inches in 1000 miles.

As long as the winds are blowing, the waters flow right on up this oceanic "hill." But between the northern and southern Trade Wind belts there is an area of calm, or at the most light and variable winds, called the Doldrums. Here, with no wind to support it, water runs eastward down the sea slope to form the Equatorial Counter Current. This is most strongly developed in the eastern Pacific but is found in the Atlantic too, flowing eastward just north of the equator. These ocean and atmospheric systems in low latitudes tend to center around the "heat equator" rather than the geographic equator. This "heat equator" is to the heat distribution of the earth what the geographic equator is to the earth's geography and is located somewhat north of the latter as determined by the maximum intensity of the sun's heating.

As the equatorial currents flow westward, the shape of the land barrier shunts them to the north and south. Outside the West Indies, the North Equatorial Current splits. Part of it is forced northwestward to become the Bahamas Current. But the Trade Winds still blow strongly from the northeast, holding the rest of the current on a more westerly course through the Antilles into the Caribbean Sea.

Meanwhile, to the south, part of the South Equatorial Current is turned down the South American coast and becomes the Brazil Current. But only about half of the water can flow this way, for the bulge of Brazil splits the current neatly. Part of it is deflected northward along the coast into the Northern Hemisphere, where it joins the north equatorial waters flowing into the Caribbean.

By now the mass of water has reached titanic proportions. It races through Antillean narrows like a swift river. Urged on by the incessant Trades and funneled by the converging passage between Cuba and the Yucatan Peninsula, it rushes headlong against the land barrier until it piles up into a head of more than seven inches. This is the "pumping system" driving the Florida Current. Forced on by this head of pressure and blocked by the mass of water trapped in the Gulf of Mexico, the bulk of the flow turns sharply north and on into the Atlantic between Miami and Cuba. Here it becomes one of the greatest rivers in the sea, reaching velocities of more than four knots and carrying a water load almost a thousand times that of the Mississippi.

When these waters turn north to begin the Gulf Stream system, they have been on their way from the eastern Atlantic for several weeks or even months. They have been warmed by the tropical sun all the way and now are carrying this heat energy northward, a striking example of how the ocean currents help balance the heat budget of the planet.

Continuing northward, the Gulf Stream picks up the water that has been diverted into the Bahamas Current. Thus it grows until, between latitudes 37° and 39° N, the stream transports more than 100 million cubic meters of water a second. That's more than 500 Amazon Rivers. It begins to veer right above Cape Hatteras, moving out from the coast and turning until it flows more or less east just off the Grand Banks. By this time, the warm blue mass of the Gulf Stream has run into the icy green waters of the Labrador Current coming from the north to cool the coast above Hatteras. As these water systems meet at sea, the Gulf Stream slows down and is cooled and slightly diluted by the northern water. It spreads out over the northern Atlantic in various current filaments that form a diffuse flow called the North Atlantic Drift which is driven partly by the prevailing westerly winds. It is doubtful that much of this ever warms the coast of Europe. The best data at this writing suggest that, by far, the bulk of the water drifts southward from the Grand Banks. It seems weakly related, at best, to currents north of the Grand Banks or the Canaries Current that flows southward off Europe, thence to feed the North Equatorial Current once more.

This circuit of the waters completes the North Atlantic gyre. There is a similar gyre in the South Atlantic formed by the South

Equatorial and weakly developed Brazil Currents with a return flow off the coast of Africa in the ill-defined Benguela Current. The circuit is completed on the southern end by another of the earth's spectacular current systems.

Between latitudes 40° and 60° South, the winds blow steadily and strongly from the west with no land to block or modify them. Driving the waters before them, they set up an ever-flowing current round the Antarctic Continent—the West Wind Drift. The Brazil Current feeds into this circumpolar system.

Like the Atlantic, the Pacific and Indian oceans have two major gyres, although in the latter they are rather vaguely developed. There is no opportunity for anything comparable to the Gulf Stream in the Indian Ocean. Instead, the shape of the land forces the North Equatorial Current down the east coast of Africa to join with the similarly diverted South Equatorial Current to form the strong Agulhas Current that flows as far as the Cape of Good Hope. But the northern part of this ocean is dominated by the monsoons, whose regular southwest-northeast seasonal shifting of the winds imposes its own current regime on the waters.

In the Pacific, there is an immense equatorial stretch with no land to divert the westward-flowing currents. Here the South Equatorial Current just spreads diffusely over the whole southwestern part of the ocean. This great gyre is completed to the south by the West Wind Drift of the "Roaring Forties," as old sailing masters called these windy regions, and on the east by the Humboldt Current flowing up the western coast of South America.

North of the equator, the Philippines split the North Equatorial Current after its long journey across the ocean. Part of the current turns south and back to join the eastward-running countercurrent. Part is forced northward where, off Japan, it becomes the Kuroshio, a somewhat weaker counterpart of the Gulf Stream. Again as in the Atlantic, this current turns eastward toward America as the Japan Current, while an icy flow from the north, the Oyashio, cuts in behind it. The gyre is completed by the flow southward down the western American coast of the California Current, which joins the North Equatorical Current off Lower California.

The circulating current systems influence the waters in the broad areas they encircle as well as those immediately connected with their flow. Nowhere is this more clearly seen than in the North Atlantic.

Desert in the Sea

In the middle of the North Atlantic gyre is a calm sunny region of legend and lazily drifting weed—the Sargasso Sea. Columbus ran into it on his first transatlantic crossing. He encountered the weed just west of the Azores, and it increased in abundance until his men began to fear they were in coastal waters and would certainly run aground. But the bottom was almost three miles below and they came through easily. Since then, and in spite of their safe passage, the legend of the menace of the Sargassum weed has grown and persisted through the years. One wonders how many sailors have carefully avoided the area because of this legend. As recently as 1952, Alain Bombard, who sailed alone on a raft across the Atlantic, reportedly planned his trip to avoid the Sargasso because he believed it to be "a major navigational hazard, a terrible trap, where plant filaments and seaweed grip vessels in an unbreakable net."

Actually, such sailors had little to fear. There is plenty of weed, but it floats in relatively small patches with open water in between. The region is really more remarkable for what it is than for what

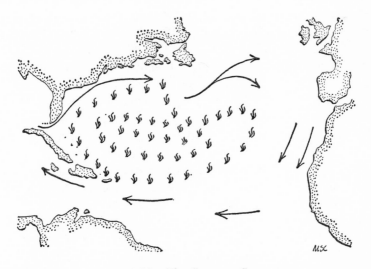

FIG. 29 : The Sargasso Sea.

the legends claim it to be. This huge, slowly rotating eddy is one of the great deserts of the sea.

The area covered by the weeds is large and somewhat variable. In late summer it is roughly an oval measuring 1000 miles by 2000 miles, with its long axis lying more or less east-west. But the Sargasso water system covers an even larger area. Dr. Columbus Iselin of Woods Hole pointed out in the 1930s that it includes pretty much the whole of the inner portion of the gyre, with the major currents as its boundaries. These impart a slow, clockwise rotation to the entire water mass.

More recently, Dr. John H. Ryther, also of Woods Hole, described the Sargasso Sea as a shallow lens of warm water floating on the distinctly colder waters of the main ocean. It is sharply separated from these colder waters by a zone of rapidly changing temperature. As far as is known, this is unique among the great gyres in the oceans. And the life that is found there is unique as well.

No one knows where the Sargassum weed comes from. It got its name from Portuguese sailors who thought that its air-bladder floats looked like small grapes they called *salgazo*. At one time weeds were thought to come from coastal areas, perhaps in the West Indies, where storms had torn them loose from their beds. Dr. Albert E. Parr, now director emeritus of the American Museum of Natural History in New York, made a thorough study of the weeds in the early 1930s. He found that 90 per cent of them consisted of two species that are naturally floating and are never found attached to rocks. Also, he estimated the standing weed crop at several million tons, far too much to be maintained by castaways from coastal beds even if these did exist. The weeds themselves seem well suited to their environment. They grow and reproduce by budding. They are vigorously healthy, often showing new leaves and young shoots. So the mystery remains. Whatever the origin of the weed, the present consensus is that it arrived in the Sargasso Sea a very long time ago and through the slow process of evolutionary adaptation has become a native of these open waters.

With little upwelling or mixing to renew its fertility, the lazily rotating Sargasso is a biological desert. Its rate of plankton production is only about one third the average for the world's oceans. Since the tiny drifting plants and animals that make up the plankton are the basic food that supports the larger marine animals, the Sargasso rates low on the over-all biological productivity scale as well.

But even deserts have their life forms. These often show curiously specialized adaptations that help them overcome the rigors of the environment. So it is in the Sargasso. Almost every clump of drifting weeds has its cargo of small fish, crabs, shrimps, octopi, and many other creatures. Each of these is marvelously adapted to living on and about the weed that gives it sanctuary in a hostile region. If they lost their grip, some of these creatures would sink uncontrollably into the depths, where they would perish.

In some cases the animals have taken on the appearance of the weed itself, so that it takes a sharp eye to spot them. There are weedlike fishes and weedlike crabs. There are sea slugs with folds of skin that enable them to blend perfectly with their surroundings. Various species of worms build houses of lime in which they float with the weeds, taking food from the passing water. There is even one air-breathing inhabitant—*Halobates,* the water strider. This adventurous character runs over the sea surface on six long hairy legs, using the Sargassum as a resting place.

But, in spite of the lively community of the seaweeds, the Sargasso Sea is a sparsely populated wilderness, a strange oceanic desert created by the pattern of wind and currents.

These current patterns give an average picture pieced together from widely scattered data. As an average, it illustrates the general movements of the surface waters and their role in transporting heat around the world. But it hints nothing of the true complexity that oceanographers now are beginning to discover. The familiar Gulf Stream is a case in point.

The Gulf Stream: A Study in Complexity

"There is a river in the ocean. In the severest droughts it never fails, and in the mightiest floods it never overflows—It is the Gulf Stream." That is the way Matthew F. Maury described this mighty ocean current in 1855, and for decades thereafter oceanographers shared this view. Just one hundred years later Frederick C. Fuglister of Woods Hole took a radically different approach. "It is evident," he wrote, "that as more detailed observations of ocean currents are obtained many heretofore unknown structural

characteristics will come to light, and the simple concept of a
major ocean current 'flowing like a river through the sea' may
become a thing of the past."

Here was the first big break with the traditional way of looking
at the surface movements of the ocean. Like the concept of the
"average man," the picture of an "average current" broke down
when it came to individual daily cases.

Scientists had known for a long time that the Gulf Stream
was more than a flow of water through a fixed channel. They
knew that it meandered and frequently shifted position, that it
threw off sizable eddies and mingled confusedly with Labrador
waters to the north. After all, the curving coast line of the South
Atlantic United States was sculptured by the stream's swirling inshore eddies. Nevertheless, the general concept was of a steadily
flowing, well-defined current—literally a "river in the ocean"—
that slowly veered northeastward.

This picture of the Gulf Stream system was based on data often
taken years apart. It showed how the waters moved on the average
over long periods of time. The question was, how much of the
natural variability of the current was left in the picture? No one
knew and few suspected how different the day-by-day situation
really was.

Fuglister became interested in the problem during World War
II while preparing charts of water conditions in the northeastern
Atlantic. That was when he first began to realize how little is
really known about the surface currents.

There were tantalizing hints in data from the International Ice
Patrol. The patrol charted water coming into and out of the
Arctic and also the position of the Gulf Stream as it flowed
past the Grand Banks and Newfoundland. Their data showed nothing like a continuous band of warm water. Instead, there seemed
to be a branching system with cool northern water between fingers
of the Gulf Stream. Also there seemed to be some kind of reverse
movement within the system, with cool water moving in a direction opposite to the warm water as a somewhat weaker flow.

After the war, Fuglister set out to learn more. Working with
L. V. Worthington and others at Woods Hole, he began tracing
the main Gulf Stream system. The hints of a branching system
in the Ice Patrol data were confirmed throughout every part of
the Gulf Stream studies. Fuglister calls this a "shingle effect" in

which a finger of water moves strongly for a way and then begins to peter out. Parallel to this and a little distance away (with variations), another current finger seems to develop and in its turn peters out. Still farther along, and again parallel, a third finger develops, and so on for all the courses the ship followed. In between these forward movements are the reverse cool currents, also in a shingle effect. This pattern of complexity showed how misleading the average currents sketched on charts can be.

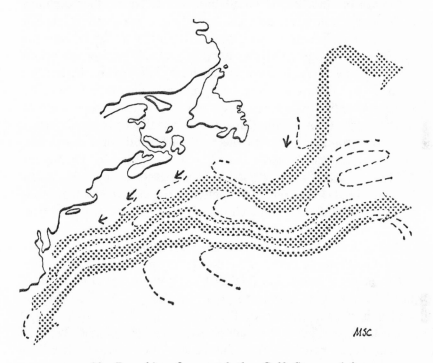

FIG. 30 : Branching fingers of the Gulf Stream (after Fuglister).

Sometimes one of the loops in the Gulf Stream's meandering course closes itself off to become an independent eddy. Since it may form from a 500- to 1000-kilometer length of the stream, it is a substantial mass of Gulf Stream water. Fuglister has traced the independent course of some of these eddies. He finds they maintain their identity for six months and longer. No one suspected that the eddies persist for so long. They appear to be a little-understood mechanism by which Gulf Stream water is carried into regions well away from the main stream. In 1966, for example, Gulf Stream water was found 140 miles off Cape Cod. That's the closest it has ever come to New England as far as anyone knows. This may well have been an invasion of a detached eddy rather than the stream itself. Fuglister thinks the eddies may play a far more important role in the North Atlantic than anyone realizes.

Meanwhile, Worthington has been trying to work out the overall course of Gulf Stream circulation. As do some other oceanographers, he seriously questions the familiar geographical notion that the Gulf Stream warms Britain. He thinks its direct influence on Europe is slight. No one has ever traced its flow in British waters. There is no clear indication how Gulf Stream water flows beyond the western Atlantic. Judging from distribution over the North Atlantic of temperature, salinity, and oxygen content, Worthington thinks Gulf Stream water sinks below the surface and flows southward far to the west and south of Britain. The main flow may get no farther north than the latitude of the Azores. There is a current moving northward and eastward past the British Isles at about 3 million cubic meters a second. It has the wrong oxygen content for the Gulf Stream. It may contain some Mediterranean water.

"What are we talking about," Worthington asks, "150 million cubic meters a second or 3 million? Anything under 10 million cubic meters a second is trivial in talking about the Gulf Stream." In these terms, it begins to look as though the Gulf Stream system is a phenomenon of the western North Atlantic. "I just don't think we know enough to say whether or not the Gulf Stream warms Europe," Worthington explains. "But this has been said for so long it has sort of jelled."

What is needed is a thorough water mapping of the North Atlantic on a month-by-month, or even a day-by-day basis to clear away this haziness with fact. The same can be said of the North Pacific and the Kuroshio. Called the "Black Current," it seems to have as much complexity as the Gulf Stream. Indeed, this is true of all the major current systems. The waters off Peru give an especially striking illustration of the potential value of understanding and predicting the vagaries of the currents.

El Niño

As South America stretches its tip toward Antarctica, it catches part of the West Wind Drift, forcing it northward in a broad languid flow known as the Peru, or the Humboldt, Current. This moves on up the west coast of the continent until, a few degrees south of the equator, it swings westward to join the South Equatorial Current. On its shoreward side are the flows and eddies which co-operate with the prevailing coastal winds in a process known as upwelling. A predominantly southeasterly wind blows surface water away from the coast. This is replaced by water moving up (upwelling) from moderate depths, bringing with it phosphates and other fertilizing minerals that nourish one of the richest populations of marine life in the world.

Life in the Peru Current is incredibly fertile. It supports millions of sea birds whose guano deposits give Peru an endless supply of high-grade fertilizer. In 1956, for example, 330,000 tons of guano were harvested. This means that the guano birds themselves caught over four million tons of a small sardine-like fish, the anchoveta. At the same time, fishermen caught 120,000 tons of the fish directly, plus a substantial haul of larger species that feed on the anchoveta. The abundance of anchoveta is truly phenomenal—and this is just one species. Imagine how luxuriant the plant and animal plankton, the base of the food pyramid in the sea, must be to support such a population!

But every so often in summer disaster strikes. The flow of the Peru Current slackens or moves out to sea. Close to shore upwelling ceases, surface temperatures of the inshore water rise to abnormal heights, and warm, less saline water moves in from the north. El Niño (The Child) has arrived. The (Christ) Child symbolizes the season.

The normal fish population dies or moves out to be replaced by tropical forms. Fishermen set their nets deeper to catch the accustomed species if they can. And the guano birds, deprived of their food, panic. Many of them abandon their fledglings and strike out blindly to the north or south. Others fly excitedly in circles, only to die of starvation on the beaches. The bird population may be reduced from a norm of about thirty million to something like five to eight million. All along the coast, rotting bodies of fish and birds foul the air. Sometimes there are so many that the hydrogen sulphide gas they release—the same gas released by rotten eggs—blackens the paint on ships, a phenomenon known (from the name of the Peruvian port) as the "Callao painter."

Originally El Niño was the name given to the southward invasion of warm water. But the phenomenon is more complicated than that. It is a complex of meteorological and oceanographic conditions that has several characteristic features, some of which may be more intense in one year than in another. Some of these features may even be normal aspects of Peru's coastal climate in the first half of the year, aspects which in El Niño years reach destructive proportions.

Conspicuous El Niño outbreaks have been reported for 1891, 1925, 1930, 1941, 1951, and 1957–58. Dr. Warren Wooster of Scripps Institution of Oceanography investigated the last of these and came up with a tentative theory of what may cause them.

In El Niño years, he says, there is a general weakening of the atmospheric circulation reflected in weakening of the southeasterly winds along the Peruvian coast. As the upwelling dies down, the surface waters are heated by the sun. Meanwhile, the northern boundary of the Peru Current moves farther south than usual and tropical waters can move down the coast. Invasions of tropical air may bring heavy rains, with flooding and crop damage, to the normally arid land. These conditions are sometimes accompanied by an outbreak of "Red Tide," a bloom of tiny organisms that poison the water and kill multitudes of fish. Other times, the normal fish population may simply move out or go deeper to stay with the water environment to which it is accustomed. Tropical species may then come in as their accustomed environment moves south. In either case, the sea birds lose their food supply.

Wooster points out that this is really more of an outline of what needs to be studied than a scientific explanation of El Niño. There are indications that the El Niño effect is related to an extraordinary change in general weather patterns that somehow weakens the Trade Winds and recurs in roughly seven-year cycles. But El Niño does not follow the cycles closely. No one knows its meteorological cause.

El Niño is usually associated with Peru. But it is a phenomenon that affects every similar upwelling coast in the world. These include coastal regions of California, southwest Africa, and western Australia. All of these have sizable or potentially sizable fisheries. If these fisheries are to be developed and managed intelligently, El Niño needs to be understood thoroughly. One region where scientists may be able to accumulate the needed data within a reasonable time is the coastal land of the East Indian Ocean, or perhaps of western Australia, where the shifting monsoons make El Niño an annual occurrence.

The shifting structure of current flows, such as El Niño or the shingle effect in the Gulf Stream, is challenge enough by itself. But oceanographers can't be content with their knowledge of the general pattern of the surface currents either. This large-scale picture still has surprises to confound the scientists and make them wary. The most recent of these has made headlines around the world during and after the IGY.

A Second "Gulf Stream"

In 1952 Townsend Cromwell of Scripps Institution of Oceanography was fishing in equatorial waters near longtiude 150° West when he noticed his gear drifting off in an unexpected direction. At that time Cromwell was working for the U. S. Fish and Wildlife Service, experimenting with Japanese long-line fishing techniques. Several miles of supporting cable had been let out with smaller fishing lines attached. Since he was in the drift of the South Equatorial Current, Cromwell expected his line to move off toward the west. Instead it headed rapidly eastward. This was the first evidence of a vast and unsuspected subsurface countercurrent.

Cromwell himself was subsequently killed in an air crash. The current, named in his honor, became a prime target for IGY investigation. John A. Knauss, then at Scripps, headed an expedition that traced the Cromwell Current halfway across the Pacific. He found it to be as mighty as parts of the Gulf Stream, flowing at 40 million cubic meters a second. "Just think," Roger Revelle observed at the time, ". . . a river in the ocean of this size, and its very existence was not known a few years ago!" The bigger part of the surprise was yet to come. Since the IGY, oceanographers of several nations have traced the undercurrent across the Pacific. They have found comparable currents in the Atlantic and

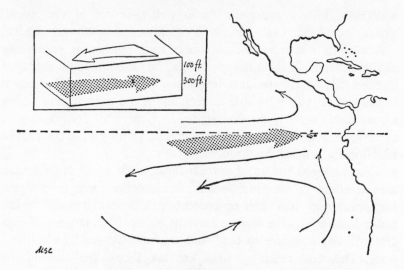

FIG. 31 : The Cromwell Current. A massive eastward flow
found beneath the westward-flowing South Equatorial
Current in the Pacific.

Indian oceans. This once unsuspected phenomenon turns out to
be a major feature of the ocean's circulation.

Knauss, now dean of the Graduate School of Oceanography
at the University of Rhode Island, says that, actually, the Atlantic undercurrent was detected in 1886. But the evidence was
neglected until Cromwell rediscovered the phenomenon in the
Pacific. As a general feature, the undercurrents are centered more
or less on the equator and flow eastward. Maximum speeds
in the Atlantic run to some three knots. In the Pacific, the undercurrent is a little slower with top speeds of just over two knots.
The undercurrent attains only about half this speed in the Indian
Ocean and is quite variable. It may be influenced by the strong
seasonal shift in the monsoon winds that dominate that region.
The fastest surface current in the sea, the Somali Current which
runs northward along the Somali coast, is strongly affected by
these winds. It flows at up to seven knots during the southwest
monsoon only to falter and die out when the winds reverse.

Unlike other major ocean currents, the water in the Cromwell
undercurrent does not differ markedly from water outside either
in temperature, salinity, or in the creatures that live within it. Yet
it, like the others, is well defined. About 200–250 miles wide by

1000 feet thick, the undercurrents flow fastest at depths of 160 to 500 feet, generally above what is called the main thermocline.

Any layer within which temperature changes much more rapidly with depth than in water above or below it, is called a thermocline. Over many areas of the ocean, the surface waters are separated from the main ocean body by such a layer. The top of this so-called "permanent" thermocline may lie from 300 to 2000 or more feet deep. It is generally the deepest and most widespread thermocline. Its changes are not linked to seasonal or other short-term influences. Other thermoclines may form above it in response to summer heating. Sometimes a transient thermocline will form near the surface during the day to disappear at night. Where it exists, a well-developed thermocline tends to seal off vertical water movements.

Although oceanographers have become widely acquainted with the undercurrents since Cromwell's fishing gear took off in the "wrong" direction, no one knows what makes the currents flow. This unsolved puzzle is basic to understanding the circulation of the sea.

But even though the experts have much to learn about the surface currents, these currents are still one of the most widely known features in the sea. They are often obvious and impressive to sailors who must navigate them, and they usually are part of children's elementary geography lessons. Yet beneath their wandering waters is a complex and considerably less-well-known circulation throughout the depths of all oceans. It operates on a scale more vast than the surface systems. It is one of the principal mechanisms by which the oceans help maintain the earth's heat balance and regulate the climate. Geophysicists will never understand the over-all workings of weather and climate until they have a true picture of these deep-water movements.

The Power of Salt and Heat

The winds that move the surface currents stir the oceans deeply. Their influence can be traced thousands of feet down. But there are other forces stirring the depths as well, forces that arise from the imbalance of water masses when some are heavier than others. This is the process of convection. Light water rises; denser water sinks. Here is a mechanism of great power—power enough to move the tremendous bulk of the oceans. It is a nice question for the theorists where wind power stops and density forces take over. Much of the circulation is a mixture of both.

Sea-water density depends on temperature and salinity. The warmer the water, the lighter it is. The more dissolved salts it contains, the denser it will be. And vice versa. It is one of the wonders of geophysics that relatively small differences in these quantities can generate the forces that move oceans.

Open-ocean surface temperatures range from about 31° or so Fahrenheit in high Arctic and Antarctic regions to around 86° in the tropics. And the difference between summer and winter temperatures at any one place is much less than the difference between these geographical extremes. In the depths, temperatures vary with water masses but generally drop off with depth so that all the deep oceans have bottom layers of about 34° or 35° Fahrenheit. Salinity likewise varies somewhat with the locale. It is higher where evaporation and sluggish or blocked circulation increase the salt concentration of surface waters. It is lower where rivers, heavy rainfall, and melting ice dilute these waters. In the Mediterranean Sea it reaches 39 parts per thousand and as much as 40 in the Red Sea, while in the Baltic it drops to 30 or less. The average salinity for all the oceans is 34 to 35, and 90 per cent of the world's sea water falls within a few per cent of that average, a tribute to the ceaseless mixing of the oceans.

The cold water that underlies all the oceans is one of the most striking features of the deep sea and one of the indicators of its far-ranging currents. Everywhere this bottom water is only a few degrees above freezing. Even in the tropics the warm upper water, which reaches down some 1500 feet, does not moderate this icy cold. This ubiquitous bottom water must come from somewhere. Its frigid temperatures show it must be formed in cold regions. Studies of dissolved oxygen content, a rough measure of its age, indicate it sinks from the surface in the far North Atlantic and around Antarctica. From these sources it spreads somehow, and at an unknown speed, over the ocean floor.

Above these deepest waters are other water masses, identified by their characteristic temperatures, salinities, and other chemical name tags. To specialists, such characteristics are as distinctive and familiar as the names on neighborhood mailboxes. These water masses are inherently stable. Spread over large areas, they show little vertical mixing, like layers in a cake. But there are also regions with substantial up-and-down movements. These are the places where the action of the density forces that drive much of the deep circulation is most apparent.

The waters around Antarctica are such a region. Here in the cold of the Antarctic winter and around the edge of the polar continental shelf, the water masses that creep under much of the ocean are born. This water is the densest known in the sea. Not only is it cooled to polar temperatures, but it is given an extra burden of salt as ice forms at the surface, throwing out the dissolved salts as its freezes. This dense water sinks to the sea floor and slowly creeps away.

Meanwhile, at the surface and a bit farther out to sea, another water mass is being formed. Here heavy rains and snowfall plus summer melting of the ice dilute the water. Even though it is cold, its salinity is reduced until it is relatively light for that region and it drifts off to the north on the surface.

The combined outflow of this Antarctic Surface Water and sinking Bottom Water brings one of the fundamental processes of the ocean into play. The outgoing water at the surface has to be replaced from somewhere. Thus a deep mass of water that has come down from the north rides up over the sinking bottom water and rises to the surface. As it rises, it brings with it fertilizing minerals that have accumulated in the depths. The result is a prodigious outburst of life that, among other things, sustains the large and famous population of Antarctic whales. Here is a mechanism that produces upwelling in the open ocean. Wherever there is a divergence of water at the surface, other water must upwell from below to take its place. And conversely, wherever there is a piling up, a convergence, of surface water, a compensating sinking must take place. In the Antarctic, there is such a convergence between latitudes 50° and 55° South where the outflowing surface water meets warmer and still lighter water from lower latitudes. The Antarctic Surface Water dips down in this region and continues northward as Antarctic Intermediate Water.

The interplay of such water masses is best known in the Atlantic. In the Arctic, cold water, made relatively fresh and light by river outflows, is formed and drifts southward on the surface until it meets the warmer, saltier, and still lighter waters of the North Atlantic Drift brought north by the Gulf Stream. Here is

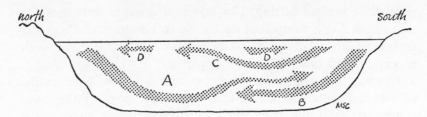

FIG. 32 : The layered flows of the Atlantic (schematic). A—Arctic water; B—Antarctic water; C—Antarctic Intermediate Water; D—Surface flows toward Arctic and Antarctic convergences respectively.

another mid-ocean covergence. Obedient to the laws that govern the currents and maintain the water balance of the seas, the Arctic water sinks and proceeds southward at great depths. Eventually it returns to the surface as upwelling in the distant Antarctic, completing a vertical circulation that is one of the principal mechanisms by which the Atlantic overturns even its deepest waters.

In the Southern Hemisphere, this North Atlantic Deep Water, as it is called, joins with other water in the southward-moving mass that rides over the northward-creeping Antarctic Bottom Water. This latter itself crosses the equator, merging eventually with the deep water of the North Atlantic. The Antarctic Intermediate Water also moves over the equator and, at depths of 100 fathoms or less, sends tongues of relatively cool low-saline water under the salty warm Atlantic Central Water of the Sargasso Sea. The over-all result of this complex interchange is a flow out of the North Atlantic across the equator of six million tons of water every second and an equal and opposite compensating flow coming out of the Southern Hemisphere. Some of this exchange is carried by swift narrow currents such as those that help originate the Gulf Stream. The rest is carried by the broad slow drifting of the layered water masses.

There is one other distinctive water mass in the North Atlantic. It comes from the Mediterranean in a vigorous exchange of water that makes the Strait of Gibraltar one of the world's famous "millraces."

The Mediterranean is one of the saltiest seas on earth. Evaporation that removes an average of 70,000 tons of water a second raises the surface salinity until, in the eastern waters, it may run as high as 39 parts per thousand—five points above the oceanic average. With winter cooling, this salt-heavy water sinks down at such a rate that rivers and rainfall can't replace it. Surface water flows in from the North Atlantic in a shallow current that brings nearly two million tons of new water into the Mediterranean every second. Beneath this, a compensating current of heavy saline water pours out over the sill at the Strait and spreads at an intermediate depth over the southeastern North Atlantic. Each of these currents carries as much water as eight Mississippis. During the last war submarine commanders sometimes tried to ride these currents to sneak in and out of the Mediterranean without giving themselves away by using their motors.

Unlike the Atlantic, where deep water from the north comprises about half the total volume of the ocean, the deep basins of the Indian and Pacific oceans are filled with water from the Antarctic. No one knows how long this water has been at the bottom of the sea or how long it will stay there. Rough estimates, based on decay of radiocarbon picked up when the water was exposed to air, give ages of from a few hundred to a thousand years. How fast the oceans overturn their waters and how their water masses circulate is another of the basic features oceanographers must learn much more about to thoroughly understand the sea.

For the most part, scientists know the layered water masses from temperature and water samples taken at different times and places by surface ships. From these usually sparse measurements, they build schemes of how deep waters circulate, based on uncertain theory and individual intuition that none of them takes very seriously. Henry Stommel of Woods Hole, one of the leading theoretical oceanographers, once put it this way: "There are a number of forces acting on the ocean and resulting in currents (winds, density differences, tides). Now which of these actually does produce any one current and how does it do it? That is the unsolved problem." Dissatisfied with previous theories, Stommel decided to try turning the situation around. A few years ago he developed a theory of deep circulations which could itself be tested by direct observations in the ocean. Herein lies the story of one of the major oceanographic discoveries of the IGY.

"Wrong Way" Current

The theory of ocean circulation is an abstruse subject. To understand it takes an expert's knowledge and a fluency in high-powered mathematics. Even the specialists didn't get down to its details before World War II. Since then, however, the theories have begun to sprout and Henry Stommel has been a recognized leader in the field. Without going into the complexities of his mathematics, it will suffice to say that Stommel built his theory around the assumption that density differences, caused by differences in temperature and salinity, and not the winds are the main cause of circulation in the depths. These differences, together with the curvature of the earth's surface and the force of the earth's rotation, in his view, determine the deep-water movements.

This was a bold departure from all previous theories. These had assumed as a matter of course that it was the major wind systems that made the deep waters circulate. Density differences could modify that circulation but could set up no sizable currents of their own. To make matters worse, in 1955 Stommel announced that his theory called for a strong southward-moving current under the Gulf Stream. This is one of the most powerful of the wind-driven currents. It had long been supposed that the influence of the wind was felt all the way to the bottom. Stommel's theory seemed to fly in the face of common sense. But within twenty-four months dramatic confirmation had come from the ocean itself.

Prior to this, Dr. Alan Faller had tested Stommel's ideas in the laboratory, using some ingenious rotating ocean models originally designed by Dr. William Von Arx. These are essentially large tubs, or segments of tubs, that are rotated to simulate the earth's spinning and are heated and cooled in appropriate places to simulate the heat balance of the planet. In one elaborate model, wooden blocks cut in the shape of the major continents can be placed on the tub bottom. In smaller versions the land barriers are simulated by simple straight walls. Currents can be traced in these models by using colored liquids.

As far as could be told with these laboratory oceans, the development of currents seemed to bear out Stommel's ideas. But that wasn't good enough. He was trying to second-guess nature, and the only way he could find out whether or not he was guessing right was to trace what actually went on in the oceans themselves. Fortunately the means for doing this were already being developed at the National Institute of Oceanography in Great Britain.

Like many another ocean observer, NIO's Dr. John B. Swallow had long been dissatisfied because there was no good way of measuring large-scale deep currents directly. Instruments then used for the purpose gave dubious results at best and had to be operated from the end of a cable tied to a ship. Oceanographers needed something akin to the wind-tracking balloons of the weathermen. Dr. Swallow set out to develop such an instrument. It was ready in time to test Stommel's theory on a joint American-British cruise made in preparation for the IGY during March and early April of 1957.

This undersea "weather balloon" is simply a neutrally buoyant float that sends out an identifying sound "ping." It is an aluminum tube affair about 10 feet long that carries weights, batteries, and a

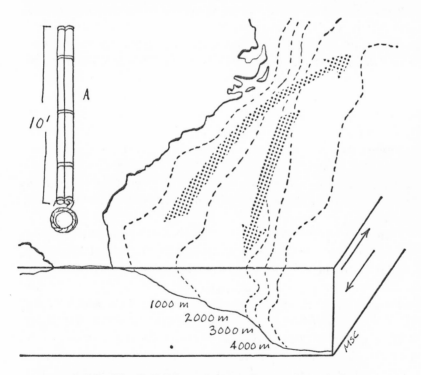

FIG. 33 : The Gulf Stream Counter Current. Inset A shows Swallow's "pinger." Ring hanging from tubes containing electrical equipment produces the sound "pings."

sound generator. By adding just the right number of small weights, the buoy can be made to float at any desired depth. In other words, it can be made neutrally buoyant without a tendency either to sink or rise. There it drifts freely along with the current, sending out "pings" by which a listener on the surface can track it.

Swallow dropped his "pinger" deep into the waters of the Gulf Stream off the Blake Plateau and followed it on the surface in Britain's research ship *Discovery II*. At the same time, L. V. Worthington in Woods Hole's *Atlantis* accurately traced the position of the Gulf Stream in that area. In all, seven buoys were released at various times. They all moved south at depths between 6600 and 9800 feet. Stommel's countercurrent had been established.

However, this doesn't prove the whole of Stommel's theory. Some oceanographers doubt that the observed countercurrent is "the" countercurrent Stommel predicted. Stommel himself points out that his theory is only a first approach to understanding ocean circulation. The Gulf Stream, he notes, "is not a river of hot water flowing through the ocean, but a narrow ribbon of high-velocity water acting as a boundary that prevents the warm water on the Sargasso Sea . . . from overflowing the colder, denser waters on the inshore . . . side." Oceanographers can't understand ocean circulation without understanding such boundary features in detail. And they can't understand currents like the Gulf Stream without detailed data on ocean circulation generally. To progress beyond the point represented by Stommel's theory, calls for effort, money, and a massive deployment of instruments far beyond any yet devoted to such studies. Without these, this branch of oceanography is at a dead end.

Commenting on this, Dr. C. G. H. Rooth, acting chairman of the Theoretical Oceanography Department at Woods Hole, used the Gulf Stream to make the point. Scientists, he said, know how ocean waters move on the average. During the 1950s, decades of data were summed up in Stommel's theory. This accounts well for what the Gulf Stream does in the steady state. This, Dr. Rooth said, is as far as oceanographers can go with the tools they have had. At this writing, they have been stuck at this point for a decade.

To understand the Gulf Stream, or any other circulation feature, Dr. Rooth explained, oceanographers must know it in all its variability. This means detailed, often daily, observations for long

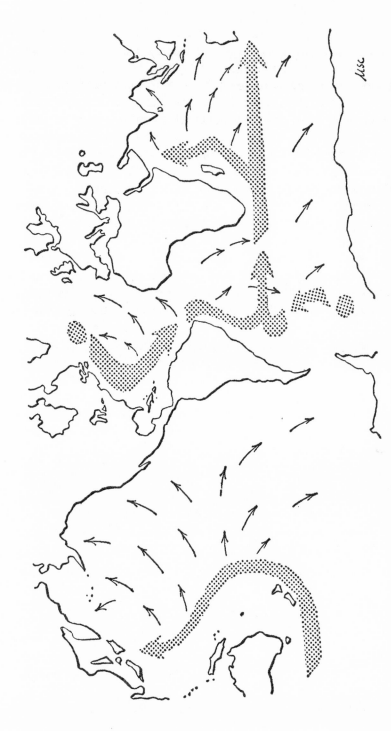

FIG. 34 : According to Stommel's theory, cold water sinks in the Arctic and Antarctic and flows along the ocean floor in relatively narrow currents from which it spreads slowly as indicated by the small arrows (after Stommel).

periods over vast areas. The most widely discussed system for doing this is a network of deeply anchored, instrument-carrying buoys. Several institutions are developing them. Some buoys would radio data ashore or perhaps relay it via satellite; others would record their data, which would be picked up regularly by ship. However it is set up, such a network would generate data at an unprecedented rate. Computerized data handling and extensive teamwork between institutions studying the data would be needed. Such a program would be expensive and ambitious beyond the dreams of oceanographers in the 1950s. Yet, Dr. Rooth said, without it, oceanographers who study circulation in the sea "might as well give up and study estuaries." A buoy program on a scale sufficient to study a large part of the Gulf Stream system may be ready by the early 1970s. Noting this, Stommel points out that "the buoy program is only one part of a many-sided approach to studying ocean circulation." Continued extensive ship surveys and perhaps aircraft and satellite surveys will also be needed. Aircraft and satellites sense surface temperatures through the infrared (heat) radiation given off by the sea. In considering a buoy program, Stommel says, "We have a measure of the task before us."

SEVEN

THE GREAT HEAT ENGINE

Every time you start a car, light a fire, or turn on a furnace you are joining in the biggest weather experiment ever. You are adding your bit to the tons of carbon dioxide sent into the air as coal, oil, wood, and natural gas are burned at unprecedented rates. Collecting in the atmosphere and warming the earth, this gas could in time substantially change our planet's climate. How fast is this unwitting experiment proceeding? What are its results likely to be? Questions such as these typify one of the biggest challenges facing earth scientists today. It is the challenge to gain an incisive understanding of the mechanisms of global weather and of climatic change. It is the challenge to use this knowledge to improve weather forecasting, to find out what man's activities are doing to the climate, to explore whether and how it may be possible to develop some degree of weather control.

The challenge is being met through mathematical equations that embody the physical laws governing the atmosphere and ocean. Used with a computer, these equations enable scientists to simulate mathematically the workings of the atmosphere and ocean with steadily increasing fidelity. This gives them, for the first time, a research tool with which they should be able to gain enough insight into the air-sea mechanism to improve forecasting substantially and explore the possibilities of changing weather and climate.

To do this, they need data on the state of the weather and the ocean all over the world. This should soon begin to be available. As of 1969, only about 20 per cent of the Northern Hemisphere and perhaps 1 or 2 per cent of the Southern Hemisphere were adequately covered. The World Meteorological Organization

(WMO) of the United Nations is working to remedy this. Member nations are establishing a joint, world-encompassing observing system called the World Weather Watch (WWW). When it is fully operating, probably by the late 1970s, the traditional manned stations on land and weather ships at sea will be supplemented by observing satellites, automatic stations on land, and automatic instrumented buoys in the ocean. Together with the mathematical models, WWW will give earth scientists the tools they need for a breakthrough to significant new knowledge of the workings of atmosphere and ocean that we call "climate" and "weather."

In using these tools, meteorologist and oceanographer work as one, for their fields of study are inseparable. From the viewpoint of weather and climate, ocean and atmosphere are intimately linked in a complex and, as yet, poorly understood manner. Together, they constitute a vast heat engine whose power source is the warming energy of the sun.

The Weather Machine

Like the motor in a car, the ocean-atmosphere engine turns heat energy into motion. In an automobile, heat is supplied by burning fuel. Much of this heat passes through the motor to be exhausted at a relatively cool temperature. The air-sea engine likewise takes in heat at the relatively warm tropics to lose most of it to space at colder latitudes and at the cold outer fringes of the atmosphere. Only a small fraction of this heat is turned into the energy of the winds and currents that keep the atmosphere and the sea in constant motion. While no one knows exactly what that fraction is, it is roughly estimated that the winds and currents at any given moment embody just under 4 per cent of the solar energy intercepted by the earth in a single day. While this percentage is small, it is slightly more energy than could be produced by all of the electrical generating plants in the United States if they were run continuously for fifty years. The currents have about 2 per cent of the energy, the wind 98 per cent.

Incoming solar energy is divided into several parts. Some of it is "deducted" before it can enter the earth's heat economy. It is reflected directly back to space by clouds and dust in the air and by the land and sea surfaces. The percentage reflected is called earth's albedo. At this writing, the best estimate for the average albedo was around 30 per cent. This varies from month to month and even from day to day as cloudiness, snow cover, and other factors change. The rest of the energy income, some 70 per cent, is used to grow plants; to heat the air, land, and sea; and to power the great heat engine.

In spite of this constant inpouring from the sun, the earth would be a far colder place were it not for the heat-absorbing gases in the air—water vapor and carbon dioxide. These invisible gases act like the glass in a gardener's greenhouse. While they let solar energy pass right on through, they absorb much of the infrared radiation by which the earth dissipates its own heat into space. This earth radiation is at much longer wave lengths than those of the solar beam. The infrared absorbing gases reradiate much of this heat back toward the ground. Without this "greenhouse effect," the earth would cool rapidly. Its surface is so warm it radiates some 10 per cent more energy than it receives directly from the sun. It would have to have a temperature of 40° below zero (C. or F.) to bring its heat loss into balance with its energy income if some of the loss were not countered by the greenhouse effect.

Much of the heat flowing through the ocean-atmosphere system is used to maintain the earth's heat balance. Because the sun heats the tropics more strongly than the poles, there is a heat surplus in low latitudes and a heat deficit in higher latitudes. Whether or not a surface area receives more heat from the sun than it loses through radiation depends on such factors as cloud and snow cover as well as the angle of the sun's rays. Generally, there is net heating between the equator and roughly latitudes 35° north and south and net-heat loss elsewhere. The excess warmth of the tropics is distributed northward and southward by winds, storms, and ocean currents to make up the energy deficit in high latitudes. Some of this energy is carried directly as heat. Much of it travels locked up in water vapor. This is the latent heat of condensation which is released when the vapor condenses to form clouds, rain, or snow. Thus every storm, however destructive from man's viewpoint, is an integral part of the heat-distributing system.

Most of the lower atmosphere's activity, which means the world's weather, is run by sources of heating and cooling at the surface. Over 80 per cent of the solar energy absorbed by the earth is absorbed at the surface. In feeding that energy into the atmosphere, the oceans play the major role. Unlike the land, which heats and cools rapidly, the sea is generally warmer than the air passing over it. Moreover, of the heat fed into the atmosphere, some 80 per cent is in the form of latent heat carried by water vapor. In the heat-engine mechanism, the atmosphere can be thought of as the working fluid of the weather. The ocean is an energy storage system of vast capacity which keeps the atmosphere going.

As pointed out in Chapter Six, the surface currents of the ocean are driven by the winds. Yet the pattern of the winds is partly determined by the pattern of heating and cooling over the earth's surface. And over most of the surface, this means the patterns of currents and water masses in the sea. The energy of the winds and the moisture of storms are also largely obtained from the ocean. More than half of that energy, in fact, comes from tropical seas. There, hurricanes and other storms pump enormous amounts of water vapor to great heights where it releases its latent heat. In forecasting weather for a few days ahead, weathermen can work with data on the atmosphere alone. But if they are to understand the basic workings of weather, if they are to uncover the mechanism that sets climatic trends, they cannot ignore the interdependence of air and sea.

What we call climate is a mode of operation of the air-sea system. The difference between an ice age and a tropical epoch is that between different working modes of this system. To understand climate, earth scientists must find out what these modes are and what causes the air-sea system to switch between them. They must learn how that system responds to changes in such basic natural factors as solar output, dust content of the air, roughness of the land, or cloud cover. And, as an added challenge, they must learn how it is likely to respond to the environment-changing activities of man.

The Big Experiment

Bosnywash and Santadiego are code names for a major climate-changing experiment. They are nicknames for the urban sprawls between Boston and Washington, D.C. and Santa Barbara and San Diego, California. In the United States, they typify the flood of pollutants with which industrialized man is filling the air. They represent areas where paving is significantly changing the character of the land surface. No one knows what effect all this may have on weather and climate. But experts suspect its influence may be far reaching.

A special Panel on Weather and Climate Modification of the National Academy of Sciences raised the question in its final report in 1966. It noted that natural rain and snow formation depend on the presence of nuclei, that is, on dust and sea salt particles on which cloud droplets and ice crystals form. Cloud seeding to increase rainfall is based partly on this. At the same time, overseeding can retard rainfall by providing so many nuclei only masses of small droplets form, without the growth of drops big enough to fall out of the clouds as rain or snow. The panel pointed out: "Europe and the United States with their exploding 'megalopolises,' now have extensive regions in which the concentrations of artificial pollutants are consistently high enough to be of possible meteorological significance. Having, by their own activities, changed the distribution and concentrations of nuclei over large areas, should we not now be concerned that we also may have changed the average frequencies and distribution of clouds, fog, and precipitation?"

And what of the long-term effect of pollution on the earth's heat balance? This, too, is of concern. Dr. Walter Orr Roberts, while at the National Center for Atmospheric Research, said that, quite apart from any effect of changing cloud cover, the clear-weather hazes due to pollution are becoming continental in extent. They could significantly cut down on the solar radiation reaching the surface. As of now, no one knows whether or to what extent they are doing this or what the effects are likely to be.

Then there is the continuing rise in the carbon-dioxide content of the air. Compared to water vapor, carbon dioxide plays a minor role in the natural greenhouse effect. But, if its concentration were markedly increased, it could conceivably change that effect enough to have an impact on climate.

According to the Academy panel, there has been a more or less steady rise in atmospheric carbon dioxide since the beginning of the industrial revolution. Its average concentration in the northern hemisphere has gone up about 10 per cent since 1900, rising from 290 parts per million to 330 ppm.

While scientists have speculated for decades about the possible climatic effects of this, it is not at all obvious what they might be. In the first place, earth's surface temperatures might not be affected by an increase in carbon dioxide at all. The Academy panel cited studies which suggest there might be a compensating change in earth's albedo or in the air's water-vapor content. For example, a change in carbon-dioxide concentration from 300 ppm to 330 ppm might be balanced by a 3 per cent change in water-vapor content to leave the greenhouse effect unaltered. It might also be countered by a 1 per cent change in average cloudiness to reflect enough additional solar heat in proper places to prevent an increase in earth's average surface temperature. Even if there were a rise in temperature, no one knows whether this would lead to a milder climate or an ice age.

The most that can be said of man's climatic influence was summed up by Revelle and Dr. Hans E. Suess now of Scripps in commenting on the carbon-dioxide increase. "Human beings," they said, "are now carrying out a large-scale geophysical experiment of a kind that could not have happened in the past nor be reproduced in the future. Within a few centuries, we are returning to the atmosphere and oceans the concentrated organic carbon stored in the sedimentary rocks over hundreds of millions of years. This experiment, if adequately documented, may yield a far-reaching insight into the processes determining the weather and climate."

But whether or not men are hastening its advent, there is reason to believe that the earth is heading into another ice age. Four times in the past 1.5 million years ice sheets have advanced in major glaciations. Four times they have staged major retreats. We now seem to be living in an interregnum between the last advance, which reached its peak 18,000 years ago, and a new glaciation that may come in the millennia ahead. If geophysicists understood the mechanism of the ice ages, they probably would be able to assess the course man's climatic experiment will take.

Frozen Paradox

The earth is by nature a semi-tropical planet. It has been relatively warm and moist throughout much of geological time. For 90 per cent of the past 600 million years, the post-Cambrian eras, its average surface temperature has been 72° Fahrenheit in contrast to the present average temperature of 58°. Tropical and sub-tropical climates prevailed to high northern and southern latitudes. Even the poles were ice-free. For such a dulcet planet, the terms "ice age" and "glacial epoch" seem paradoxical. Yet every so often the heat engine that maintains the climatic balance shifts gears, and ice sheets creep over land and sea.

There have been three of these glacial epochs since Cambrian times and several before that. They seem to have come at more or less regular intervals of 300 million years. Each has lasted only a few million years and may have been split into several distinct ice ages when glaciers alternately advanced and retreated. The last glacial epoch had five such advances and retreats. The Quaternary period, which includes the Pleistocene glacial epoch which began 3.0 million years ago, has already had four ice ages. A fifth ice advance may come sometime in the future, although the present climate is gradually warming up. Dr. Hurd C. Willett of the Massachusetts Institute of Technology, a meteorologist who has specialized in climate trends, estimates that the world at present has come two thirds of the way between the climatic extreme of an ice age and the warm peak of an interglacial period. What causes the periodic icy departures from the earth's normal climate? Why does the great heat engine shift gears? This is another fundamental question for which geophysicists can only guess at the answer.

There has been a plethora of theories to explain the shifts of climate—far too many to detail them here. Most of them, however, shake down into one of three general types. They either explain climate shifts by astronomical changes in the earth's relation to the sun; by strictly geophysical causes such as migration of continents and poles, the uplifting of mountains, or the spreading of volcanic dust; or finally by solar effects—that is, changes in the energy of the sun. Any fully satisfactory theory must account both for the onset of a glacial epoch and for advances and retreats of ice ages within that epoch. No single theory yet proposed has done this adequately. Often a theory that explains in detail how ice ages develop within a given epoch is vague about how the epoch itself got started.

This is true of so-called "astronomical" theories that feature cyclical changes in earth's relation to the sun. There are three ways in which this relation changes. The shape of the earth's orbit slowly changes so that the distances with which the planet swings closest to (perihelion) and farthest from the sun each year alter. This is a long-term effect that repeats itself every 60,000 to 120,000 years. Then the earth's axis of rotation changes its tilt with respect to the earth's orbit in a cycle of 40,000 years. It also wobbles so that at times, such as the present, the Southern Hemisphere is tilted toward the sun at perihelion. Then, 13,000 years later, the Northern Hemisphere will be favored. These cyclical changes alter the amount of sunshine reaching a given latitude at a given season, and some scientists think they explain the ice ages. For example, Wallace Broecker of Lamont uses them to explain Pleistocene climatic fluctuations for the past 200,000 years. His colleagues Ericson and Wollin disagree. They find no correlation whatever. Also, astronomical changes don't show how an ice epoch begins. Some other factor, such as geological change, is needed.

Most geophysicists today do not believe there is enough evidence to support ice-age theories based on such geophysical effects as major shifts of the poles or the drifting about of continents either. But mountain building is something else again. C. E. P. Brooks, the great British climatologist, has noted that, just as the earth's normal climate is warm and moist, its normal geography is one of low-lying continents and widespread seas. And, just as the climate has been periodically interrupted by glacial epochs, the geography has sometimes been drastically altered by epochs of mountain building. Brooks and others have thought the effect of the uplifted land in altering the circulation of air and oceans would be a sufficient cause for glaciation. Critics such as Willett point out, however, that, while there has never been a glacial epoch without continental uplift and mountain building, there have been epochs of uplifting with few or no glaciers. The current view is that, while uplifted land masses are probably a necessary base for the ice sheets, they can't cause glacial epochs by themselves.

Geologically disturbed periods could well set the stage for an ice epoch. Then, rugged mountain chains are thrust across the wind currents. The oceans are confined more closely in deep basins rather than being spread out in broad, shallow seas. This could establish wind and current modes that favor ice ages. Mountain building might also involve enough volcanic activity to fill the air with dust, cutting down on the sunshine reaching earth's surface. It might also stimulate unusual amounts of rain and snowfall as dust particles acted as condensation nuclei. Some scientists have speculated along these lines. But there is little evidence to support them. Uplifted continents may establish a topography in which the air-sea system can operate in a glacial mode. But something more is needed to get an ice age started. Perhaps variability of the sun is the key factor.

The question remains: What makes the sun change its energy output? Dr. Ernest J. Öpik of Armagh Observatory in Northern Ireland has made a detailed study of this question. He notes that it would take relatively small variations in solar output to do the job. He estimates that an 8 per cent cutback from the present solar output would be enough to drop the earth's average temperature to the 41° Fahrenheit of the coldest ice ages, while a modest 9 per cent increase in output could raise the temperature to the "normal" 70° average. Öpik has suggested a mechanism that would make the sun act up this way.

The nuclear furnace in the core of the sun "burns" hydrogen as fuel. But the sun is made up of many other materials as well. As the fuel in the core is "burned," fresh hydrogen slowly diffuses in from the surrounding outer layers. As it diffuses, it leaves behind heavier elements which tend to concentrate and, like a cloud of smoke, to block radiation from the core. Because of this, the core heats up and begins to expand. To do this, it has to work against gravity. The net result is that so much energy is spent in the expansion that the sun actually has less heat than usual to send into space. This means that a 10 per cent rise in heat production in the core could, according to Öpik's calculations, cut down the over-all heat output by an equivalent 10 per cent. When this happens, earth's heat engine gets less energy and a new ice age begins.

According to Öpik, this process should occur at intervals of a few hundred million years and should last for a few million years. This would seem to fit the timetable and duration of the major glacial epochs nicely, but it does not explain the alternating advances and retreats of the ice during an individual epoch. Öpik thinks there may be minor variations in solar output, like the flickering of a candle, that might account for the different ice ages within a given glacial epoch.

There are certain similarities between general climate shifts of all types that support this theory. For example, Willett describes all climatic changes, from major glacial epochs to minor fluctuations of a few decades or less duration, as changes of essentially the same nature, changes that tend to run in cycles. The difference between them, he says, is merely one of degree. Also, he points out that all climatic cycles seem to be world-wide. When the weather swings colder in the Northern Hemisphere, it swings colder in the Southern Hemisphere as well, and vice versa. Any glacial theory, he says, has to explain why all climate cycles seem to belong to the same family and why they are always world-wide in scope. As far as he is concerned, variations in solar output seem the most likely explanation.   •

Whatever the ultimate cause of climate change may be, our present climate is very sensitive to changes in average temperature. A drop of only four degrees might be enough to bring on an ice age. It would mean a climate cool enough so that summer melting might not be able to remove the winter's accumulations of ice and snow and the glaciers would grow and move southward. On the other hand, the British geophysicist Sir George Simpson has dissented from the assumption that the temperature has to drop to start the glaciers growing. Instead, he has argued that the temperature would have to rise. He pointed out some thirty years ago that the chief result of a general cooling might be a drop in the moisture content of the air and a damping down of the atmospheric circulation. This could cut down snow and rainfall so much that ice would be unable to accumulate in spite of the cooler summers. Moreover, the Arctic seas would freeze, cutting down even further the amount of moisture and snowfall in northern latitudes. A general warming would have an opposite effect. Increased evaporation from the oceans would load the air with moisture. Winter snowfalls would be heavy—too heavy for summer melting to keep up with—and glaciers would start to grow. There would be more cloudiness, helping to increase the amount of incoming sunshine reflected back into space. If the warm-up continued strongly, summer melting would, of course, predominate and the ice sheets would again melt. But a slight warming, according to this theory, could conceivably start an ice age. No expert today understands the climate mechanism well enough to confirm or refute this theory.

Once an ice epoch is underway, the air-sea heat engine seems to have two preferred modes of operation—glacial and nonglacial. When it is set in either of these modes, it tends to persist in it. When it switches modes, it does so abruptly. The Pleistocene ice ages have set in rapidly and broken up quickly. This suggests that uplifted topography and other causes of an ice epoch adjust the heat engine for operating in either of these modes. Yet other causes decide which mode is in effect. Some geophysicists such as Broecker think the switching is caused by variations in solar heating due to astronomical factors. Perhaps flickering of the solar "candle" would do it. One recent theory locates the switching mechanism within the air-sea system itself.

Ocean Thermostat

It would seem obvious that during an ice age the polar waters of the Arctic Ocean would be frozen as solidly as everything around them. However, by turning their backs on the obvious and working out what might have happened had this ocean been open during the past four ice ages, two geophysicists have come up with a remarkable theory of climatic change in which the sea acts as a kind of thermostat. They also conclude that the earth is heading inexorably into still another ice age in spite of its present warming trend. The geophysicists are Dr. Maurice Ewing and Dr. William L. Donn, professor of geology and meteorology at Brooklyn College. Here is the way they think the ocean thermostat may work.

Given the start of a glacial epoch, Ewing and Donn think that an ice-free Arctic Ocean is the trigger for a Northern Hemisphere ice age. Its waters would provide a copious source of moisture for Arctic glaciers to grow. This would mean a radically different weather pattern in the far north than is found there today. The Arctic is cold enough now to form glaciers. But there is so little snowfall that summer melting can more than keep up with the winter accumulation. With an ice-free Arctic Ocean warmer than the surrounding land and moistening the air, the situation would be different. Heavy snowfall would outpace summer melting. The snow would build up into glaciers, changing into steel-hard ice under its own weight. As the ice sheets grew, they would tend to make their own climate. They would reflect much of the incoming solar heat, for their albedo would be high. This would further retard summer melting. Thus the ice sheets would flow slowly southward, eventually engulfing regions as far south as New York and Paris.

Meanwhile, the growing ice sheets would cool the Arctic. Cold winds would blow from them over the Arctic Ocean. Icebergs would calve off and melt in the water cooling it further. At some point, the Arctic Ocean would freeze, cutting off the northern moisture supply. From that point on, the growth of ice sheets would be fed only by moisture from oceans to the south. Ewing and Donn think this would be mainly the North Atlantic. They note that the ice reached as far south as 40° north latitude in North America. But it only came down to about 60° N. in Siberia which has desert to its south. The main contribution of the North Pacific seems to have been to the glaciation of western North America.

Eventually, the ice sheets would reach a point of equilibrium in which melting is just balanced by growth due to precipitation. This precipitation would slowly decline as the Atlantic waters continued to cool. Evaporation over the ocean would diminish as the water temperature fell. The ice age would reach its end when the precipitation no longer balanced the melting at the ice sheets' margins. Ewing and Donn think that, for the North Atlantic especially, the temperature would be lowered enough for the precipitation deficit to continue as the ice sheets shrank. At the same time, melting at the glacial margins would be accelerated. The wet lands and dirty ice found there would have a much lower albedo than new snow and would absorb much of the solar radiation falling on them. Once started, Ewing and Donn think the ice retreat would be rapid. As sea levels rose, more warm Atlantic water would reach the Arctic. Eventually, the Arctic Ocean would unfreeze. It would be ready to start the ice cycle all over again.

The scientists think that the Pleistocene Epoch itself was started by migration of the poles during the Tertiary Period. The North Pole moved into the Arctic and the South Pole drifted into Antarctica where they were thermally isolated from the world ocean. This set up the present climatic patterns with distinctive zoning in which high-latitude temperatures are at the glacial threshold. It was a sharp contrast to the warm, equable climates that had prevailed. The two scientists note that the climate began cooling in the late Tertiary. They think Antarctica was the first area to be glaciated and that it has remained glaciated ever since. This, they say, would have a global effect on climate. Cold bottom water formed in the Antarctic at the ice sheets' edge reaches at least to 35° North. The increased albedo of the ice would reduce earth's heat income. Also, lowering of sea level as the Antarctic ice sheet grew would reduce the heat absorbing area of the sea. All of this, according to Ewing and Donn, sets the stage for the cycle of ice ages and warm interglacial periods of the Pleistocene. These, they feel, are controlled by the mechanism already outlined. It, too, would be global in influence. The two scientists think that enough solar heat would be reflected by the ice sheets and by clouds in areas of heavy precipitation to significantly cool the earth as a whole. Thus, the ice-age cycles controlled by the ocean thermostat of the Northern Hemisphere would pace glaciation throughout the world.

Ewing and Donn point out that their scheme requires neither a variable output of the sun nor changes in heating due to astronomical cycles in earth's orientation. Glaciation in the Northern Hemisphere is switched on and off by increases and declines in precipitation. And these are controlled by the ocean thermostat.

The two scientists do not explain in detail how this Northern Hemisphere process affects glaciation around the world. Some other scientists feel that there is little evidence that one hemisphere can control another in this way. They would like a more detailed explanation of how albedo changes in one hemisphere would communicate their influence to the other hemisphere. Critics also object that Ewing and Donn have little evidence that the North and South poles migrated to start the Pleistocene Epoch in the first place. However, this objection has weakened since the theory of continental drift has been revived as explained in Chapter Four. Among other things, the indications that the magnetic poles have wandered, strengthens the case for wandering of the geographical poles. On the average, earth's magnetic axis tends to lie in more or less the same direction as the geographical axis.

In any event, the ocean thermostat presumably could work whether the Pleistocene "refrigerator" were turned on by polar migration, solar fluctuations, or some other factor. It would not account for all climatic cycles, which Willett thinks should have much in common. But it might account for the simultaneous advent of ice ages in both hemispheres. As in the case of other ice-age theories, however, the available data are inconclusive. The mechanism of the Atlantic thermostat is a novel but unproved speculation.

Meanwhile our own climate at the moment is growing warmer. The polar icecaps are melting, and the sea, currently rising at the rate of two feet a century, is slowly encroaching on the land. This could have serious implications for coastal regions the world over.

The Advancing Sea

During the IGY, scientists scaled mountains to sample glaciers, bored deeply into the Greenland and Antarctic icecaps, and floated about the Arctic Ocean on ice islands. From these and later investigations they bring back a common story—everywhere the ice is melting, but no catastrophic rise in sea level is yet in sight. On the other hand, this may be only the prelude to a thoroughgoing thaw if the present warming trend continues.

According to very rough calculations of the United States Weather Bureau, the rate of warming of the earth's surface right now is something like two or three degrees' rise in average temperature per century. What causes the warming is not known. It may be a solar effect, an already noticeable result of the increase in atmospheric carbon dioxide, or something completely unsuspected. The climate has run to cycles of warming and cooling ever since the last ice age. The over-all result has been a significant warm-up over the past eleven thousand years. The present warming trend, which dates from the turn of the century, appears to be more closely related to one of the short-term cycles of warming and cooling than to the over-all long-term warm-up.

Just before the start of the IGY, Öpik calculated that if the Greenland and Antarctic icecaps were completely melted they would yield 4,860,000 cubic miles of water. Spread over the entire sea, this would amount to a water layer 186 feet thick. When IGY explorers probed the Antarctic icecap, they found so much more ice than had been expected that former estimates of how much ice there is in the world may have to be increased by something like 40 per cent. If the ice of Greenland and Antarctica did melt during the present warming trend, this could add well over 200 feet to world sea levels.

Fortunately the Greenland and Antarctic icecaps, which have most of the world's ice, do not seem to be melting nearly as quickly as the mountain glaciers or the Arctic sea ice. But this is no guarantee for the future. The Arctic sea ice has shrunk 12 per cent in total area in the past 15 years and now averages 6 feet thick. That is about half as thick as it was in the late nineteenth century. It may one day begin breaking up. Since it is already floating in the ocean, its melting will have little effect on sea levels, just as a melting ice cube in a brimming glass of water won't make the glass overflow. On the other hand, with one to two per cent of the world's water locked in their frozen masses, concomitant melting of the icecaps and glaciers of even a few per cent could significantly affect sea levels.

Actually the sea already has risen a good deal since the great thaw set in after the last ice age. At its peak the ice drew the oceans down by perhaps as much as 500 feet, according to maximum estimates. The sea has gained back at least 300 feet of that drop in level and seems to be gaining more all the time. It is not known whether the post-glacial rise came in an initial spurt which has since tapered off or whether the oceans have been steadily rising for the past eleven thousand years. Furthermore, the sea-level picture is complicated by compensating changes in the sea bottom itself.

The rocks below the earth's crust are more rigid than steel to forces that act on them for only a short time. But under prolonged pressure they flow like viscous pitch. If water is added to the oceans above them, they sag under the increased load. The density of this rock magma is about three times that of water, so when extra water is added the sea bottom yields by one third while sea level rises by two thirds of the amount of added water.

What is true for the sea is true for the land, whose relatively light rock masses float in the viscid magma. The burden of the ice sheets, which reached several thousand feet in thickness, depressed the land. When the ice melted, the land floated up again. One can see this happening today. Stockholm, for example, is rising a foot and a half per century, while the north Baltic coast of Sweden, where the ice stayed longer, rises over twice as fast. The general uplifting of Scandinavia indicates a former ice burden of 5740 feet average thickness.

This "give" under the land and ocean floor is called "isostatic adjustment." It complicates the sea-level picture by dropping ocean bottoms and raising at least some shore lines all at the same time.

Moreover, it is a slow process. The delayed adjustments in the earth's crust may take 20,000 to 30,000 years to run their course. Because of this, it is hard to foretell what the melting of today's icecaps would eventually lead to. But this much seems certain: if the warm-up continues over the next century, low-lying coastal areas like those around New York, Los Angeles, or London will be in danger of flooding.

On the other hand, men may not wait for nature to run her course. They may grow impatient for the slow melting of the Arctic to free northern sea routes. They may try to intervene in the workings of the heat engine to adjust climatic trends to their own liking. Weather and climate control is on the horizon. Even though they are aware of their ignorance in this field, men may become impatient to try it.

"Adjusting" the Heat Engine

While any present-day schemes for changing climate are either pipe dreams or precocious visions, experts foresee a day when serious proposals along this line may be made. The steadily improving ability to simulate the air-sea system on a computer, coupled with the growth of global weather observations, should soon enable earth scientists to judge how sensible such proposals might be. Commenting on this, Roberts has explained that "the odds of our learning to control weather on a continental scale are very, very small. On the other hand, as long as there exists a chance in 10,000 . . . the potential returns are so great we can't afford to neglect it." He added that this is why he thinks "the most important demand from the viewpoint of society that we can make on the computer is the investigation of the atmosphere."

Thawing out the Arctic Ocean is a favorite project with would-be climate tinkerers. It is typical of many grandiose and loosely considered schemes that have been suggested. Some would bring on the thaw by damming the Bering Strait and pumping in warm water from the Pacific. Others suggest spreading carbon black on the ice to absorb heat and speed up melting. They don't blink at the formidable logistics of getting enough carbon black and of spreading it around adequately to do the job. Certainly there would be an immediate payoff in ice-free northern harbors and trans-Arctic shipping routes. Perhaps average temperatures might rise several degrees Celsius at latitudes of London, Moscow, or New York as some proponents suggest. On the other hand, Ewing and Donn would expect the start of a new ice age.

Most earth scientists take such schemes with a grain of salt. They are generally put forward more to stimulate thinking than as serious engineering proposals. Neither the establishment of the World Weather Watch nor the computer studies of the next decade are likely to lead immediately to any degree of weather or climate control. But they should give earth scientists the tools with which to find out whether or not such control is at all possible. They should enable them to test any control schemes on the computer so they can design experiments with the real atmosphere with some assurance that these won't backfire.

All of this is tremendously challenging. Yet it may turn out that the most pressing aspect of that challenge lies in man's inadvertent modification of weather and climate through air pollution and changes in the land surface. No one knows what these are doing to climate and weather. Finding out is high-priority research for meteorologists and oceanographers. The NAS Panel on Weather and Climate Modification noted: "If pollution becomes heavier and much more widespread, our attention *must* turn to the question of effects upon . . . weather and climate. If we accept the . . . possibility of continued growth of pollution, the present is none too soon to begin the required detailed scientific examination."

EIGHT

WATERS OF LIFE

To the multitude of marine organisms, the oceans are literally the waters of life. Except for the bordering shore areas, the rigors of the land—extremes of weather, temperature, and aridity—are unknown in the climatically stable oceans. At the same time, dissolved minerals and the natural aeration of the circulating surface waters make them an ideal growing medium for the plant life that is the basis of all life in the sea. These waters seem in some respects to be almost an extension of the living organisms themselves. They carry food to sedentary and passively floating creatures. They bring together sperm and ova to fertilize the eggs of many animals. They cradle, nourish, and resettle the young of countless species. And in ways biologists are only beginning to understand, they distribute traces of potent chemicals that some organisms make to prepare the water for certain favored succeeding organisms or, conversely, to exclude competitors.

With most of its inhabitants protected from harsh atmospheric extremes and with many of them virtually bathed in their food supply, even a layman can begin to appreciate how the sea supports a rich variety of animal life. That variety can only be suggested here by outlining the basic principles and relationships that underlie this wealth of life and by briefly introducing a few of its interesting representatives.

Perhaps one of the first things one should note is that while the oceans are all interconnected their inhabitants are not everywhere the same. Populations and their characteristic species vary widely from place to place, often with no apparent obstacles to their intermingling. Like the land, the sea has its barriers to animal migration, except that they tend to be more subtle. Most of them are merely differences in such things as temperature or salinity, or are related to the play of the currents. Immersed all their lives in sea water, many marine creatures are attuned to its chemical and physical composition, sensitive to slight variations.

For those animals that live near the bottom, topography can be a barrier too, just as it is on land. The Wyville Thomson Ridge that separates deep-water Arctic and North Atlantic forms in the area northeast of Scotland is a case in point. But for the most part, the lives of the creatures that inhabit the seas are governed by the characteristics of the water. Nowhere is this more evident than in the collective life of that community of assorted floating plants and animals known as the plankton.

The Wanderers

"Plankton," meaning literally "that which is made to wander," is one of the most expressive scientific names that has been borrowed from the Greeks. To wander is exactly what these floating plants and animals are made to do. They are either too small or their swimming powers are too feeble to resist the flow of the currents, and they are carried willy-nilly wherever the waters go.

There are countless billions of microscopic plants and equally countless numbers of tiny animals feeding on them. There are larvae of fish and of many other marine creatures in various stages

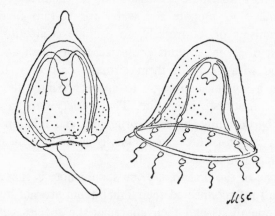

FIG. 35 : Two of the tiny transparent jellyfish (medusae) of the plankton. *Steenstrupia nutans* (left) about 17 times life size; *Phialidium hemisphaericum* (right) about 10 times life size. Medusae are the larvae of sessile polyps.

of development. Here and there miniature jellyfish are floating. These are called "medusae" and are the reproductive form of certain sedentary polyps. Tiny arrowworms move about, feeding on fish larvae and similar small prey, while others of the planktonic wanderers feed on them. All told, there are representatives of every major phylum of the animal kingdom, at least in the larval stage. They include one order, the Radiolaria, known only in the marine plankton. According to Professor (Emeritus) Sir Alister Hardy of Oxford University, one of the world's outstanding authorities on marine life, "it is no exaggeration to say that in the plankton we may find an assemblage of animals more diverse and more comprehensive than is to be seen in any other realm of life."

This diverse assortment of organisms is united by two necessi-

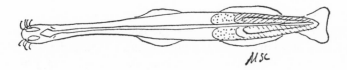

FIG. 36 : An arrowworm, one of the Sagitta.

ties of their common experience—their status as passive drifters and the need to keep afloat in a fluid medium. The latter is the common environmental influence behind many of the curious shapes the plankters have evolved.

The problem of floatation can be solved in several ways. Planktonic fish eggs, for example, contain small drops of clear oil. When they hatch, the young larvae live for a time on what is left of the yolk carried in an attached sac and are in turn buoyed up by the oil drop. Another way of solving the problem is to increase surface area without appreciably increasing weight. This gives the organism a greater frictional resistance to sinking. Some species have spines. Others have filmy appendages of protoplasm. Still others have various arrangements of fine hairlike projections. They float like thistledown on a summer breeze.

The effectiveness of such floatation devices has been graphically demonstrated by species of an organism called *Ceratium* (a Dinoflagellate), which can adjust the length of its hornlike projections to meet varying conditions of viscosity. Warm water is less viscid than cold, so that an object of given shape and density will sink twice as fast in tropical waters as in polar seas. If these organisms are carried into relatively warm water, they compensate for the loss in viscosity by growing longer horns. If later they re-enter cooler water, they shed the excess length, always adjusting their bodily resistance to the present need.

In one way or another the diverse collection of wanderers called the plankton is the first link of almost all food chains in the sea. Fish ranging from fingerlings to the great basking shark feed directly on the small planktonic animals. Others eat the fish that eat the plankton. Many animals of the shore and shallow-water bottom just stay put and strain out whatever planktonic food the water flow brings them. Intermingled with the living plankton is a good deal of dead and decaying organic matter. This detritus also feeds some of the animals and the bacteria found in the plankton itself.

In deeper waters there is a continual rain of detritus and the larger remains of dead and dying organisms from the upper sunlit planktonic zone. This feeds animals at intermediate depths, while a host of hungry mouths are waiting on the bottom. Some bottom animals look like plants, spreading branching, food-gathering arms. There are also shellfish of many types and other creatures, all equipped in one way or another to collect this rain of nutriment. These in turn become food for worms, starfish, sea urchins, crustaceans, and many other roving bottom animals, as well as for bottom-feeding fishes like the cod, haddock, and plaice. The latter, in their turn, become an important element in man's diet.

Whatever escapes larger mouths is attacked by bacteria, which break down the organic materials into basic minerals, phosphates, and nitrates. These are returned to the sea, where in time they may again reach the upper waters and be taken up by plants to enter the food cycle once more. Indeed, this brief sketch of the food economy of the sea should properly start with the plants. With their photosynthetic ability to use sunlight to make organic substance, they are the primary energy source for all the rest of marine life.

The Grass of the Sea

Nobody knows exactly how much plant material is produced annually in the ocean. Its total tonnage must be immense. In a good year the world's fishermen land something like eight to ten thousand million pounds of herring and related fish. Many of these are of small size—sardines, anchovies, pilchards. California pilchards, for example, run five to ten to the pound. The total number of individual fish caught probably runs to tens of thousands of millions. Birds and other fish must catch equally large numbers, while vast numbers aren't caught at all. Then there are the other food fishes caught in large quantities and the multitude of species that are never touched by man. Truly there are inestimable numbers of fish in the sea, let alone other animals. The vegetable production that ultimately feeds these fishes, a production that must be many times their total weight, is at this stage of knowledge beyond precise reckoning. Yet, except for the relatively insignificant amounts of seaweed growing along the shores and the floating weeds of the Sargasso Sea, this great bulk of vegetation consists of minute one-celled plants. The "grass" of the sea has to be harvested with a fine cloth net and studied under the microscope.

This situation reflects a basic factor in the life of plants floating in the ocean; namely, the importance of having a large surface area in ratio to volume. For one thing, the larger this ratio, the more resistance there is to sinking. But even more important, the more area there is in relation to its bulk, the more readily can an individual plant absorb sunlight filtering through the water and take up enough of the nutrient materials, which may be present only in minute amounts, to meet its needs. Here is a decisive evolutionary advantage favoring smallness of size. Plants might evolve other means of buoyancy, such as the bladder floats of many seaweeds. But in the competition for light and food, the ability to absorb these readily is what counts. Hence the rise of the microscopic phytoplankton, as the planktonic plants are called. A cube the size of one of these plants has hundreds of times the surface-to-volume ratio of a cube one inch on a side.

One of the most abundant groups of the phytoplankton are the diatoms. Encased in transparent silica shells, they glisten like jewels in little crystal caskets. Some species have the shape of perfect little pillboxes. Others are more rectangular or elongated, rodlike and needle-shaped. Every plant is an individual separate cell. Yet many species, as they multiply by dividing in two, remain joined together in long chains. Sometimes these chains look like diamond bracelets. Sometimes they have hairlike appendages that assist their floating, making them look like multi-footed animals.

These little brown-green plants are the only type of alga that forms a siliceous exoskeleton. The skeleton or shell is in two parts called "valves," which are joined by "connecting bands." They can be thought of as fitting together like the top and bottom of a pillbox. Under an ordinary compound microscope the shells of some species do indeed look like little glass boxes intricately patterned with perforations, pits, and striations which form "designs" characteristic of individual species. The electron microscope, which can magnify images hundreds of thousands of times, shows even

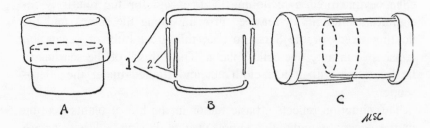

FIG. 37 : Many diatoms are shaped like pillboxes, as in A. The closely fitted tops and bottoms are made in several parts, as in B. The two end plates are the valves. The vertical sections are the two circular "connecting bands" which help fit the whole together. This is the simplest of the varied and often complex diatom structures. As they grow, the little pillbox diatoms may divide or may become extended cylinders, as in C.

more intricate detail. Some species have several systems of increasingly smaller pits and holes and more than one layer of silica. Others have valves made of little threads woven together like baskets. These intricate structures, coupling strength with lightness, allow the diatom to present a far greater surface area of protoplasm to the water than would be the case if it were merely encased in a neat little box.

When a diatom divides, each of the two new individuals keeps one of the old valves, growing a second one to complete its shell. This process is completed before separation takes place, the new valves being grown within the old and fitting tightly into them to form the bottoms of the "pillboxes." Since the new valves are formed inside the old, one of the individuals so formed will be smaller than the original cell. Thus in a series of such divisions the average size of a population of diatoms will get progressively smaller. This gives a considerable size range to any particular species. Sometimes a given population can be identified and traced in its planktonic wanderings by its regular decrease in average size. But there is a limit to this, for the plants can't go on dividing to the vanishing point. Eventually, after dividing a number of times, a diatom cell discards its valves entirely. New valves, two or three times as large, are then formed inside its swelling protoplasmic mass, which in this form is called an "auxospore." In this way, the original size is recovered.

This sequence of division with occasional regrowth is the only definitely known way in which diatoms multiply. Hardy reports that they may have a sexual phase as well. In some species tiny specks called "microspores" have from time to time been seen forming within the cell wall. These may be gametes (sex cells). But Hardy says this has not yet been established.

Diatoms can also take on a form known as the "resting cell" if living conditions become severe, especially in winter. The old set of valves is again discarded, while the protoplasm concentrates into a tight mass around which a new and differently shaped thick-walled shell is formed. Thus protected, the now-dormant cell sinks into deeper water or even to the bottom to await the spring.

The diatoms share the ocean meadows with a second large group of plants belonging to the assemblage of organisms called "flagellates." These are characterized by one or more whiplike appendages with which they swim or which they can use to create small currents. With the exception of some little-known planktonic bacteria and two or three species of yellow-green algae that grow as large as a millimeter in diameter, the flagellates comprise the rest of the phytoplankton. They are a strangely assorted group. Keeping themselves from sinking out of the sunlit upper water by whipping about their flagella, they live both by photosynthesis and, in some instances, by capturing particles of food like animals. Even the experts aren't sure whether certain species are plant or animal or both. Most of them found in the plankton, however, are definitely plants, living by photosynthesis and in many cases actively seeking the light with the aid of a small red "eye spot." In some species the eye spot has been elaborated into a complex organ with a lens and pigment cup.

The more notable of these curious plants are the Dinoflagellates. Some of these are brilliantly luminescent, making the sea sparkle at night or causing the breaking waves to flash with cold blue-green fire. *Noctiluca* is probably the most brilliant and is also one of the few dinoflagellates that lives more like an animal than a plant. *Ceratium,* mentioned earlier for its ability to regulate its body resistance to sinking, can also give a spectacular performance. When organisms like these abound, nets, fish, oars, and other objects that disturb the water will seem coated with fire as millions of individual Dinoflagellates are set aglow, their light coming from chemical reactions stimulated by the agitation.

Dinoflagellates are distinguished by having two flagella. One runs along a beltlike groove encircling each individual, while the other trails behind like a propeller. Between the two, the little plants waltz round and round as they propel themselves forward through the water. Many species also have distinctive spines, one pointing forward and two projecting backward from behind the groove of the transverse flagellum. The bodies of these plants are encased in a cellulose wall of little plates arranged like a mosaic.

By fixing the energy of sunlight in forms that make it available to animals, the microscopic diatoms and flagellates support the rest of ocean life. At the same time, an abundance of oxygen and carbon dioxide dissolved from the air and the nutrient minerals

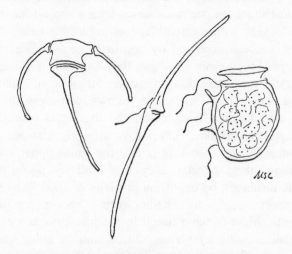

FIG. 38 : A few Dinoflagellates. Two species of *Ceratium* (left) about 200 times life size; and *Dinophysis acuta* (right) about 400 times life size.

carried in solution make the sea an ideal place in general for these plants to grow. Nevertheless, there are limiting factors. For one thing, plants usually need light. While some species have been found at great depths, phytoplankton generally flourish in what is called the "photic zone." This is the upper few hundred feet of water into which sunlight readily penetrates. Another important factor is the local distribution and availability of the nutrient minerals and other chemicals needed by the plants. If any of these is in short supply, it will limit the plant growth, no matter how plentiful the others may be. The variations of these necessary chemicals, both geographically and seasonally, explains much about the variations in abundance of the phytoplankton.

March of the Seasons

One way to illustrate the regulatory influence of these chemicals is to consider the seasons in the temperate waters of the North Atlantic. Here, as the buds begin to swell on land and the crocuses appear, there is a prodigious outburst of plant growth. Within a fortnight the diatoms that have been resting through the winter increase some ten thousandfold. As the season advances and summer comes, however, the vernal abundance of plants steadily declines, only to be followed by an equally sudden, though shorter and somewhat less intense, outburst in the fall. After that the population again declines to its lowest ebb of the year as the plants wait out the winter. This sequence is readily explained by the distribution of the essential fertilizing nitrates and phosphates.

During the winter the upper waters are thoroughly stirred by wind and storms and by the convection set up as water cooled at the surface becomes relatively dense and sinks. Dissolved minerals are distributed fairly evenly through the upper few hundred feet, and the temperature becomes uniform throughout this depth. As the days lengthen and light intensity grows, there is a moment when conditions again become favorable for plant growth. The necessary nitrates and phosphates being available, the spring outburst commences.

But as the season advances, the uppermost waters are warmed. They become relatively light—light enough to float on the cool denser water below—and a thermocline develops that seals off vertical mixing. The depth of the thermocline includes most if not all of the photic zone, where the plants are living and reproducing. This means that the supply of phosphates and nitrates can't be replenished. These minerals are relatively thinly distributed at any time. Together with iron, strontium, and silicates, they account for only 6 per cent of the salinity of the sea. Thus the minerals in the layer sealed off by the thermocline are thinly spread to begin with and are soon used up, bringing plant activity to a halt. Unable to keep pace with the persistent grazing of animal plankters, the plant population drops sharply through the summer.

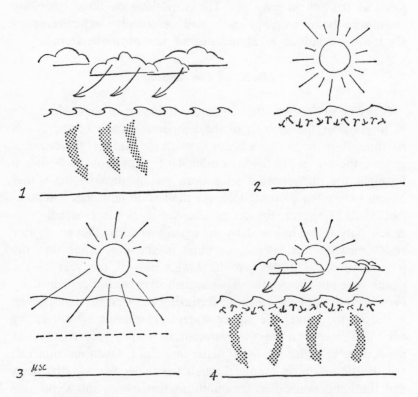

FIG. 39 : March of the seasons. Winter storms and winds stir the waters deeply, bringing nutrient minerals to the upper layers (1) where, as the light intensity increases during spring, an outburst of planktonic life begins (2). As summer comes, and a thermocline seals off vertical mixing, the minerals are depleted and the plankton declines (3). Then the gales of autumn again stir the waters, bringing fresh minerals up from below and the plankton bursts forth again until the winter light becomes too weak to support photosynthesis (4).

In the autumn the cooling air and increasing gales again stir the waters, destroying the thermocline and bringing a new supply of minerals from below. The light is still intense enough to encourage growth, and the plants burst out in their second orgy of reproduction. Then their numbers again decline as the light becomes too weak to support active photosynthesis.

These seasonal ups and downs illustrate the crucial role of the fertilizers, a role that affects the geographical abundance of the plants as well. In tropical waters, for example, the light favors plant growth the year round. Yet the more persistent thermocline of these latitudes tends to prevent mixing of the surface waters and the replenishment of the vital minerals. This is why tropical phytoplankton is generally less abundant than that of temperate and polar waters in spite of the greater variety of tropical species. In like manner, wherever upwelling currents bring up the phosphates and nitrates that have been accumulated near the bottom by the action of bacteria, the seas abound in phytoplankton and in the animal life it supports.

But this is not the whole story. There are indications that marine plants and animals are favorably, or in some cases adversely, affected by traces of unknown chemicals. Some of these may act like vitamins in the diet of land animals and seem to be just as essential. Indeed, vitamin B_{12}, Cobalamin, which is present in sea water, is known to be necessary to several of the marine flagellates and at least one of the diatoms.

Dr. E. J. Allen of the Plymouth (marine biology) Laboratory in England ran an experiment almost fifty years ago which vividly illustrated the presence of these largely unknown trace chemicals. He tried to grow phytoplankton in artificial sea water that was made up according to a very precise analysis of the real article. But the plants would not grow until about 1 per cent of natural sea water had been added to the medium.

The succession of plants and animals in the plankton suggests that individual species may release something into the water that inhibits their own growth or favors the growth of a successor. Perhaps some species release chemicals that inhibit or exclude predators and competing species. Certainly the use of poisons is widespread in the marine world.

Toxic species are found in many classes of marine organisms, including the plankters. Dinoflagellates that cause the red tide are notorious, especially *Gymnodinium brevis,* a problem in the Gulf of Mexico, and species of the genus *Gonyaulax,* which often make shellfish poisonous. Under conditions not yet fully understood, a bloom of such organisms reddens the sea. It is known as red tide. When it appears, the water is poisoned. Fish swimming through red tide die in masses, fouling the sea and adjacent beaches. It looks as though the Dinoflagellates wanted the water to themselves. Dr. Robert Endean of the University of Queensland, Australia, an authority on marine toxins, thinks antibiotic activity may be widespread in the sea. Antibiotics, he says, may be a means by which organisms, especially sedentary creatures, prevent encroachment on their territory. Even at the microbial level, antibiotic activity seems important. Something in sea water tends to kill all types of land bacteria and to exclude certain bacterial classes. Yet some bacteria thrive. They provide food for many tiny animals, break down dead organisms into nutrients, and may release as-yet-unidentified chemicals important to planktonic life. Synthesis of growth factors by land bacteria is well known; it is reasonable to expect marine bacteria to play a similar role in the sea.

Scavengers of the Sea

Bacteria play such an important role in ocean life that they deserve a brief section of their own. They thrive in all parts of the ocean, from the surface to the greatest depths. They can eat organic matter in any state, solid or liquid, suspended or dissolved. Because of this, they are regarded as the principal scavengers in the sea. Moreover, they make such good work of it that, according to Dr. Claude ZoBell of Scripps, one of the few marine biologists in the world studying bacteria today, the ocean can be described as the world's largest and most efficient septic tank. As by-products of this activity, the bacteria produce carbon dioxide and the phosphates, nitrates, and perhaps other chemicals that maintain the fertility of the sea or affect its life cycles.

Although bacteria are found throughout the water, pelagic (free-floating) species are most abundant in the photosynthetic zone at the surface, while the greatest abundance of all marine bacteria is at the bottom. There these tiny organisms build up reserves of fertilizing minerals and serve as an important food supply for bottom-grazing animals such as protozoans, worms, sponges, mud-eaters, and the like. In shallower parts of the ocean there is a good deal of solid organic matter raining down to sustain bacteria. In the abyss, where such material is scarce, the bacteria probably feed on dissolved matter carried to great depths by currents.

The full story of marine bacteria has yet to be understood. Even the mere existence of bacteria at great depths is a major research puzzle. ZoBell points out that "most of the scientific observations on the effect of hydrostatic pressure . . . have been made on organisms that normally live at one-atmosphere pressure. Deep-sea organisms, living at 700 to 1000 atmospheres, have received scant attention in this regard." Many bacteria normally found in soil, sewage, or fresh water are injured by pressure equal to that at depths of about 5000 feet and lower. Yet bacteria and some high organisms have been found in the deepest trenches.

ZoBell calls these pressure-loving bacteria "barophilia," a term he coined in 1949 when working with Dr. Frank H. Johnson of Princeton University. The existence of such microbes deep within the sea was demonstrated by ZoBell and Dr. Richard Y. Morita, now at Oregon State University, from material gathered during the Galathea Expedition (1950–52). They isolated bacteria that grew in a medium of sea water, peptone, and yeast at pressures of 600 to 800 atmospheres. Yet the bacteria would not grow at one atmosphere. In 1964, ZoBell recovered bacteria in sediments taken from depths of roughly 32,700 feet in the Philippine and Marianas trenches. In 1966, he found more bacteria in sediments from depths of 30,350, 31,100, and 31,600 feet in the Japan-Bonin Trench five hundred miles south of Japan. He explains that oceanographers "now know that bacteria are present in the great ocean deeps, but we must do further research to learn whether bacteria are active at such depths." To what extent, he asks, do bacteria serve as food for deep-sea animals? How do pressure-loving microbes differ from surface bacteria that can't stand up to high pressure?

Then there is the question of the bacteria's role in food cycles of the sea. How fast and by what chemical processes do they turn dead proteins into nitrates and other nitrogen compounds to fertilize the sea? Dr. Akira Kawai and Isao Sugahara of Kyoto University, who shared in the 1966 cruise off Japan, have found nitrates in sediments at great ocean depths. This is at least circumstantial evidence that bacteria are carrying out their fertilizing activity even under high pressure.

The sea is like a great chemical vat teeming with life. The water in that vat is a fairly good solvent. It facilitates a complex chemical interaction between the bacteria, plants, and animals of the plankton, to say nothing of higher forms, that is only dimly sensed today. This is a challenging area for research that will have to be explored if men are ever to farm the sea; that is, to regulate its ecology to grow food crops, as they now do that of the land.

To return to the marine food system itself and to the little floating plants that are its basis, it is obvious that these plants can pass on the energy of sunshine only if they are first converted into a form that higher animals can eat. This is the role of the grazers, the so-called "key industry animals." These are the marine analogue of the field mice and the deer, the cattle, sheep, and other vegetarians that turn the grasses of the land into animal protein that meat-eaters can consume.

The Grazers

The grazers of the sea are almost as small as the microscopic "grass" they feed upon. They are all part of the drifting animal plankton—little crustaceans, small larvae, and many other forms, collectively called the "zooplankton." This is the term biologists use to distinguish these drifters from the more powerful animals, such as the fishes, whales, or squid, which can swim in any direction they please. The latter are known as the "nekton." There is still another specific name for bottom dwellers. These are called the "benthos."

The most prominent of the grazers, and indeed of the whole zooplankton, belong to the class Crustacea, and of these the members of the subclass Copepoda are overwhelmingly the most numerous. Copepods, the "oar-footed"—so named because of two long appendages at the head that wave about like oars—swarm the seas in countless numbers. Like all grazing animals, they are less numerous than the plants on which they feed. Where these latter are numbered in millions, the former are numbered in thousands or tens of thousands only. Yet Hardy thinks it no exaggera-

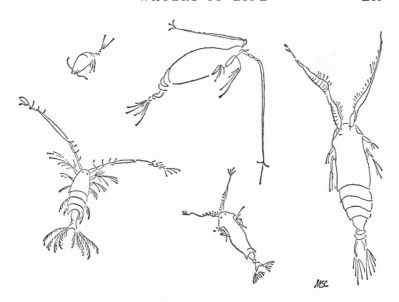

FIG. 40 : A selection of Copepods. *Temora longicornis* (upper left); *Arietellus insignis* (lower left); *Gaetanus pileatus* (upper middle); *Anomalocera patersoni,* female (lower middle)—preceding all about 3 times life size. *Anomalocera patersoni,* male (right), is about 8 times life size.

tion to state that there are more copepods in the world than all other multicellular animals combined, including the insects.

The planktonic copepods are generally small—about the size of a pinhead or, at most, a grain of rice. They are the main link between the microscopic energy-fixing plants and the flesh-eating consumers of the sea. These little crustaceans reproduce profusely and rapidly. Ten days is enough to cover the life cycles of some species. Thus they can quickly increase their numbers to exploit a bloom of diatoms or flagellate plants. This in turn makes the vegetable abundance available to other animals so that, in the general economy of the sea, a wealth of phytoplankton is usually reflected in a wealth of animal life.

There isn't space to list the other considerably less numerous grazing animals here. However, one curious creature should be described, for his amazing filtering apparatus first revealed the existence of exceedingly tiny flagellate plants that escaped the meshes of the finest tow nets. These minute flagellates, which are very numerous, now can be cultured in the laboratory. But their existence was first discovered toward the end of the last century when the German planktologist Dr. H. Lohmann began studying the filtering mechanisms of a class of animals called Larvacea, whose most prominent members in the plankton belong to the genus *Oikopleura*.

Oikopleura has a small body with an undulating tail that is about four times as long, the whole measuring something less than an inch. It secretes an elaborate "house" made of thin, transparent, gelatinous material. This first appears as an elastic envelope which

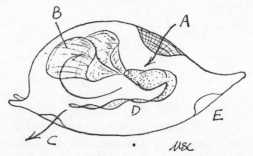

FIG. 41 : *Oikopleura* in its wonderful house. A—water-entry gate; B—filters leading to mouth; C—water exit; D—*Oikopleura;* E—emergency exit.

the animal separates from its body with flicks of its tail. Then, undulating this tail to create a flow of water, it inflates this fragile envelope around itself like a balloon. And what a marvelous balloon it is! It has a grille that prevents all but the finest particles from entering with the currents created by its tail. Once inside, these particles are sieved out by a pair of conical nets leading to the owner's mouth. Lohmann found that these nets, with meshes closer than the finest man-made gauze, trap flagellates measuring only one or two thousandths of a millimeter in diameter. One can only marvel at the evolutionary processes that have produced so efficient and intricate a mechanism.

The history of the Larvacea is something of an evolutionary wonder too. They belong to the phylum of the tunicates, many of which are sedentary animals called ascidians. *Oikopleura* and other Larvacea are transformed larvae of ancient bottom-living animals similar to ascidians. Through accelerated development of their reproductive organs, the larvae became sexually mature while still in the free swimming state and have dropped the immobile adulthood of their ancestors. This remarkable transformation was pointed out by the late Professor Walter Garstang (1868–1949) of the University of Leeds. It was part of his larger theory of the evolution of animal forms through modification of the young, the most important biological principle to come from studies of the plankton.

"Larval Forms"

When Garstang began his researches, one of the widely held biological theories was the so-called "biogenetic law" associated with the name of the nineteenth-century German zoologist Ernst Haeckel. "Ontogeny recapitulates Phylogeny," said this "law." In layman's language this means that the development of the young of any species (ontogeny) is a synopsis of the evolutionary history of the adults of its type (phylogeny). Thus the metamorphosis of tadpole into frog was supposed to be a key to the amphibian's evolution, while the gill pouches of the human embryo bore mute testimony of ancient aquatic ancestors. Garstang rejected this view and replaced it with a dynamic principle of his own. "Ontogeny does not recapitulate Phylogeny," he told the Linnean Society of London in 1921. "It creates it."

Believers in Haeckel's law thought of evolution as proceeding through gradual changes in adult forms. Garstang, who was intimately acquainted with the host of larvae that drift with the plankton, knew that evolutionary forces were a potent influence in the life of the young larvae as well. Far from being a mirror of adult evolution in the past, the development of larval forms is a field of evolutionary change in its own right. Here, he surmised, was a route by which the gradual molding of evolution could make drastic changes almost at one sudden jump.

Many of the planktonic larvae come from sedentary bottom-living or shore-dwelling animals. By drifting with the water they spread their otherwise immobile species like the wandering seeds or fruits of rooted plants. Garstang realized that, instead of representing a primitive adult stage long discarded, planktonic larvae often showed remarkable adaptation to their mode of existence.

Natural selection tends to favor two major characteristics of these larvae. On the one hand, there are advantages in modifications that enable them to remain floating and drifting as long as possible, thus spreading their kind widely. Yet there are competing advantages in changes that facilitate their maturing quickly to give birth to offspring before falling prey to an enemy. Garstang showed how the forms of many planktonic larvae compromise and adjust between these two rival needs. Here was evolution acting directly on the young in an unmistakable manner. He called this process of evolutionary development through modification of the young "paedomorphosis."

Within the framework of this general process, it is easy to see how forms like the Larvacea have originated. As previously mentioned, there is an advantage in the rapid onset of maturity so that the animal can get on with the main business of propagating its kind. This is offset against the competing advantages of being able to float with the plankton as long as possible to achieve maximum distribution. These factors favor an accelerated development of the reproductive organs in relation to the rest of the body —a phenomenon called "neoteny." Thus the Larvacea have dispensed entirely with the bottom-living adult form and have become true planktonic animals, maturing and reproducing as they drift along. In their case, the change-over seems to have been made in two stages. They have directly evolved from larvae of a creature called *Doliolum,* which had already become "pelagic" —that is, an inhabitant of the open sea.

Garstang's ideas have spread slowly among biologists. He never got around to writing a comprehensive statement. Instead, his ideas were presented between 1921 and 1949 in four serious scientific papers and in a number of informal verses which seem to be his natural mode of expression. The latter are colorful and engaging statements of many of his central ideas and have been published posthumously in a little book appropriately entitled *Larval Forms.* The following, entitled "Oikopleura, Jelly Builder," is both typical and to the point:

> Oikopleura, masquerading as a larval Ascidian,
> Spins a jelly-bubble-house about his meridian:
> His tail, doubled under, creates a good draught,
> That drives water forward and sucks it in aft.

> A filter in front collects all the fine particles—
> Micro-flagellates and similar articles—
> Which pour in a stream through a jelly-built tunnel
> Into his mouth and its mucilage funnel.

The funnel begins with his endostyle gland,
Which flicks mucus up to his circular band:
The stream through his mouth trails it out into threads,
And the whole is rotated as fast as it spreads.

In effect this rotator's a neat centrifuge
That lets out the water and keeps in the ooze:
The water's sucked outwards by paired water-wheels,
The residue serves him with plentiful meals.

Now although Oikopleura sits by himself
In the midst of his house on a jelly-built shelf,
He's firmly attached in front by his snout,
And never lets go till his house wears out.

But his body behind is completely free
And bathed by the water that comes from the sea
Through two lattice-windows let into the walls,
Which limit the size of incoming hauls.

Into this water-space the effluents flow
That start from the spiracles' outward throw:
And lest water-pressure the bubble should burst,
A tubular valve in front blows first.

What shall we say of this marvellous creature
Who breaks all the rules by his composite nature?
The puzzle increases the more it's observed
How far from the track of his fellows he's swerved.

When his jelly-house starts as a lump on his back,
His tail is the finger that stretches it slack:
He probes with its tip between body and test
And loosens the parts which too closely are pressed.

Then, after windows and traps are all ready,
The tail pops inside and, with motions more steady,
Sets the pump working, the water streams in,
The jelly-house swells, and the fishings begin.

We believe we can satisfy any scrutator
That anatomy, house, and pharyngeal rotator
Are pure Doliolid in all their relations,
With highly original specialisations.

His tail is the problem and also the base,
For nothing will work if this you erase:
It seems that, from lack of metamorphosis,
He's larva and adult in half and half doses.

Like Haeckel's biogenetic law, most of Garstang's ideas were speculation. They deal with subjects that are difficult if not impossible of experimental proof. On the other hand, his concept of paedomorphosis changed biologists' outlook on the processes of evolution. It once was thought that when evolutionary lines became too highly specialized they were doomed, like the dinosaurs, to extinction. Now, while this remains a possibility, it no longer is thought inevitable. However specialized the adults of a particular line may become, their younger stages still are capable of change and adaptation. Then, by the process of neoteny, they can produce a new evolutionary line to become perhaps a whole new order, class, or even a phylum. In this way, Garstang speculated, the vertebrate line which led to man himself once arose from the paedomorphic transformation of the larvae of sessile bottom-dwelling animals.

"This is the major contribution that Garstang made to zoological thought: to have first shown that such a possibility is not unreasonable," comments Alister Hardy in the introduction to *Larval Forms*. He adds, "I, for one, am confident that the coming generations of zoologists will judge it to be among the more fundamental conceptions given to our science in this century."

To return to the planktonic animals, there is one more feature that should be outlined, for it is probably the most puzzling and at the same time the most widespread characteristic of these wandering creatures. This is their habit of daily commuting over vertical distances that may amount to several hundred feet.

The "Commuters"

Every day as the light waxes and wanes many animals of the plankton undergo a curious vertical migration. At night they climb upward toward the darkened surface, only to sink downward again with the rise of the sun. Some species regularly travel several thousand feet. This is a considerable effort for these weakly swimming animals. Yet it must have a profound significance in their lives, for the migratory habit has been evolved independently by almost every major group of the zooplankton. Moreover, it has been found in deep-water planktonic animals as well as those drifting within a few hundred feet of the surface. Nobody knows just what the mechanism or significance of this strenuous migration is. It may be connected with feeding and, even more importantly, it may to some extent release the tiny drifting animals from their bondage to the currents.

The problem is far too complicated to go into its details. Many investigations have been carried out by a number of marine biologists over the past half century, each of which has only added to the complexity of the picture. However, one can outline that picture roughly by noting that, as far as operating factors are concerned, the movement up and down of particular intensities of light appears to be one of the most important influences. Many animals seem to prefer a particular light intensity, and they tend to follow the zone of this intensity up and down in the water as the daylight comes and goes. For example, Dr. George L. Clarke of Woods Hole and Harvard University has found that the vertical migrations of certain copepods correlate more closely with the movements of light intensity than with any other factor in their environment. But at the same time he found a great variability in behavior. Other factors, perhaps the varying constitution of the water or of the food supply, also seemed to be operating. This is typical of such studies. Sometimes animals that usually stay below in the daytime are found in abundance in sunlit surface waters. There are also indications that hunger may help set the pattern of reaction to light. Certain animals tend to seek the light when hungry, presumably in order to feed on the plant life in the upper waters, and to retreat from it when sated.

Whatever the factors that control the vertical migrations, there is the correlative question of what advantage these migrations are to the animals themselves. Hardy has suggested that this may be a way by which the drifting animals use their weak swimming powers to gain a limited freedom of movement. In the ocean, where water masses tend to sort themselves into layers, conditions change much more markedly in a vertical direction than they do horizontally. Swimming a few hundred feet left or right would usually make little difference to a tiny plankter. But a few hundred feet change of level would probably bring it into an entirely different water mass, often into an oppositely flowing current.

The animal is like a balloonist who can control only his vertical movements, spilling some ballast to go up or valving out a little gas to go down. If the balloonist wants to change his speed or direction, he has to go up or down until he finds a favorable wind. There is often a velocity difference of one or two miles per day between the surface currents and those a dozen or so fathoms down in the ocean. Trying to swim along itself, a planktonic animal would get practically nowhere in relation to its water mass. By dropping down a hundred feet in the morning and rising to the surface again in the evening, an underwater "balloonist" may well travel a mile or more in relation to the surface.

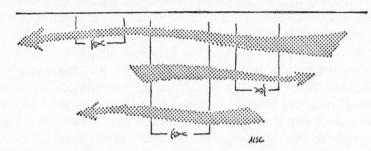

FIG. 42 : Although planktonic animals are poor swimmers, vertical migration helps them travel. By dropping down or rising a few dozen feet, a plankter may enter a current that carries it several miles horizontally in a day to a new feeding ground.

In this way, the little animals can move fairly quickly. If food is short in one place, the next evening may find them in a richer area. Usually the surface waters are moving faster than those deeper down, so that the animal actually is left behind when it drops out of the surface waters. Nevertheless, it is traveling relative to those waters. The animal itself probably knows nothing of this. It is merely responding to whatever mechanism induces its daily up-and-down migrations. Yet the practical effect is that the animal continuously samples a new environment. This also gives the weakly swimming animals some power of choice. If an environment is uncongenial, they can swim down out of it and move on. Conversely, if they find themselves climbing into unfavorable water at nightfall, they can hold back as the current carries them along.

Thus Hardy's suggestion points up a major advantage of the otherwise mystifying habit of vertical migration. A given assemblage of plants and animals are not condemned indefinitely to travel along together. The drifting of the animals is not quite so passive as it once appeared, for they can, in a sense, hunt about for new environments and new food supplies. It is little wonder that this migratory habit has become widespread among the zooplankton.

For some of the tiny animals, color also calls a tune to which they dance to their advantage. In 1962, H. Dingle of the University of Michigan, then working at Woods Hole, reported that some species of copepods and crab larvae are sensitive to red and blue light. In reddish light, their movements in the water are not especially vigorous. Stimulated by blue light, the dancing grows lively, particularly in horizontal directions. As you would expect, this behavior is shown by species that live within the photic zone rather than by zooplankters that come near the surface only at night. The color sensitivity may help the little animals in finding food. The drifting plants on which they feed tend to filter out the blues to leave an illumination enriched in red. This suppresses the animals' dancing when food is abundant so that they remain in the area. If food is scarce, and the light somewhat more bluish, the vigorous horizontal dancing starts. It helps disperse the animals to other areas where, perhaps, the dining is better.

This chapter has been devoted largely to the plankton because it is believed to be the base, the ultimate food source, of all other life in the sea. This life, however, in one form or another, has spread to every part of the ocean. That is the subject of the following chapter.

NINE

THE RANGE OF OCEAN LIFE

Wherever oceanographers have looked, from the abyssal depths of Pacific trenches to the half-land, half-water world of the shore, they have found living creatures. An impartial observer from another planet would probably quickly grasp a fact that has only begun to be apparent to land-oriented man—the most characteristic life forms of the earth are the marine organisms. In some form they inhabit over 70.8 per cent of the earth's surface throughout all levels of a water envelope many times thicker than the thin zone of life on land. It would take a book in itself to describe this vast and, to the landsman, alien biosphere. The interested reader should consult one or more of the excellent books on the subject listed in the bibliography. However, the range and variety of this marine life can at least be indicated by highlighting certain of its aspects, such as the life of the shore. This is by far the most challenging environment into which marine life has extended.

The Rigors of the Shore

From the viewpoint of a marine organism, the shore of the ocean is the threshold of outer space. Except for the lowest reaches of the lowest tides, the protective stability of the water is gone. At least part of the time the shore-dwelling organisms have to endure the harsh extremes of the weather, drying in the air or flooding with fresh-water rains, freezing in the winter and baking in the summer. Like astronauts who orbit just outside the earth's atmosphere, shore creatures live on the fringes of a hostile, alien environment. Unlike man, however, they have had many hundreds of millions of years to adapt to this rugged existence. The results of this adaptation are evident to any visitor to a rocky shore, where the fairly well defined life zones on the rocks tell a similar story of adaptation to varying degrees of exposure along all the temperate coasts of the world.

Biologists distinguish between several zones of differing degrees of exposure. These are usually named for one of their typical organisms. Thus the zone farthest from the water, where the exposure is greatest, is sometimes called the "Littorina zone" after the hardy little snails that live there. The middle and lower levels,

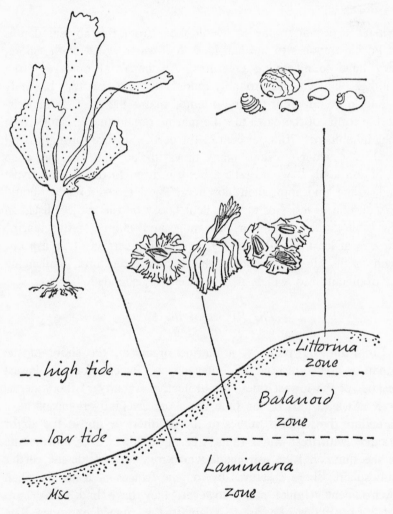

FIG. 43 : Major life zones of the shore.

which are covered by water for at least a short time every day, may be called the "Balanoid zone" after its characteristic barnacles. Similarly, the region below low tide to the seaward edge of the underwater seaweed forest is often called the "Laminaria zone," using the Latin name for the kelps that grow there. These are the typical major zones for a temperate rocky shore, although experts may make many finer distinctions.

As far as the shore dwellers are concerned, the boundary between land and sea is usually marked by a black zone of blue-green algae. There may also be a few lichens and some green algae. But the dark plants predominate at the extremity of the ocean world, only occasionally wetted by the spray from breaking waves or by the highest high tides.

The shore below is an area of evolutionary transition between sea and land. Although all of its creatures are tied to the ocean, some of them have gone far in making the slow change-over that will enable them to cross the algal border to a terrestrial mode of life. Consider the snails, for example. The ancestors of all land snails once came from the sea. Today one can see others of these mollusks at evolutionary way stations along the rocky shore.

In a zone extending from above the highest high tides down to where there is about 50 per cent exposure to air, the rough periwinkle (*Littorina rudis*) is found. It is most likely to be seen in cracks and crevices of the rock, browsing on the algae. This particular snail has all but broken its ties with the sea. It has a gill cavity equipped with blood vessels to "breathe" oxygen from the air almost like a lung and can go a month without contact with the water. But more significantly, it has broken one of the strongest ties of all those that bind an animal to the water—the need to use the sea for reproduction and dispersal of its species. The rough periwinkle has become viviparous, bearing its young within its own body until they are ready to be born as tiny snails, miniature replicas of the adult form.

However, no one factor such as ability to withstand exposure to air or breaking of the reproductive tie with the water constitutes the crucial break with the sea. It is the combination of such factors that enables a one-time marine animal to cross the border to the land. In these terms, the rough periwinkle is farther along the evolutionary road to terrestrial living than is its companion in the dry upper zone, the tiny snail *Littorina neritoides*. *Neritoides* can stand even drier conditions than can *rudis,* venturing high up and even a little beyond the algal threshold. But like many another sea creature, it sheds its eggs directly into the water, in this case during the highest of the spring tides.

Farther down the slope, in a zone from 65 per cent or more exposure to air down to the low-water level, the common periwinkle (*Littorina littorea*) abounds. It often lives at the upper reaches of its range, where it is covered only briefly during high tides, showing it is well adapted to cope with exposure. Yet it too sheds its eggs into the sea and so has much farther to go toward adapting to land conditions than its viviparous cousin. The smooth periwinkle (*Littorina obtusuta*) also lives in this lower zone with a range comparable to that of *littorea.* It can stand only brief exposure and is usually found only where seaweeds afford protection against drying as well as a handy food supply. But, while *obtusuta* cannot venture very far into the drier zones, it has already significantly reduced its reproductive dependence on the sea, for it lays its eggs in moist gelatinous masses attached to the seaweeds on which it lives.

In these and other ways some of the snails mark a road of transition between marine life and that of the land. On the other hand, others of the shore dwellers, such as the mussels and the ubiquitous barnacles, are totally water creatures. Even though some species have adapted to living in the drier zones, there is no suggestion of evolving toward a terrestrial life. They are entirely dependent on the ocean. They strain out the food particles the water brings them and in season commit their larvae directly into the sea.

This is a quite different mode of life from that of the browsing snails. Exposed to waves and surf, these sedentary filter feeders have to be securely anchored. Mussels literally tie themselves to the rock with many tough threads. Barnacles are even more firmly attached. When a barnacle larva is ready to leave the drifting life of the plankton and settle down as an adult, it cements itself to a firm substratum, if it is fortunate enough to find one. Then it quickly builds up its characteristic lime cone. The animal itself is encased in a shell of chitin, the same material that covers many insects. But its main protection is the lime "house." This consists of six closely fitted plates which form what looks like a miniature volcanic cone. The top is closed by a door of four plates which opens when the animal is feeding and closes when the tide is out. These stout little houses withstand the heaviest waves, although the grinding of winter ice may scrape a barnacle-covered rock clean.

Like the snails, different species of barnacles show a preference for different zones of dryness. One species with a difficult Latin name, *Chthalamus stellatus,* is generally found high up among the hardier snails, where it is wet by only the highest water of the highest tides, although it ranges in decreasing numbers down to the 10 per cent exposure zone. Thanks to its small size and very firm attachment, this rugged little animal is able to thrive on wave-beaten rocks where even the larger barnacles seem unable to establish a hold.

Just below the dry upper zone is the beginning of the preferred region of the common acorn barnacle (*Balanus balanoides*), which ranges over the middle part of the shore. At the lower part of its range, extending almost to the low-tide level, is found a still larger barnacle, *Balanus perforatus.* As with many other shore animals, this latter barnacle may be found well up in the dry regions. But it seems to prefer the lower, wetter zone. Thus the preferred range of the different species reflects their individual abilities to cope with exposure.

Exposure of greater or lesser extent is of course a constant, perhaps the dominant, fact of life to all of these shore creatures at whatever level they are found. To return to the analogy of the space traveler, for these creatures the threat of exposure to air is comparable to the threat to man of exposure to the harsh conditions of space. And, like the space traveler in his ship, many of them have solved the problem by keeping a little bit of their natural environment about them. They have protective shells into which they withdraw when the tide flows out. Barnacles close their doors and mussels shut their bivalves. Some of the snails also secrete mucous films to seal off the opening of their shells. Others of the snails, like the dog whelks and limpets, press the openings tightly against the rock.

Limpets are especially well adapted to do this. Instead of the usual spiral snail shell, a limpet has a single flattened lime cone about the size of a thumbnail. It looks somewhat like the upper half of a small turtle shell. Each limpet seems to have its particular "home" on the rock, where the surface has been gouged to fit its shell exactly. When the tide is in, a limpet ranges over a small area of rock, feeding on larvae that settle on its territory. But with the ebb of the water, it returns to its particular home. There it remains tightly pressed against the rock. Waves that may roll its spiraled cousins about slide harmlessly over its streamlined surface. Some of the sea water is held in a groove running around the inside of the shell, so that the limpet keeps its native moisture securely locked within.

On rock faces beaten by waves and vigorous surf, only the hardier of the animals abound. Whatever seaweeds do manage a foothold are sparse and stunted. In quieter areas, however, the rocks will be covered with a heavy growth of weeds whose species, like those of many animals, show a zonation according to their ability to survive exposure. All of these shore plants are members of the algae. As already mentioned, those found farthest from low water are microscopic plants clinging to the rock as a film. They furnish food for some of the snails that live along the border with the land.

Farther down the shore, where the degree of daily exposure is less, the algae grow bigger. To give a quick listing of typical species, the hardiest of these rockweeds in its ability to endure exposure and the one found highest is the channeled wrack (*Pelvetia canaliculata*). It is out of the water 90 per cent of the time. Some days it is not wet at all at the upper edge of its zone. Just below is the preferred range of the related and almost as hardy spiral wrack (*Fucus spiralis*), which flourishes from levels of about 80 to 60 per cent exposure. The channeled wrack is a European plant, so that on a North American rocky shore the typical downward sequence of the rockweeds begins with *spiralis*.

The bulk of the shore area, from levels of 50 per cent or so exposure down to 15 per cent, is populated by the bladder and knotted wracks (*Fucus vesiculosis* and *Ascophyllum nodosum*). Of the two, the knotted wracks predominate wherever there is adequate protection from pounding waves. Below all of these and beginning just beyond the lowest of the low-water levels is the Laminaria zone of the kelps. These great broad-fronded plants grow upward from 10 fathoms or more of water to become the largest of the seaweeds.

As in the case of the animals, this is not an exhaustive list of the seaweeds, nor will the species mentioned be found in all places. But it is typical of the algal forests along temperate shores. Compared to land vegetation, the seaweeds are simple plants. They have no need of roots, for when the tide is in they are bathed in a solution of all the minerals and water they need. A grasping organ or "holdfast" provides for attachment to the rock. There is no need for supporting trunks and stems, either, for the water supplies all the support that is needed. Gas-filled swellings on some of the seaweeds help them rise in the water.

At high tide the swaying fronds of these various algae make a weirdly animated forest in which and on which a host of sea animals live and feed. When the tide is out, much of this once-lively forest lies limp over the rock. Then it offers shelter to many animals from the eyes of enemies and from the drying action of the air. Because of this, the life of the shore tends to be richest where the rockweed forests grow.

There are other sheltered places among the rocks that moderate the harsh shore environment too. Tide pools provide a refuge for many animals ordinarily seen only below low-water level. They make handy aquaria where one can watch starfishes, sea urchins, snails, fishes, crabs, anemones, sponges, and many other creatures. Individual rocks also provide shelter beneath them. Here one can often find a host of small animals such as crabs and various worms.

Because of its variety of sanctuaries, a rocky shore supports a richer marine life than does sand or mud. With the latter there is no firm substratum on which to hold against the pounding of waves and surf. What animals do live there are usually buried in the mud and sand. Worms, snails, bivalves, crabs, shrimps, and other burrowers can make a go of it. There are even some plants, microscopic diatoms, living among the sand grains in the wetter zone. But unless one is willing to dig and sift, sand and mud are not as easy an environment in which to observe the life of the shore as are the rocks and tide pools.

This brief outline scarcely begins to sketch the broad picture of shore life. Again the interested reader is referred to one of the pertinent books in the bibliography. However, it does indicate something of the nature of the most rugged environment into which marine life has extended itself. The second most rugged ocean environment lies at the opposite extremity of the marine world in the cold and unilluminated depths of the abyss.

The Great Life Zone

The largest single biological habitat on the earth is found in the deeper waters of the ocean. One doesn't usually think of the ocean depths in this perspective. For most of us they are far removed from the land and shallow-water world we know. Yet something like 60.8 per cent of the earth's surface, 86 per cent of the area covered by ocean, lies a mile or more under water. Except for sealed-off basins such as those of the Arctic Ocean or the Mediterranean or Caribbean seas, these deep waters are interconnecting. The only topographic barriers are those surrounding holes and troughs of exceptionally great depth. These are indeed isolated from one another and are comparable, in their way, to mountaintops on land. Yet even in the deepest trenches, wherever oceanographers have specifically investigated, they have found living organisms. Thus the deep-ocean basins can be thought of as one continuous zone of life. Except for those creatures living near the surface, it is a world monotonously characterized by cold calm water, chronic food shortages, and perpetual darkness broken only by the ghostly lights of its many luminescent organisms.

One way briefly to consider this vast deep-sea realm and its host of strange creatures is in terms of some of the broad characteristics of its life patterns. In this connection the terrific pressures that in Forbes's day were thought to preclude life at any great depth seem to be far less critical in setting these patterns than are such things as light, temperature, the calmness of the water, and the food supply.

Many of the deep-sea organisms are what biologists call "pelagic"—that is, they live swimming or drifting in the water. Organisms that need light live in the sunlit wave-tossed upper waters, the so-called "epipelagic" region. The creatures considered here prefer twilight or utter darkness. They live in the "bathypelagic" region from the limits of light penetration down to the bottom. Many live principally in the dusk of the upper bathypelagic waters, often migrating into the food-rich surface waters at night.

The diminished light intensity has a marked influence on the coloring of these animals. Where there is plenty of daylight many of the planktonic creatures are transparent. Other animals, too thick to see through, are camouflaged to merge into their surroundings. Fish often have dark blue-green backs that blend with the color of the depths when seen from above. Seen from their own level or from below, their silvery sides and bellies reflect the color of their surroundings. But in the dusk and darkness of the deep, protective coloring means the ability to melt into the perpetual night. The characteristic pigments are black, dark brown, red, and orange. Colored with the latter two, some of the most brightly hued animals in the sea live in this bathypelagic world. They are as invisible there as their drably colored companions, for the long, red rays of sunlight are the first to be absorbed in the water. Red light virtually disappears after about 300 feet even in the clearest water and on the brightest days. Beyond that, blue rays penetrate deeper than green. By 5000 feet, virtually all traces of daylight vanish. The bright colors that would be such a disadvantage in the well-lighted surface waters are as effective as the blacks and browns in matching the surroundings a few hundred feet down. It is no accident that the most characteristic deep-water crustaceans are large scarlet prawns.

As the light disappears with increasing depth, one might expect the faculty of vision to become less useful and, as in the case of cave animals, to disappear. There is some tendency for eyes to diminish in size with depth, and blind fishes are well known. On the other hand, it is impossible to generalize about the role of vision in deep-water life. There are some large and very well-developed eyes on animals that dwell in the perpetual night. Some deep-living fishes even have telescopic eyes. These protrude from their heads, often fixed in an upward direction, with parallel lines of vision. Do these help their owners see falling food outlined against the lighter background above? Do they and other eyes of deep-water animals serve to pick up the flashes of luminescence that are the only light in the depths? No one knows. While luminous flashes of other animals may be an object of vision, for some of these fish the most highly developed light organs are found on species that live around 1600 feet, in the twilight zone rather than in complete darkness. As with bioluminescence itself, which will be considered farther on (page 236), marine biologists don't yet understand completely the significance of light and vision in bathypelagic life.

Temperature is another important life factor. Indeed, with some animals it seems to be temperature rather than light conditions that keeps them at intermediate depths. These animals collect in large numbers around well-developed thermoclines which in the tropics and subtropics may lie at depths of 800 to 1700 feet. This in turn makes the upper bathypelagic levels a good feeding ground, attracting such swift predators as prawns, fish, and squid. Thus temperature conditions as well as those of light seem to pattern life at intermediate depths.

There is a violent reaction to temperature change when animals caught in biologists' tow nets in deep waters are hauled to the surface. They almost always arrive on deck in a moribund state. For fishes with swim bladders the disaster may be due to pressure. A swim bladder is essentially an elastic chamber, a "balloon," inside the fish which is filled with gas and with which the fish regulates its buoyancy. Adjustments in gas pressure are slow, so that a fish is helplessly bloated if raised from the depths too quickly. But many deep-sea fish have no swim bladder. For them it is the temperature shock that is fatal.

Adapted as they are to cold water, some bathypelagic animals are found much higher in cold polar waters than anywhere else in the ocean. This is the key to what was once a biological conundrum. Identical species of certain planktonic animals have been found in both Arctic and Antarctic surface waters but nowhere in the immense stretches of ocean surface in between. Biologists were unable to explain this anomalous bi-polar distribution until it was recognized that the cold water at deep levels provides an unobstructed channel. Pressure is no barrier to the distribution of these animals, but warm surface temperatures are, driving them into the depths of temperate and tropical seas.

Yet another factor affecting the life and form of deep-water animals is the relative calm of the water. Remote from even the wildest storms, the deep-water movements are gentle compared to the waves and agitation of the surface. Animals are able to develop delicate structures under these undisturbed conditions. Their bodies are sometimes so flimsy, they don't survive a net haul to the surface.

Some of the fishes and squid, for example, have bodies encased in thick gelatinous sheaths like the substance of a jellyfish that are quite fragile and yet have a practical advantage in the undisturbed water. Such water-saturated tissues have almost the same density as the surrounding sea water. They are more or less

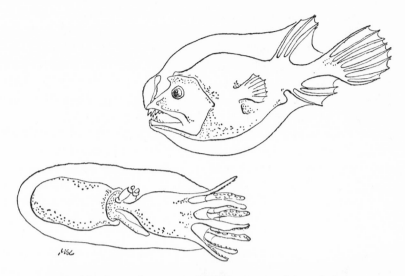

FIG. 44 : Some deep-sea animals are encased in gelatinous sheaths whose water-saturated substance has almost the same density as sea water, making them neutrally buoyant. The octopus *Amphitretus pelagicus* (below); one of the *Haplophryne* angler fishes (above). Both are shown 2 to 3 times life size.

neutrally buoyant, enabling an animal to maintain its level in the water with a minimum of effort. This in turn has the further advantage of helping an animal conserve its strength in a region where food is scarce.

Of all the factors listed at the beginning of this section, the distribution of food is probably the most important. It is food, or rather the lack of it, that makes the deeper parts of the ocean such a difficult place to live. The creatures there are at the slim end of the food chains that start in the rich phytoplankton of the surface. As far as is known today and except for those organisms that feed directly on plants, grazers, and other creatures near the surface, life in the depths depends on the sinking of dead or dying organisms or on animals that make regular extensive vertical migrations. Even though some of the deep-water animals don't eat the falling material themselves, the animals they prey upon do. In this way the general food distribution is downward from the primary phytoplankton producers to the ultimate consumers in the abyss.

This downward distribution of food with an attendant thinning out in deeper waters of the amount of life it can support is the scheme that has been generally sketched by marine biologists. However, some experts suggest that deep life may have independent food sources as well. Phytoplankton has been found at great depths, growing by nonphotosynthetic processes and living on dissolved organic matter. Bacteria, too, thrive in the deep. A few observations by men who have gone into the depths also suggest there are deep-food sources. One of these men, Captain Jacques-Yves Cousteau, outlined this possibility after diving some 4000 feet to the floor of the Mediterranean in the French Navy's bathyscaphe *F.N.R.S.3* in December 1953.

The "Living Soup"

Cousteau was interested, among other things, in the deep-scattering layers (DSLs). These are one or more sound-scattering layers that echo sounders have recorded at moderate depths. Rising at night and sinking by day, a DSL seems to be a biological phenomenon. Its echo can be as distinct as that of the sea floor, hence it is sometimes called a "false bottom." DSLs occur in all oceans, most commonly at depths of 300 to 2000 feet during the day. They are hard to detect in Arctic and Antarctic waters. Yet they have been found beneath the Arctic ice pack. Here, in the land of the midnight sun, they have a yearly rather than a daily cycle. They stay deep throughout the summer, rising toward the surface when the long Arctic night comes. The DSLs now are thought to be due to small animals. But in 1953, no one knew what caused them.

Cousteau had hoped to find this out when he dived in the bathyscaphe. But when he passed through the level where the DSL should have been he found no exceptional concentration of animals. Instead it appeared that there was a steadily increasing concentration of small living organisms the deeper he went. The two French naval officers, Commander Georges Houot and Lieutenant Pierre Willm, who have operated the French bathyscaphe to depths of up to two and a half miles and more have observed this phenomenon too. It also tallies with the few observations made in the early 1930s by William Beebe and Otis Barton in their bathysphere. This was a steel observation chamber suspended from a surface ship by cable which reached depths of several thousand feet.

Cousteau described his observations in *The National Geographic Magazine* as follows:

Houot and I agree that bathyscaphe dives upset some traditional ideas of the sea. For us, at least, the problem of the deep scattering layer is now restated in entirely new terms. So far as we can see, there is, biologically speaking, no DSL, but rather a great bowl of living soup extending on down and growing thicker the deeper into the "tureen" we go. Both Beebe and Barton, the two men who have previously looked out into the deeps, have reported that the density of organisms seems to increase with depth; but so far little attention has been paid to their statement.

The cycle of marine animal life is supposed to depend directly on phytoplankton . . . This [photosynthetic] activity can take place only in the layer penetrated by sunlight, usually to a depth of 600 feet, often not more than 200 feet.

Below this life-giving realm of the sun, says classic theory, the animal population thins out in the dark and the cold, where living creatures are supposed to depend on the plant life at the top, in a vastly complicated web of existence. Yet against this notion are ranged the direct observations of five men who have been to the depths—Beebe, Barton, Houot, Willm, and myself. I cannot propose an explanation of why reality does not match the simple, attractive theory. But there must be somewhere an unsuspected link in the cycle of marine life yet to be discovered.

Hardy suggests that Cousteau's "soup" may consist largely of dead rather than living organic matter. Some of it may be slowly sinking shells of dead planktonic organisms. The greater part, Hardy thinks, may be the cast-off skins of planktonic crustaceans. Some of the particles may also be aggregates of material formed from dissolved organic matter. Such particles can be made in the laboratory by bubbling air through sea water that is free of suspended matter to start with. Since Cousteau made his observations, a number of bathyscaphe divers have seen the submarine "snow," the cloud of particles extending virtually to the bottom. But biologists have by no means accepted this as a major food supply for deep-living animals. Also, Cousteau was wrong about the DSL. While some DSLs may be due to layers of "snow," gas-filled swim bladders of tiny bathypelagic fishes and gas-filled floats of certain siphonophores now are known to cause many of the layers. Other tiny animals may also be involved.

The viewpoint adopted in this chapter is that of the classical theory concerning the food cycles and distribution of life in the sea. Yet Cousteau's speculations should be borne in mind. As more firsthand studies are made and as oceanographic research intensifies, traditional concepts based on scattered sampling from surface ships may be shaken.

Recent discoveries of deep-living phytoplankton underscore this point. In the summer of 1965, Prof. E. J. Ferguson Wood of the University of Miami found algae as deep as 12,000 feet east of the Island of Rhodes in the Aegean. Earlier reports of deep-living plants had been discounted by many biologists. They skeptically suggested that the plants were caught in shallow water as the sampling nets were hauled in. This time, Dr. Wood proved definitely that he had taken his plants at great depths. In that same summer, Robert O. Fournier, a graduate student at the University of Rhode Island, found tiny plants in the North Atlantic at depths of 3300 to 16,500 feet. Their abundance was one hundred times greater than that of any organism previously reported for these depths. Mr. Fournier notes that earlier deep-sea studies, using inadequate research methods, had found relatively few deep-living organisms. This established a trend of thought. It was reinforced by ignorance of how widespread the lightless way of life may be for plants in the sea. The ability of dissolved organic matter in the water to support them was unappreciated. Now this viewpoint is being challenged.

To return to the food distribution, as it is conceived today, the downward-raining particles are thought to become both scarcer and larger the deeper one goes. Small bits of refuse are eaten in the higher waters or disintegrate more rapidly than the larger ones. Also, the latter have less surface in relation to their volume and sink more quickly. Thus the animals sustained by the sinking particles tend to become fewer and to some extent larger too. Planktonic animals, for example, are found at all depths. But, as far as the evidence of biologists' tow nets has shown, they tend to be both sparser and larger in the depths than at the surface. The largest copepods are bathypelagic animals. In like manner, the largest representatives of many other animal types known at the surface are found in the depths.

On the other hand, and again so far as is known from what biologists have caught with their nets, there is a limit set to size by the scarcity of food. Deep-living animals are not thought to attain whalelike dimensions. The conditions of deep life seem to be such that food comes in relatively big meals at long and irregular intervals. Many of the animals have adapted to these conditions by evolving enormous mouths, extensible stomachs, and other devices for preying on creatures as big or bigger than themselves, while their overall bodies have become relatively slight.

The Weirdest Fish in the Sea

The bathypelagic fishes can be truly grotesque. It is impossible to convey their weird appearance in words. The accompanying sketches of a few species illustrate the strange forms that have evolved in the depths—forms that are closely related to species well known in shallow waters.

Most of these fishes are dark-colored—black, dark brown, or blackish violet. They have little luster and in some cases have no scales. Their bodies are generally loose and flabby, with poorly developed bones and muscles. This doesn't seem to be a disadvantage, for, as pointed out previously, the calm water enables such flimsy body structures to survive.

The most striking common feature of these fishes is their enormous mouths. Consider the Stomiatoids, for example. This suborder is one of the largest groups of deep-living fishes. They generally have extended bodies ranging from a few inches to over six feet in length, with rows of light organs arranged like portholes along their sides. They have well-developed eyes below which are red and green light organs. Luminous filaments hang from the chin or throat of many species, occasionally running many times the length of the fish itself. But the outstanding feature of these fishes, and one that gives a fearsome look, is their huge jaws armed with great teeth. In one species—the viperfish—the teeth are too large to fit inside its mouth and remain outside when its jaws are shut.

Another curious feature of bathypelagic fish are the "fishing rods" that some of them have developed. The creatures that employ these devices are appropriately named angler fish. They are related to the common angler or "devilfish," a bottom-living, shallow-water animal well known to trawler fishermen. The devilfish lies half buried, "angling" with a filament that emerges from just behind its head and ends in a little tuft. It plays this in the water like a fisherman's fly, luring quite sizable fishes close enough to be snapped up.

Like the common devilfish, some deep-sea anglers lurk on the

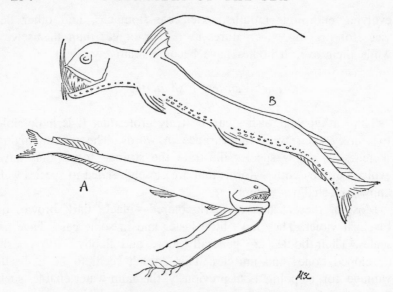

FIG. 45 : Two Stomiatoids: *Chauliodus sloanei,* viper fish (above), 1½ times life size; *Flagellostomias boureei* (below), roughly life size.

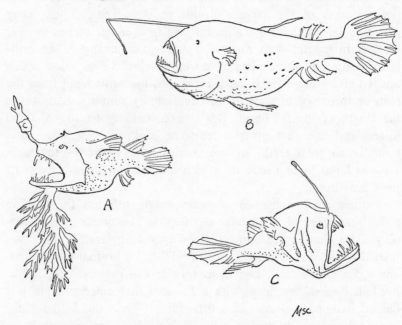

FIG. 46 : Some angler fishes: A—*Linophryne arborifer;* B—*Ceratias holbölli* with male attached; C—*Melanocoetus cirrifer.* (Shown ⅓ to ½ life size.)

bottom. A number of small species also live among the Sargassum weeds. However, the nearly 100 species of bathypelagic anglers form a special suborder of their own, the Ceratioidea, that live most abundantly below 6000 feet. These grotesque little fish show their deep-water character in their enormous mouths, very extensible stomachs, and relatively small bodies. They often are globular-shaped, as broad as they are long, with the head accounting for nearly a third of their length. They are generally black and scaleless, with small, poorly developed eyes. Their jaws are armed with long spikelike teeth that fold back when their mouths are closed. These folding teeth make it easy for prey to enter an angler's mouth. But once the teeth have caught, it is difficult, if not impossible, to get back out again. One wonders what happens when an angler fixes its teeth on an animal that is too strong for it.

Although some of these angler fish grow to be a yard long, most of them are only a few inches over all. They are poor swimmers and apparently lurk in the dark, quiet water, waiting for a meal to come along. Some have luminous chin barbels. Their most characteristic feature is their angling device, which usually ends in some kind of light organ and probably resembles a tempting crustacean or other morsel that attracts unsuspecting prey.

These angling devices are an interesting example of the evolutionary transformation of an organ and its migration to another part of the body. They are really the first fin ray of the dorsal fin. This ray is modified in some way on many fishes—into a poisonous spine, a tactile filament, or an adornment for courtship display. But in these angler fish not only has it been transformed into an angling device and provided with a light organ, it has migrated from the back to the very tip of the head. Biologists are certain of this migration because, upon dissecting one of these fish, they can trace the motor nerve controlling the angling device back to a segmental nerve that emerges from the spinal cord at the point where the ancestral fin ray once stood.

The angler fish are remarkable in still another way and one which illustrates a crucial problem for animals living in the darkness; namely, that of finding mates. Wide-ranging swimmers probably meet other members of their species often enough in their wanderings for this not to be too great a difficulty. Distinctive light organs may help in mutual recognition. But for poor swimmers like the anglers that lurk about waiting for prey to come to them, it would be fatal to rely on such chance contacts. They have a unique solution. The males of their species have become parasites and live permanently attached to the females.

Since the young of species are more numerous than the adults, young males as a group are much more likely to meet up with females than are older fish. Thus, in the angler fish, evolutionary forces have favored an early union of the sexes that links male and female even before the males are sexually mature. The result is a strange parasitic relationship. The relatively small male bites into the female at almost any part of her body. Their tissues fuse and their bloodstreams form one circulatory system. Permanently attached to and nourished by the female, the male then becomes sexually mature, ready to fertilize the female's eggs whenever necessary. Sometimes two or more males are found attached to one female.

The anglers just described are all bathypelagic. However, one of the strangest of the deep-living anglers is a bottom fish. It was discovered in the course of the Danish deep-sea expedition made in the research ship *Galathea* (1950–52). It represents a new genus and species and has been appropriately named *Galathea-thauma axeli* after the chairman of the expedition's committee, H.R.H. Prince Axel. This angler has its lure inside of its mouth. It is a large forked light organ suspended from the roof of the mouth. The fish apparently lies on the bottom with its mouth open, enticing its meals with its glowing lure.

Cold Light

The ability to produce light is widespread among marine creatures. The glows and flashes of luminescent organisms pattern the eternal night of the depths just as they often do the nighttime surface of the sea. Dr. George Clarke, who has made extensive studies of marine luminescence, reports that numerous and brilliant light flashes have been detected at great depths by deep-water photometers. In *Oceanus,* the Woods Hole magazine, he says that "since our records at a depth of one mile show flashes occurring as frequently as five or more per second, we now know that the deep sea is not continuously enveloped in inky blackness but at times, at least, must present the appearance of the night sky on the Fourth of July." In some cases, such as lures of angler fish or the

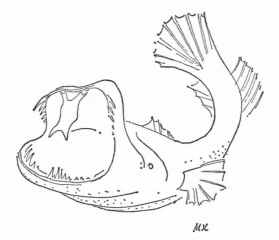

FIG. 47 : Bottom-dwelling angler *Galatheathauma axeli*. Caught by the *Galathea* expedition, it was named for the expedition's chairman, Prince Axel. Note forked light organ in mouth.

protective luminous clouds of deep-water squid and crustaceans, the purpose of the light seems obvious. But in many other cases, biologists do not yet know what significance the lights have for their owners.

The luminous animals are the most efficient light producers on the earth. If human engineers could do anywhere near as well in turning energy into useful light, the lighting portion of our electric bills would be substantially reduced. An electric lamp gets hot because much of the energy it consumes is lost as heat. But as little as one per cent of the energy animals use to make light is lost this way. Theirs is the coldest light known, produced by a chemical process that has been evolved by at least some marine representatives of almost every major group in the animal kingdom.

In some cases, the ability to produce light is merely the ability to discharge a luminous slime. In others, specific organs called "photophores" are involved. They are wonderfully efficient little lanterns with a lens and a concave reflector and can be turned on or off at will. Hardy describes them as being "as good a parallel to the bull's-eye lantern as the camera is to the eye."

In still other cases, marine animals that have not developed light organs of their own have made a home for luminous bacteria on certain areas of their surface. One fish, *Photoblepharon*, has a patch of these bacteria below each of its eyes. When the fish wants to turn off its lights, it draws a fold of skin over the luminous patches.

The really remarkable thing about all these luminous devices is that they have been evolved so widely among marine creatures. Even the intricate little photophore lanterns have arisen independently and with quite similar designs in a number of different types of animals, such as fishes, prawns, squid. To appreciate why this is so remarkable, one needs to understand how slow and bumbling the processes of evolution generally are.

Biologists think of the mechanism of evolution as a blind, haphazard process rather than a purposeful striving on the part of an organism to develop in this or that particular direction. From time to time and in the normal course of events, slight inheritable changes arise in any type of creature. These changes, "mutations," are then passed on to offspring. If a change confers some advantage, it will tend to be preserved and spread through the species over a number of generations. If it is a disadvantage, however, so that the animals affected are handicapped, perhaps in the competition for food or for mates, the mutation usually dies out. Then too, there are many changes that are merely indifferent. These may or may not be preserved.

In the case of the well "designed" photophores, there must have been a series of changes in the organs involved, each conferring some advantage on its possessor, which led finally to the structure of lens, reflector, and nerve-controlled light-producing mechanism. Whatever the advantage or advantages are, they must have a fundamental significance in ocean life. The apparently haphazard process has led to similar results in too many animals for it to be otherwise. But what can that significance be?

Some animals quite obviously use their light to see by. Certain squid and fish, for example, have luminous organs so placed in relation to their eyes that the field of view is illuminated at least for short distances. One stomiatoid is able to throw a beam of strong blue light in front of itself for some two feet. Yet the most characteristic arrangement of photophores is along the under sides of animals whose eyes look in different, even opposite, directions. Perhaps the lights form distinctive patterns by which members of a species recognize one another. This would be useful both for mating purposes and to avoid eating one's own kind. But then what is the advantage of the brilliant fireworks produced at the surface by tiny organisms such as certain Dinoflagellates? These little organisms don't have vision. Indeed, one would think that their luminescence, stimulated by any agitation of the water, would make them more easily spotted by creatures that eat them. Here the luminescence may be just a by-product of reactions to the agitation of the water. Then there are defensive uses for luminescence. As previously mentioned, many deep-water prawns and squid eject luminous clouds. These serve the same purpose of covering the animal's retreat as do the ink clouds of shallow-living squid and octopi.

In the cases cited here and in many others, the usefulness of light to certain animals is obvious. There are mechanisms for luring prey, for defense, for seeing in the bathypelagic night, and so forth. Yet none of these uses is really of fundamental importance to wide areas of marine life. None can account for the frequent occurrence of the photophores. Even the crustaceans and squid that use luminous "ink" for defense also often have patterns of photophores whose use is anything but obvious. Here again, in some species they may serve as recognition patterns. On the other hand, and in spite of a number of studies by various biologists, the use of these lights for recognition has never been established as a general rule.

In fact, the only general observation one can make about the occurrence of photophores or of the ability to produce light in any fashion was first made by Johan Hjort in *The Depths of the Ocean,* a book published in 1912 which he coauthored with John Murray. Hjort noted that among pelagic animals bioluminescence is as widespread as vertical migration. Moreover, taking the pelagic animals as a whole, there is a correlation between the habit of migration and the ability to produce light.

This suggests that the light itself may be of only secondary importance. It may be the by-product of a chemical process that helps these animals in their migrations, that enables them to endure the drastic change of environment between the surface and the depths. Some animals then put the light to use. In a similar vein, Drs. William D. McElroy and Howard H. Seliger point out that early life forms arose when the air was oxygen-poor. As oxygen became more abundant, many organisms would evolve ways to get rid of it because it would be poisonous to them.

The Johns Hopkins scientists suggest that one way to do this would be to bind the oxygen chemically in a waste product such as water. This process would release energy, perhaps in the form of light. In this way, the ability to produce light may have arisen widely long ago. Later, as higher animals evolved, some creatures developed uses for the light. Photophores and other luminescent organs were evolved. For other organisms, luminescence remained merely incidental. But this is only speculation. Except for the cases where a specific use is obvious, the significance of cold light remains one of the unsolved puzzles of the sea.

The Deepest Life

Another unanswered general question about deep-water life is when and how the depths were populated. It once was thought that the deep basins had remained undisturbed since the remotest era, providing a refuge where ancient animal types could go on living even though surface conditions had changed. Yet most abyssal animals seem clearly related to modern shallow-water forms. There are indications that sweeping changes may have taken place in the deep sea itself. If this is true, when did they take place, how did they affect life? Biologists do not know. Whatever happened, that life today has extended itself to the remotest ocean depths.

At whatever depth marine biologists have looked they have found life, even on the floors of the deep-ocean trenches. Since the *Galathea* Expedition, the first expedition fully equipped to dredge for the deepest life, nearly 300 species have been found in the trenches. Yet, in the early 1950s, no one knew what to expect. As in the explorations of the *Challenger,* there was the thrill of probing the unknown, the same wonder as to whether anything living would be brought up, the hope that some new and strange creature would be found. One of the deepest trenches then probed was the Philippine Trench, where the *Galathea* biologists fished up bottom-living animals from a depth far greater than they had been found before. Here is how the late Anton Bruun, expedition leader, described that record haul:

There, deep down in the clear water, was the faint outline of the large triangular bag of the sledge-trawl. It was pitch-black night, but the quarterdeck lay bathed in the beams of our spotlights. Standing by the trawl gallows, watching the trawl breaking surface, was the fishmaster, his arm waving in a slow circle.

At the winch all eyes were intently following the motions of his arm, as they slowed down and then came to a stop, the hand raised as a signal to stop hauling in. It all went with the fine rhythm of experienced teamwork, but the occasion was a special one: it was the first time that the indicator had stood at zero after reaching 12,163 metres [39,907 feet], the full length of our wire.

During the work of taking in the trawl and the two small dredges that had been fixed to the trawl frame (it took a few minutes but felt like an eternity), we prepared for the disappointment of seeing a bag without any bottom animals in it; for a failure, in short. We comforted ourselves with the thought that it was the first attempt with the full length of our new wire, that everything had gone like clockwork all night, that the wire was safely home and we should be able to make a fresh attempt . . . Then the facts came out in rapid succession. "There's clay on the frame!" somebody cried. "It's been on the bottom!" And then: "There are stones in the bag!" Everybody on board who could leave his job gathered around the big dishes while nervous fingers unloosed the cords so that the contents could be carefully removed. We hardly noticed the red prawns, luminescent euphausids, or black fishes; we all knew these to be pelagic animals, caught on the way up through the free water masses. But there, on a rather large stone, were some small whitish growths—sea-anemones! Even if no more animals had been found, this would still be the outstanding haul of the expedition. It was proof that higher animals can live deeper than 10,000 meters [actually 10,190 meters or 33,433 feet]. Is it surprising that all were overjoyed? And that pleasure became excitement when out of the greyish clay with gravel and stones we picked altogether 25 sea-anemones, about 75 sea-cucumbers, five bivalves, one amphipod, and one bristle-worm? It was an unexpectedly rich variety of bottom-dwelling animals. . . .

. . . We [eventually] found a whole little animal community. All the large groups of invertebrates were represented—polyps, worms, echinoderms, molluscs, and crustaceans. The known depth limit of life had been pushed some 2.5 kilometers lower down; and whereas it might have been doubted whether we should find anything in the Philippine Trench, there is now no reasonable ground for supposing that life cannot also penetrate the few hundred meters further down to the new record depth . . . in the Mariana Trench . . . [Life has been found there and in other trenches.]

One of the hopes that has gone with fishing the deeps has been that of finding survivors from a remote geological age. The dinosaurs died out on land. Perhaps, it was suggested, the calm and supposedly unchanging waters of the abyss had provided a refuge for survivors from past eras in the sea. Yet except for a few rarities like Neopilina, an ancestor of the snails which has been found in the Pacific, and the coelacanth, the search for "living fossils" has been disappointing. And even the celebrated coelacanth suggests that the search has been in vain.

This strange fish had been thought to be extinct for fifty million years until a specimen was found off South Africa in December 1938 and identified by the South African ichthyologist J. L. B. Smith. Several others have been found since then. At the time, it was widely assumed that the fish was a true "living fossil." In their heyday, three hundred million to fifty million years ago, the coelacanths were a widespread animal group that inhabited fresh water as well as salt. Their characteristic form, with short stubby fins that look more like paddles than true fish fins, hardly changed during that long period, nor indeed in the fifty million years since then. When the first modern coelacanth was found it seemed obvious that, as surface conditions changed unfavorably, the remnants of the coelacanth line had retreated to the depths.

But Smith himself does not think this was the case. For one thing, he says that the specimens caught have been too well built and vigorous to be true deep-water creatures. Most abyssal animals are dead on arrival or die shortly after being hauled aboard. Moreover, when the first coelacanth was caught, the haul included

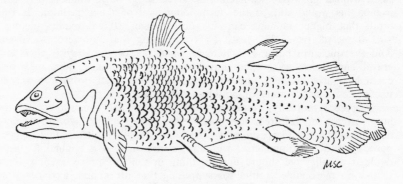

FIG. 48 : Coelacanth.

several tons of sharks. Even among shallow-water fishes, only the hardiest can survive the crush of such a netful. The fall in being dumped on deck and the pressure of the heap usually finish off the rest except for an occasional tough shark. The coelacanth, 5 feet long and weighing 127 pounds, was on the bottom of the heap. Yet it snapped viciously when approached and lived out of water for several hours. "No deep-sea creature could have endured all that and lived," says Smith.

Then too, the modern coelacanth doesn't look like a deep

dweller. It is blue in color, which suggests shallow water. Also, it is well armored with scales and ruggedly built. Smith thinks it may live in rocky areas, perhaps among reefs below the main action of waves and surf. Far from being a "living fossil," a degenerate form that evolution has passed by and which has taken up shelter in the depths, the coelacanth seems to have become well adapted to modern marine life without the need for the drastic evolutionary changes that so many other animal lines have undergone.

In recent years some biologists have begun seriously to question whether the depths are really as good a haven for evolutionary refugees as they were once supposed to be. The animals generally found there are directly related to well-known shallow-water forms. Also, there are indications that the abyssal environment itself has undergone more sweeping changes than had been believed. In his book on the coelacanth, *The Search Beneath the Sea,* Smith writes:

> It is by no means certain and not even likely that the fishes that live in the depths, or their ancestors, went there to escape competition with other fishes. My work has repeatedly shown the enormous stretches that even feeble fishes have colonized, and all the evidence indicates that fishes tend to move and seek new places to live, just like other creatures. All the types we know from the deeps are derived from ancestors who lived in waters of ordinary depth, and though most deep-sea fishes are of course greatly modified to suit the special conditions, all are clearly related to surface forms, none of which are any markedly better equipped to withstand "competition" than the ancestors of the deep-sea forms. In the depths bodies are soft, bones are light, eyes are enormous or have become obsolete, and huge jaws are filled with long fangs, often barbed. There is no valid evidence to support the idea that any of them retired to the depths to escape competition.

At the "Symposium on the Deep Sea" held during the 1959 annual meeting of the (American) National Academy of Sciences, Robert J. Menzies of Duke University reported that, geologically speaking, deep-living species seem to be surprisingly young. Menzies is studying the smaller organisms, some of which are microscopic. These are much more abundant than the larger animals, making it easier to get a statistically valid and representative picture of their populations.

"With each cruise," Menzies said, "was the hope that the presumed constant deep-sea environment would yield its trilobite, possibly only a millimeter in length. Each trawl sample, however, showed this not to be the case—that is, even the little fellows of the fauna were morphologically like the big ones; namely, closely related to shallow-water genera and species."

Except for bottom-living Foraminifera, whose forms can be traced back to the Paleozoic era, Menzies found that the average geological age of the deep-sea organisms decreases with increasing depth. Even the Foraminifera don't upset this general rule. Menzies thinks that their apparent great age may be due solely to their simple structure. In other words, the forms now living in the deep may be of recent origin. But because they are so simple, they differ little from the Foraminifera of past eras.

Menzies suggests three possibilities to account for the apparent youth of the deep-sea fauna. First, there may have been no deep sea prior to the Mesozoic era, which began some 230 million years ago. This echoes the theories of geologists who think the bulk of the ocean water is of recent origin. Although he suggests this as a possibility, Menzies himself thinks it unlikely.

A second possibility is that there actually was a Paleozoic deep sea but that its animals were killed off by changes in circulation, sedimentation, and food supply. As still another possibility and one which he favors, Menzies suggests that there has always been a deep-sea fauna which has suffered repeated extinctions and repopulations, so that the animals now living there originated from shallow-water forms within the past seventy million years.

If this latter proposition is correct, then the deep-water environment has been far from stable throughout geological time. The temperature record of the oxygen thermometer as read by Emiliani indicates that this may have been the case, for it shows temperatures of the deep-sea bottom to have been eight to ten degrees Celsius higher in the Eocene, forty to sixty million years ago, than they are today. In this connection, Menzies notes that most deep-living animals now are cold-water creatures. Except for a rare form like Neopilina, the few relatively warm-water animals among them may be the only kind of "living fossils" one will find—not ancient forms that found sanctuary in a changeless environment, but survivors of a geologically recent and uniformly much warmer deep sea.

Certainly there is reason to think there were massive changes in marine life at the end of the Mesozoic. In 1965, Professor Emeritus M. N. Bramlette of Scripps reviewed the evidence indicating mass extinction of planktonic plants and animals and of some high animals at the end of that era. It looks as though sudden catastrophe overtook these organisms. Dr. Bramlette thinks a key factor in this was reduction of nutrients from the land. This, he says, would have been due to the land having been heavily eroded after a long period without much uplift or mountain building to renew the higher elevations of the land from which minerals would be carried to the sea. Many higher forms of life must have shared the disaster that struck the plankton at the base of many marine-food chains.

However, not all biologists agree that the deep-sea animals have moved into the abyss and trenches in geologically recent times. Two eminent Soviet biologists, in particular, have taken specific issue with Menzies. They are Prof. Lev A. Zenkevich of the Institute of Oceanology in Moscow and Prof. Yakov A. Birshtein of Moscow State University. They maintain that "The colonization of the abyssal zone by animals has extended over a very long geological time. The recent deep-sea fauna contain species which immigrated into the abyssal zone at different periods. . . ." They point out that the percentage of older forms, if not the total number of species, in the abyss is larger than in coastal waters. They think, therefore, that the abyssal population is older, on the whole, than that of the continental shelves. They call the abyssal zone "a refuge where, as in caves . . . archaic forms are preserved almost unmodified."

At this writing, the question of when and how the depths were populated is an open one. A significant number of ancient forms may yet be discovered in the abyss. Perhaps geological research will trace more certainly the history of the ocean environment, confirming or disproving that substantial changes have taken place within its deep waters.

It is interesting that this fundamental question in marine biology is tied to the equally basic question in marine geology of when and how the oceans originated. And, as in the case of geology, the recent evidence argues against the long-held notion that the ocean basins have been stable throughout geological time. Future research in marine biology and geology thus have a fundamental question in common.

TEN

THE PROMISE OF PLENTY

The ocean is like a grab bag stuffed with riches out of which man has been taking only those few packages he can lay hands on easily. There are living riches that represent a large and relatively untapped food resource. There are mineral riches spread thinly throughout the water or scattered about the sea bed. One of the bright promises of oceanography is that an increase in scientific knowledge of the sea will help man to exploit systematically the resources of the marine grab bag.

Probably the most dramatic and far-reaching aspect of that promise today is the prospect of substantially increasing the world's food supply. There is no need to emphasize here the widely reported statistics on humanity's burgeoning population. Mankind faces the bleak outlook of continuing chronic hunger for a majority of the earth's people unless food supplies can be multiplied. Seen in this light, the ocean offers an opportunity man can no longer afford to ignore. Taking food from the sea now is largely a matter of hunting. With research and capital investment, the yields of fishermen could be increased. But, however productive it may be in its own terms, hunting is an inefficient way to exploit a food resource. Aquaculture, the systematic farming of the sea, is largely a scientist's dream. But when it is fully developed, it may well be as revolutionary an advance over fishing as agriculture has been over hunting on the land. All of this is of tremendous significance for a hungry world.

Yet when it comes to enjoying the vast food resources of the sea, chickens have had the edge over people. Like people, they find fish protein a nutritionally potent addition to a basically cereal diet. Adding a small percentage of fish meal to poultry feed boosts egg and meat production. It has been a major factor in keeping poultry prices down and pushing up the demand for fish in the United States. This is why chickens, unlike the world's protein-hungry people, benefit handsomely as mankind's harvest of food from the sea grows three times as fast as its population.

In 1964, to quote statistics of the United Nations Food and Agricultural Organization (FAO), livestock feeds accounted for some 40 per cent of the 51.6-million-(metric)-ton world fish and shell fish production, 45 million tons of which came from the sea. The latter included 40.54 million tons of fish. A metric ton is 2205 pounds. To Dr. Wilbert McLeod Chapman, Director of the Division of Resources of the Van Camp Sea Food Company, and a leading American authority on marine-food resources, the fact that so much fish protein is fed to animals is an outstanding para-dox of the thriving seafood industry. He notes that men already have the capability to increase greatly seafood production; by fully exploiting the kinds of food resources now used with presently available technology, the world's annual fish take could be raised to 200–250 million tons. The food challenge posed by the sea is no longer simply that of discovering presently unknown riches, he says. It is a challenge to do for people what has already been done for chickens—to make fish protein available to those who need it in a form they will accept and at a price they can afford.

Feeding the Hungry

The food potential of the sea needs to be considered in its proper perspective. Dr. Bostwick H. Ketchum, Associate Director for Biology and Chemistry of the Woods Hole Oceanographic Institution, says it "frankly is a lot of nonsense" to think the oceans might solve *all* of man's food problems. "To meet the main food need," he explains, "it is better to expand carbohydrate (grain and vegetable) production on land." He adds that "a really fundamental part of the food problem is lack of animal protein." In areas with chronic malnutrition, the need is generally for animal protein to balance inadequate diets rather than for food in general. In meeting this need, Ketchum agrees that "the sea is of tre-mendous importance."

Dr. George Borgstrom of Michigan State University made some interesting calculations in the 1950s which illustrate the point. At that time, he noted that seafood is sometimes dismissed as insignificant because it represents only a small proportion of the world's food calorie consumption. "What has been forgotten," he said, "is that fish account for 12 per cent of the world's animal protein. They are especially important in a country like Japan, where they make up less than 3 per cent of the calorie consumption, but 74 per cent of the animal protein."

According to Borgstrom's calculations, the United States at that time would have had to increase its daily farming by 30 per cent to make up for the protein it receives from fish. In Japan, this figure would have been 990 per cent; in Portugal 165 per cent; in Norway, 143 per cent; and in the Philippines, at least 200 per cent. The point Borgstrom made is valid today. In this perspective, an increase in seafood production would be more significant for the world's diet than an equal increase in traditional land crops.

The ultimate protein potential of the sea is far beyond that of the 200–250 million tons a year Chapman thinks could be harvested in conventional seafood. It is set by the basic production of carbon-fixing plants, mainly of the phytoplankton. Chapman estimates that some 19,000 million tons of carbon are fixed annually by life forms in the sea. This supports a production of some 2000 million tons a year of animals suitable for harvesting by man. The 1964 harvest, the harvest Chapman used in his analysis, represented only about 2 per cent of the total. Chapman wryly notes that "in fact, the amount used by man is less than the probable error in the above estimates."

Many shellfish feed on seaweeds and phytoplankton. Anchovies, which made up about a quarter of the 1964 marine-fish catch, are also herbivores. Some other important food fish, such as sardines and herring, are partly vegetarian and partly carnivorous. But man eats many fish that are several links down the marine-food chains. Man takes a large discount in terms of the ocean's primary food production in using such animals. This gives rise to the recurrent question: Can the harvest be made closer to the base of the food chains? Can men profitably fish for plankton?

The Vision of Plankton Fishing

After his trip across the Atlantic on a raft, Dr. Alain Bombard said that the plankton he had eaten "tasted like lobster, at times like shrimp and at times like some vegetable." Thor Heyerdahl, who fished for plankton from his raft *Kon-Tiki*, called it "good eating." However, there is a tremendous difference between survival rations for men adrift on a raft and a plankton fishery that could supply a sizable population regularly. Yet the idea is tantalizing.

Every step along a food chain involves losses. In the food chains of the sea, where there are a number of steps between the plankton and man, these food-energy losses are considerable. At best, there is only 20 per cent efficiency in going from grass to milk on land. At one of the richest fishing grounds, Georges Bank, it takes an estimated 1000 pounds of phytoplankton to put a pound of flat fish on the table. This is rather poor efficiency even for food chains in the sea. With some species, under favorable conditions, 10 pounds of plankton to a pound of edible fish may be the norm. Even this represents a tenfold loss. Most of the food the higher marine animals eat goes into activity and body maintenance. Only a small percentage is used for body building. In terms of energy and food bulk, the resources of the sea are most abundant at the level of the plankton. The question is whether or not, in this form, they can be made readily available to man.

The picture is rather discouraging. Plankton is patchy, both in occurrence and in quality. One of the biggest problems would be to find ways of collecting it and concentrating it in useful quantities. In ordinary coastal waters in temperate latitudes, for example, fishermen would have to filter a volume of water equal to something like sixty times the volume of a large living room to get the equivalent of a pound of beans. They would also have to be constantly on guard against poisonous species and other unwanted plankters.

Of course plankton fishermen would be selective in their fisheries. They would hunt out species of high-food value that occur in large masses. There is no doubt such plankters exist; whales and many fishes, both large and small, feed on them exclusively. Dr. Lionel A. Walford, director of Sandy Hook Marine Laboratory, has reported that a basking shark had a thousand quarts of copepods in its stomach when caught. Sir Alister Hardy calls attention to the krill of the Antarctic Ocean. These shrimplike euphausiids swarm in huge masses. They are the only food of the southern blue and fin whales, the largest mammals in the world. Sir Alister suggests that some of the krill masses could be netted to help feed another and somewhat smaller mammal— man.

Plankton of a kind you might consider "good eating" is abundant. But, except for special cases such as that of the krill, this does not mean it would be abundant enough in any one area to be profitably harvested in bulk. The heavily fished waters of the North Sea have a standing crop of zooplankton that is estimated to be over 10 million tons wet weight. It is also estimated that, in a good year, North Sea fishermen average something over fifty-eight tons of herring per hundred hours. They would have to strain about 58 million tons of North Sea water to gather an equivalent amount of plankton.

It will take detailed, specific research to determine whether man can hope to exploit the plankton—research on plankton itself, on possible fishing methods, on processing, and on breeding. Kansas wheat is very far removed from the wild grains our ancestors harvested. Likewise, through specific research and a thorough understanding of life processes in the sea, it might one day be possible to breed special food crops of plankton which could be grown under controlled conditions in enclosed waters. That is a challenge for the distant future, if ever. Based on today's sketchy knowledge and the kind of statistics for the distribution of plankton cited here, the attitude of experts is bearish. They regard the dream of plankton fishing as a chimera. "It is better," Ketchum advises, "to rely on the eat-and-be-eaten food chain in the sea." When you think of all the water that would have to be handled to harvest plankton commercially, the fish and other familiar seafood animals are seen in new perspective. They are an army of unpaid workers doing the filtering for us, working around the clock and concentrating the planktonic food in a form convenient to man. Thus the world's protein hunger must be met in the foreseeable future by hunting the hunters and herbivores of the sea. As Chapman points out, there are enough of them to make satisfying that hunger a goal well within reach of mankind.

Improving the Fisheries

In winning food from the sea, a modern fishing fleet is a marvel of efficiency. With the help of echo sounders, fish concentrations are more easily located than ever before. Once found, they are intensively exploited by fishing boats that pass on their catch to factory ships if they do not have processing facilities on board themselves. In either case, the fish are cleaned, frozen or cooked, and packed for shipment almost as soon as they are caught. If the fishing grounds are rich, the packed fish can be sent to port by relay vessels while the fleet stays on the job. Sometimes, at least with Soviet fleets, new crews are sent out by special liner and the relieved crews brought home without interrupting the fishing. In addition to the older nets and trawls, the boats also are using new means to capture fish, including use of lights to attract fish and electric currents to guide them.

Electricity has long been used in fresh water to attract and repel, to guide and stun fish; but there had been a serious technical problem in using it in the sea. Because of its salinity, sea water is a much better conductor of electricity than is fresh water. Also, there are no natural boundaries in the open ocean comparable to river banks or shallow lake beds which confine an electric field generated in fresh water. These things made it difficult and costly to use electric fishing at sea because the usual techniques would require too much power. Then, in the mid-1950s, the International Electronics Laboratories of Hamburg, Germany, solved the power problem by using pulses, rather than a continuous flow, of current. Although these pulses may run to several thousand amperes, power needs were cut from several thousand kilowatts to as low as ten kilowatts.

The system consisted basically of a three-foot diameter flexible tube with a positive electrode and a light at its underwater end. Fish, attracted by the light, were directed toward the tube's mouth by the current pulses. A pump sucked the fish up the tube and into the ship's hold. Since this system was first demonstrated, various electric techniques have begun to be employed in commercial fleets. In 1967, for example, the Soviets were using a system of lowering electrodes from the fore and aft sections of

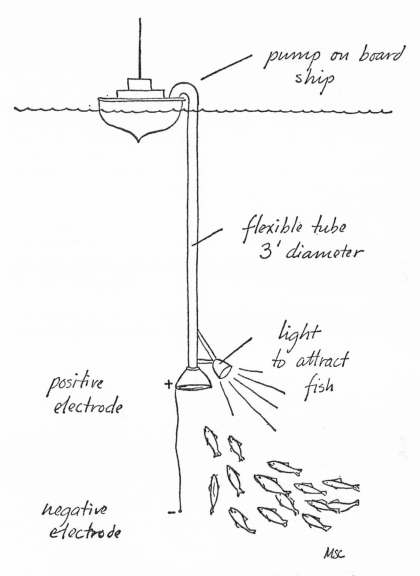

pump on board ship

flexible tube 3' diameter

light to attract fish

positive electrode

+

negative electrode

−

MSC

FIG. 49 : Electric fishing (schematic). With this system, developed in West Germany, fish are attracted by a light, and guided by an electric field toward a tube through which they are pumped into the trawler's hold.

a ship. Directed by the electric field toward the positive electrode, fish enter a trap there and are pumped aboard.

At this writing, the modern fishing fleet, making full use of the latest technology and scientific knowledge of fish habits, is exemplified mainly by the crack long-range fleets of Japan and the Soviet Union. Often, these fleets sweep into the accustomed fishing areas of technically backward countries to reap a rich harvest, packing it up and sending it home before the eyes of the natives. American fishermen are prominent among these envious bystanders. For, when it comes to developing the food resources of the sea, America at the end of the 1960s is a technologically backward nation.

This is reflected in a few statistics. In the Georges Bank area off New England, the total catch rose from 1.8 million metric tons in 1955 to 3.2 million tons a decade later. But the American share dropped from 27.3 per cent to 10.3 per cent in 1965. Meanwhile, Soviet fishermen moved into the area in force. As many as two to three hundred Russian trawlers have been seen in the area at one time. As a result of this intensive effort, the Russian catch in this one region rose from 5000 tons in 1964 to 82,000 tons a year later, eclipsing the American catch of 55,000 tons. This hurts New England pride because the fishermen see it happening. The over-all statistics are even more unfavorable. In 1967, the U.S.S.R. caught 5.8 million metric tons of fish compared to a U.S. catch of 2.4 million tons. To meet its needs, the United States imports fish products. In 1965, for example, 2.8 million tons of seafood products including $505,000 worth of Russian wares were imported. The Russians are moving ahead swiftly; they have tripled their annual catch over the past twenty years while the American catch has dropped off slightly. While the United States has built mammoth new industries in such glamorous fields as atomic energy utilization and space flight, it has allowed its fishing industry to languish in a prison of archaic restrictions.

The American fishing industry has a long history. Over more than two centuries a solid crust of institutional barriers has been built up which prevents that industry from moving ahead. To state the problem in oversimplified terms, most ocean research in the United States is carried out at the federal level while fisheries regulation is done at the state level. Because the twain seldom meet, the American fishing industry now is restrained by archaic laws which constitute the biggest barrier it must surmount to become efficient and modern.

Fishing methods, types of equipment, and sizes of catch are regulated by each of the fifty states individually, and states have jurisdiction only within United States territorial waters. Beyond these, rules for American fishermen are laid down by the Federal Government. But a state can prohibit the landing of fish which are not caught according to its regulations. This is an effective way to regulate the fishermen who do business in a given state. The result is a legal tangle which discourages development of uniform fishing practices. Even more damaging is the fact that it often hampers fishermen by enforcing outmoded standards and forbidding effective use of modern equipment. The Federal Government and many of the states now are aware of the situation and are seriously working to remedy it. But it takes time to weed out bad laws and build a modern, legal framework because the present legal structure is so firmly entrenched.

Some of the old laws had a social purpose, such as spreading work among fishermen. Often intended to promote good conservation practices, they have codified practices no longer scientifically valid. Sometimes the laws were to give a state's own fishermen a commercial advantage. Generally, such laws have outlived their purpose. To cite a few examples, California has had a law forbidding the use of anchovies to make fish meal and oil. As a result, Chapman says his company takes anchovies off Peru. They use about half a million tons of the ten-million ton annual Peruvian anchovy catch. Another California law has forbidden trawling nets with mesh smaller than 5½ inches. This is too big for hake. Yet hake are a big resource off California and the Russians regularly fish for them there. Then there is the State of Washington law preventing the use of echo locators to find fish. Perhaps the most frustrating rule of all is a Federal law passed in 1792 requiring that all fishing vessels authorized to operate from American ports be built in the United States. Because American shipbuilding costs are prohibitive, this effectively blocks fishermen from buying well-equipped, modern vessels. In 1966, a Gloucester fisherman would have had to pay $5.2 million for an American-built ship. This compared to $1.8 million for the same ship built in Germany. Even a 50 per cent subsidy from the Federal Government is not enough to enable fishermen to close the cost gap.

Meanwhile, American seafood companies, as opposed to fishermen, slip from the legal net by operating abroad. They fish in foreign waters, process their catches in foreign factories, and import the finished products. These are generally fish meal or some other fish-based food for pets and livestock. In 1964, four large American seafood companies, by themselves and in their world operations, caught, processed, and sold over a million metric tons of fish. Hence the paradox that the American seafood business flourishes while the domestic fishing industry flounders.

In taking food from the sea, the United States has been its own worst enemy. It could afford this luxury because its people are well fed. Many other countries with underdeveloped fishing industries aren't so fortunate. Like the United States, they often hamper their fishermen with restrictive codes. Unlike the United States, they badly need the protein that seafood could provide. They have the example of Peru to show how much is to be gained by removing artificial restrictions on their fishermen.

Peru used to prohibit reduction of anchovies to fish meal and oil because it wanted to protect the food source of the guano birds. These birds provide a high-grade fertilizer for Peruvian farmers that can be gathered at costs far below the prices of the world fertilizer market. When the prohibition was removed, Peru's annual fish catch soared from 120,000 metric tons in 1956, to slightly over ten million tons in 1967. The fish meal and oil provided a valuable export. At the same time, there has been no noticeable drop in guano production. There seems to be enough fish for both birds and men.

In trying to boost fish production, each country has its own particular problems. Each situation has to be tackled individually. Yet self-imposed limitations are a common factor holding back fisheries development. This is why the United Nations programs aimed at fisheries development often have to start by trying to remove legal and cultural roadblocks. Sometimes, as in the case of Peru, these are based on a mistaken sense of conservation. Sometimes, they are imbedded in the local tax structure. One of the commonest practices is to discourage use of modern vessels and equipment to protect fishermen using traditional methods and ancient gear.

Once the self-made limitations are swept away, there remains a formidable job for marine science and technology. This includes modernizing the fishing fleets of needy nations, extending basic scientific knowledge, and developing satisfactory ways to get fish products to the consumer.

The need for more scientific knowledge is critical. To substantially boost fishing yield, fisheries biologists need both to sharpen their ability to predict where fish will be found and to identify entirely new fisheries. Also, as present fisheries are intensively exploited, biologists need to understand fully the life cycles of the fish and the factors that affect them so that they can set sensible limits to prevent overfishing. Today, biologists don't know all the relevant factors they should consider to manage a fishery so as to make the most of it. Obvious restrictive measures, such as regulating the size of the catch of adult fish, are not necessarily the answer. For many fish, it is not the number of fish left to spawn that determines the size of the future population. There are many, largely unknown, influences affecting the survival rate of infant fish that seem in combination to be critical. Man's fishing is only one of these. Unless a particular stock is being quite obviously overfished, there is no guarantee that leaving more adults would increase the stock of young fish.

Consider the mackerel. Every year these important food fish lay eggs by the billions. A relatively few adults would be enough to keep the species abundant if most of their offspring reached maturity. However, the mortality rate by the time the young fish grow to two inches has been estimated at as much as 99.9996 per cent. The great mackerel fisheries may depend on the survival of a few ten thousandths of 1 per cent of the annual spawning. What is more important, the difference between good and bad years in mackerel fishing may be a difference of only one or two ten thousandths of 1 per cent in the survival rate.

What determines survival? Probably it is a variety of combinations of water conditions, availability of planktonic food, currents, occurrence of predators, and the like. An understanding of the life cycle and ecology of such fish as the mackerel would undoubtedly suggest a number of ways to increase survival to help achieve good fisheries year after year, as well as aiding in forecasting their occurrence. Also, as sea conditions which influence fish migration and concentration are better understood, modern aids can be more effective in locating favored fishing grounds.

In this connection, Charles F. Luce, former Under Secretary of the Interior, has noted that earth satellites could be valuable fish-finding aids. Already, aircraft make rapid surveys of water-surface temperatures off some coastal regions. Airborne sensors measure infrared (heat) radiation from the water and, from this, determine temperature. Fishermen can then use the up-to-date temperature charts to aid in locating likely places for certain kinds of fish which prefer water of certain temperatures. Satellites can likewise measure surface temperatures. Also, Luce notes that experiments are underway to use satellites for "radar detecting of surface-water disturbances caused by surface-feeding fish schools, estimation of wave height by radar, detection of chemical fish trails at the surface left by migrating schools of fish and direct spotting of large marine mammals by high-resolution photography."

Knowledge of fish ecology is also needed to find the new fishing grounds which will be essential to making a really substantial boost in world-fish yield. Among the most promising areas to look into are coastal regions with offshore currents that induce massive upwelling which, in turn, brings nutrients to the surface. The fish-rich area of the Peru Current is one region of upwelling which is already being heavily fished. The Benguela Current, running up the African west coast, defines another promising region. So does the Somali Current.

The Somali is a monsoon current that runs along the east coast of Africa from south of the equator to Arabia. It was extensively explored during the International Indian Ocean Expedition (IIOE). From June to September, the season of the southwest monsoon, this current flows strongly northward, reaching speeds as high as seven knots. During the reverse season, the northeast monsoon of December to March, the Somali disappears. But when it flows, it is sometimes stronger than the Gulf Stream. It seems to be a northward extension of the Indian Ocean South Equatorial Current which flows westward at all seasons between 5° S. and 15° S. From these latitudes, the Somali flows for a thousand miles along the East African coast before turning eastward around 6° N. to 10° N. There are extensive areas of upwelling when the current flows northward. Even when it dies out during the reverse-monsoon season, other areas of upwelling then are found off India's east coast.

The IIOE investigations indicate that rich fisheries might be developed in the Somali Current region and in some other parts of the Indian Ocean. Some two million metric tons of fish a year now are taken from the northern two thirds of that ocean. IIOE studies suggest that the area could yield ten times that much, and perhaps more, on a sustained basis. While this is encouraging, the IIOE findings need to be followed up with detailed studies to define the potential fisheries. Knowledge of most of the offshore fish stocks still is patchy. Then there is the problem of equipping countries on the Indian Ocean to take advantage of any fishing grounds that are found. Dr. N. K. Pannikar of the Indian National Institute of Oceanography points out that this requires major help in four technical areas. His country, and others bordering the ocean, need modern fish-finding aids such as echo-locators and helicopter patrols. They need a continuing research program to pin down the factors such as water temperature or oxygen content that affect fish distribution. They need help in developing new fishing techniques, such as attracting fish by light or guiding them with electric currents, in ways suitable for use in the Indian Ocean. And, of course, they need large-scale aid in building modern fishing fleets.

To this list, you can add one all-important shoreside requirement—the need for cheap, effective means of preserving the catch. This is a problem for the food technologist rather than the ocean engineer. Yet it needs to be mentioned for, unless it is solved, there will be little point in helping protein-hungry countries increase their exploitation of the sea. In such countries today, only those who live near the sea benefit much from its produce, for these countries are generally hot lands, and the rate of fish spoilage there is appalling. Boats spend a minimum of time on the fishing grounds, yet spoilage is considerable even during the few hours journey to shore. Once there, the fish must be sold within a day or it has to be thrown out for fertilizer. There often is no question of transporting it inland. Ice is of some help, but it melts fast and is expensive to produce. Canning is often no answer, either, since canning industries tend to be rudimentary at best. Freezing and refrigeration would be ideal solutions technically, and indeed, an FAO team recommended them for Thailand in the 1950s. But after consideration, the Thai National FAO rejected them as being impractical: rough roads would soon wreck transportation equipment and high capital costs would make it hard to sell the products at a price Thailanders could afford.

Fish meal for people may be the answer, at least in the fore-seeable future. It could be made by grinding up many kinds of fish. The meal itself or protein extracted from it would be as nourishing for people as it is for chickens. Unfortunately, the kind of meal used for livestock is impractical for humans. It contains fishy oils, which soon go rancid. While livestock don't mind them, rancid oils are objectionable and sometimes poisonous for humans. Recently, ways have been found to take the oils out of fish meal, so that it is virtually odorless and taste-free. Two such processes developed in the United States were approved by the United States Food and Drug Administration in 1967.

In Sweden, a factory for industrial production of fish-protein concentrate has started operation at Bua. Here, the pharmaceutical firm, AB Astra of Södertälje can turn out 10,000 tons a year. Also, in Britain, the Torry Research Station at Aberdeen has developed a protein extract from sprat meal that seems to be wholesome and to keep well. Such fish meals and protein extracts made from them would mix well in breads, gruels, or tortillas. They could be pressed into cakes. With a little fresh fish or other additive to give them flavor, they could be used to thicken curries and other sauces to balance a rice meal.

Estimating present world protein shortages is rough guessing at best and forecasting future shortages is even more uncertain. Nevertheless, an estimate made in 1964 by the U. S. Department of Agriculture is instructive. For the year 1970, the USDA foresaw a world deficit of animal protein of 6525 thousand tons in terms of nonfat dry milk equivalent. That is the same as 3012 thousand tons of fish-protein concentrate. In addition, there should be a shortage of plant protein equivalent to 6714 thousand tons of dry beans or peas. There is a significant difference between the two types of protein. While you can get all the protein food value you need from nonfat dry milk or fish-protein concentrate, plant proteins such as those of dry beans lack some of the essential nutrients. This is why a balanced diet usually includes animal protein as well as plant protein unless a well-planned assortment of plants is used. Citing the USDA forecast, Chapman notes that the total expected 1970 protein deficit, both of animal and plant protein, could be made up by 7 million tons of fish-protein con-centrate. That would require an increase in world fish production of 45 million tons a year. Then there is the need for edible oil.

The USDA anticipates a world fat shortage of 3101 thousand tons by 1970. Chapman points out that, in producing the 7 million tons of fish-protein concentrate, at least a million tons of edible fish oil would also be made. In other words, a mere doubling of the 1964 catch would satisfy the world's expected protein hunger in 1970 and go a long way toward meeting its need for fat—if the food reached hungry people rather than livestock.

Given the determination to do so and sufficient aid to the needy countries, meeting the protein deficit is a modest goal in terms of developing the ocean's food resources. Since World War II, world fish production has been doubling every ten years and has recently been increasing some three times faster than has the population. In the long run, meeting the world's food needs demands a complex effort both to check runaway population growth and to strengthen the lagging economies of the developing nations. But, over the short run of the next decade, the food resources of the sea could well meet the world's need for protein. This still begs the question of whether men must be restricted to merely the wild stocks of the sea or will someday be able to farm the sea and husband its resources as they now do the livestock of the land.

Farming the Seas

In taking food from the sea, modern men are little better off than were their ancestors in gaining a living from the land before farming was invented. While fishermen today have sophisticated aids in finding their quarry, like their hunting forefathers on land, they are at the mercy of natural fluctuations in the abundance of their game. If fish could be domesticated and farmed like cattle on the range, it would take some of the uncertainty out of the seafood supply. Such marine farming now is a bright long-range promise on the research horizon. Given adequate research and the self-discipline to preserve the salt marshes, estuaries, and other shore-line areas that would be the marine "farmsteads," aquaculture can become widely practical over the next decade.

If men are to develop sea farming, they will need the equivalent of the land farmer's agricultural-experiment stations. These stations, usually run by governments, are the chief agencies that have turned scientific knowledge into practical farming techniques. Agriculture has, of course, been developing for thousands of years. But the great advances it has made in recent times have come through the practical application of scientific knowledge. This has been the work of the experiment stations, which carry practical research to the point that it can be turned over to farmers for immediate use. There are few comparable laboratories for aquacultural research today. Yet such an agency is probably more vital to practical development in this field than it has been in land farming.

Agriculture could and did develop to a fair degree without the aid of science. Man is, after all, a land dweller. His domestic animals and his food crops were selected from wild stocks with which he had long been familiar. When man began developing agriculture, he was not working with an unknown, alien environment. He had a heritage of practical knowledge to draw upon, knowledge gained through long ages of food gathering, and common sense was at least a workable guide.

How different it is with the ocean. Here the only heritage of common-sense knowledge are the traditions of fishermen and of the few fish farmers or shellfish raisers whose total effort is insignificant compared to the fishing of wild stocks. To develop aquaculture on a scale large enough to make a meaningful contribution to the world's food supplies is a job that requires both a comprehensive and fundamental research effort to understand the alien marine environment and practical research that will turn the new knowledge into workable sea-farming techniques.

The primitive aquaculture practiced today—fish farming, shellfish raising, seaweed cultivation—illustrates this point. This type of marine cultivation generally makes use of protected waters such as bays, estuaries, swamps, brackish-water lagoons, passages protected by barrier islands, and the like. It is from these easily enclosed areas along the edge of the sea that full-fledged sea farming will likely spread out in the future.

In the simplest operations, the sea farmer corrals animals into a diked or fenced enclosure, perhaps letting them swim in with the tide. Without feeding them or fertilizing the water, the farmer lets them grow for a suitable period. This at least helps protect the animals from predators and ensures that the farmer knows where they are when he wants them. In more elaborate operations, the animals are fed directly or fertilizing minerals are added to the water to encourage the growth of natural-food organisms while predators are controlled. In some cases, the young fry of fish such as mullet or whitefish are caught in the open sea and raised in an enclosure.

Hundreds of thousands of acres are cultivated in this way, largely along the coasts of Asia. The brackish-water zone is especially valuable. Less salty than the open sea and fed by mineral-rich water from the land, this zone is the habitat of valuable shellfish such as oysters, clams, and mussels. Indeed, oyster farming is already quite profitable and for some time has been highly successful in Japan and western Europe. It now is beginning to develop in the United States, especially along the northeastern seaboard. David H. Wallace, Director of Marine Fisheries for the New York State Conservation Department, estimates that the bulk of the world oyster production during the 1960s has come from farming. As early as 1962, the oyster farms accounted for 75 per cent of the world annual harvest of 500,000 metric tons.

Raising marine fish as one does cattle is another matter. Open-ocean farming is virtually nonexistent. There has been some work, especially in Europe, in transplanting young fish to more favorable waters for growth, which has often been quite profitable. There have also been scattered attempts to regulate the environment in closed or protected areas such as bays to encourage fish growth as mentioned earlier. But, on the whole, true marine-fish farming is in its infancy. Nevertheless, experiments in Britain have shown that technical problems in marine-fish husbandry can be overcome.

A research team led by J. E. Shelbourne at the Fisheries Laboratory at Lowestoft on the North Sea coast of England has developed a reliable way of rearing certain bottom-living flatfish such as plaice and flounder. First, they learned to grow them from eggs to the stage of fingernail-size fishes in tanks. This gave fisheries biologists, for the first time, a tested way to raise fish for experiments as well as developing techniques important for fish farming. That was in 1962. Since then, the United Kingdom White Fish Authority and the Ministry of Agriculture, Fisheries, and Food have been supporting research on hatching and rearing of marine fish that points the way to farming.

Biologists at hatcheries are experimenting with different conditions for rearing the fish, while other biologists are beginning to try out different techniques for growing bottom fish to marketable size. They experiment with fertilizing enclosed or partly enclosed sea-water areas to stimulate the growth of tiny plants and animals upon which the growing fish feed. They are also using cooling water from larger power plants. Normally, growth falls off during the winter, but this water is warm enough to stimulate a high rate of fish growth all year long. In a warm-water environment, the fish probably will grow to edible size in two to two and one-half years instead of the normal four years. One uncertainty is whether or not the fish can tolerate the chlorine which is put in power-station cooling water to prevent fouling by marine growths. Two experiments underway at this writing have been encouraging. They were being carried out by the White Fish Authority at Carmarthen in Wales and at the Hunterton nuclear power plant in Scotland. The fish do not seem to mind the chlorine; they have been growing rapidly.

Yet another encouraging approach is the development of desirable strains of "domesticated" fish. The cattle on land are far removed from their wild ancestors. Likewise, fish stocks can undoubtedly be bred to have desirable qualities for farming. For example, hybrids derived from crossing plaice with flounder are vigorous and grow faster than their parents, while producing high-quality meat.

The growth of food fish, especially of bottom-living fish, may also be aided by cultivating the sea bed to get rid of unwanted animals competing for the food supply. Dr. Gunnar Thorson of the Zoological Museum in Copenhagen has estimated that, on the feeding grounds off Denmark, starfish and other invertebrates that feed on the same food animals as do the fish, leave the latter only 1 or 2 per cent of the available food supply. From man's viewpoint, these invertebrates are like weeds in a garden. If enough of them can be removed to give the fish 20 per cent instead of a mere 1 or 2 per cent of the food supply, the yield of fish in a given area could be increased ten times over what it is today.

To do this will take research. It will take fundamental studies to determine which and how many animals can be eliminated from an area without upsetting the necessary balance of life. It will take practical research to develop techniques and machinery to do the weeding. The time will probably come when large areas of the continental shelf will be cultivated, as one now cultivates the land, by dragging some sort of combing or filtering device along the sea bed to weed out unwanted animals or perhaps by using some form of chemical control analogous to selective weed killers.

Adding fertilizers to protected waters is a promising way of stimulating sea-food production. But it would cost too much to try this in large areas of the open sea. Oceanographers point out that, fortunately, this may not be necessary for boosting the productivity of many offshore and presently fish-poor areas. The sea has all the nutrient minerals needed if you can get them into the sunlit zone where the phytoplankton grow. Where there is natural upwelling, as off the coast of Peru, minerals are constantly brought up from the depths. Plant growth is abundant and the area is rich with fish and animal life. Oceanographers envision some kind of artificial upwelling in regions that now are deficient in phosphates and nitrates but that otherwise might support a rich population.

One scheme that has been widely and at least half seriously discussed is the salt-water siphon. In most shallow parts of the sea, if a vertical pipe were set up and water started flowing through it, either upward or downward, the flow would continue indefinitely. Surface water is usually saltier than the deep water. If the two types of water were at the same temperature, the saltier of the two would also be the heavier. Surface water stays on top because it is significantly warmer than water deeper down. However, when water flowed through the pipe in either direction, it would tend to be warmed or cooled by the water surrounding the pipe. Thus bottom water started up the pipe would arrive at the surface with more or less the same temperature as the surrounding water. Because it is less salty, it would flow out of the top of the pipe. Likewise, surface water flowing down the pipe would be heavier than the surrounding water when it arrived at the bottom and would keep on flowing downward. In either case, once the water were started on its way, it would keep on flowing. If done on a large scale, this would overturn enough water to bring substantial amounts of minerals to the surface. Another way to cause this overturning might be to use a nuclear reactor to heat the bottom water, making it rise by convection.

Schemes such as these sound like science fiction. Yet as early as 1959, the Brown committee of the National Academy of Sciences, which outlined promising research lines in marine sciences, considered the concept of artificial upwelling "promising enough to recommend that grants be given, first for feasibility studies, then for detailed engineering development of promising proposals, and finally for pilot-scale trial of devices which are developed." Now, more than a decade later, the idea has yet to be tested. It remains an example of the kind of imaginative technology that will probably be needed to make large-scale sea farming an economical proposition.

Although it could become an important aquacultural technique, artificial upwelling, by itself, would not always be enough to make an area fertile, There are trace chemicals in the sea that are as important as the phosphates and nitrates. These largely unknown substances, which occur in minute amounts, are essential to plant growth and also have a direct effect on animals. These substances must be isolated, identified, and their effects understood if large-scale aquaculture is to be developed on a scientific basis. In some instances, it may take only a small injection of one or more of these substances into surface waters to increase substantially their productivity. Then too, there may be bacteria or other organisms whose activity is essential or inimical to the primary plankton growth in which future sea farmers will be interested. These organisms too, must be sought out and, where necessary, controlled or employed.

"Comprehensiveness in marine-biological research is not a luxury," writes Lionel Walford in his book *Living Resources of the Sea*. He adds:

Our use of the sea as source of food and other biological raw materials is technologically and philosophically about two hundred years behind our use of the land. . . . But why put up with such antiquity? Why should not technologies and philosophies advance? If we learned how to use sea resources fully and scientifically, the material rewards should well compensate for all the investment that would be required for the learning. There is no way of evaluating these rewards now. Nor can anyone honestly promise that they will in fact be forthcoming, any more than anyone could have promised the ultimate use of atomic energy. There is no simple, direct short cut to a full understanding of the proper uses of the sea. The most economical, efficient way to reach that understanding is not to try to do it penuriously. If we really desire to exploit the sea fully, if it is knowledge that we need for that purpose . . . then we had better make the necessary costly investment and put full effort into the job of acquiring that knowledge.

So far, the support of this kind of research has indeed been penurious. The regular budgets of marine-research institutions have been too taut to support a comprehensive, biological research program, while support from governments and the fishing industry has been spotty. The latter tend to support research only when directly related to specific fisheries' problems and often only when one or another fishery is in trouble. Scientists have sometimes been called in when it was too late for the slow processes of research to be of much practical help. However, with the increasing interest now being shown in oceanography in many countries, this situation is rapidly changing. Both national programs and the kind of co-operative exploration represented by the IGY and the International Indian Ocean Expedition are beginning to carry out the rounded biological research that Walford says is so badly needed.

Meanwhile, the basic question about the future of fish farming —will it pay?—awaits an answer. Among other things, the answer depends on finding cheap ways to feed the fish. Agricultural-feed manufacturers haven't even considered this yet. Alan Benton Bowers of the University of Liverpool Marine Biological Station at Port Erin says it is too soon to try to judge the economic prospects. He thinks it would be "a great mistake" either to try to apply economic criteria too soon or to be too optimistic about the immediate future of fish farming. He says, "It may be ten years before useful crops can be produced; it will be many more years before the full potential of the new science of marine-fish farming can be adequately assessed."

It is time, however, to take steps to remove a major legal factor that retards development of aquaculture, the lack of suitable "farmsteads." Rights even to inshore waters are vague. American would-be sea farmers, especially, have no assurance that animals they raise will not be taken by someone else. "What belongs to everyone, is harvested by no one," David Wallace of New York State's Conservation Department explains. He notes that "sea farming [generally farming of mollusks] has advanced most where individual or corporate rights have been granted by government." He puts this legal problem high on the list of obstacles that must be removed before marine farming can begin to develop on a large scale. Prof. Nelson Marshall of the University of Rhode Island agrees. He is one of the leading exponents of shellfish farming along the American northeastern coast. Even for such highly salable crops as oysters, he points out, successful farming has gone hand in hand with a firm guarantee of the farmer's exclusive legal right to harvest the crop he has nurtured. By 1967, about a dozen shellfish farms were operating in southern New England and New York State. Noting this, Professor Marshall points out that "the major developing programs are not in Rhode Island. They are in areas where people can lease or own [sea] bottom lands with assurance of continuing control." Rhode Island local authorities have been reluctant to break with the tradition that inshore waters are public property with the animals in them being free for the taking.

Equally important with the need to give the sea farmer firm ownership of the crop, is the need to preserve suitable areas for future farm sites. Salt marshes, small bays, and estuaries are, in many cases, the places where both shellfish and true-fish farming will start. It will be a long time before men learn how to fence the open sea, if they ever do it. The inshore areas are important as breeding grounds for marine animals and they are the scene of a vital part of the ocean-life processes. Yet they are constantly being lost through pollution or being filled to create building sites. To those who believe in the future of marine farming, this is as wasteful as it would have been to make dumps out of Kansas wheat fields.

C. G. Matthiessen of The Marine Research Foundation, Inc., makes this point, citing the potential capacity of a sea farm to outproduce the best of cattle ranches on a pounds-per-acre basis. A four-to-one ratio in favor of shellfish or future fish farms is often estimated. But Matthiessen thinks the modern technique of vertical oyster culture makes the ratio much higher. In this technique, oysters are grown on strings suspended from rafts. The entire water body is used rather than just the bottom. He says that such oyster farming has yielded up to 50 bushels of oysters for a single 50-square-foot raft over a two-year period—roughly 150 pounds of meat a year. It represents a ratio of one thousand to one over a cattle ranch in pounds of meat per acre per year. With such prospects as this for raising a high-value crop, Matthiessen says that shellfish farming is already an economically attractive alternative to filling in estuaries for housing. It also underscores the folly of thoughtlessly ruining, today, the potentially valuable sea-farm sites for other types of aquaculture in the future.

Compared to hunting the wild fish of the sea, marine farming will be only a secondary factor in helping to feed mankind for a long time to come. But as a source of high-quality fish of certain desirable species such as plaice or flounder, fish farming could, within a decade, become practical. For some animals that have been overfished or decimated by pollution, such as oysters along the eastern United States, farming already is the only guarantee of a continuing supply. "As is the case with lumber," Professor Marshall says, "we have come to the point with shellfish where the natural resources have been exploited. As we must now look to tree farms and replanting programs for our forest products, we must learn to 'farm' our shellfish, using careful management backed by scientific knowledge." This will also be part of the rationale for the fish farms of the future.

Meanwhile, the world is growing as hungry for minerals and metals as it is for protein. Here again, men are beginning to look to the wealth of the sea to help meet their needs. Vast supplies of minerals, especially of oil and natural gas, lie under the sea bed, while the mineral resources of the oceans' 328,740,000 cubic miles of water should be virtually inexhaustible. Every stream and river reaching the sea carries its load of dissolved minerals. Some of these are leached from rocks or soil. Some come secondhand from man. Metals corroding in junkyards are slowly converted to other forms through the action of wind, rain, and chemical change. Eventually, many of them find their way into the water flowing seaward. Rich phosphate fertilizers mined from rock once laid down by the sea and spread on farmlands, likewise go through a series of steps to end up in the ocean treasury. One way or another, the mineral wealth of the land gradually migrates to the sea. There it remains in solution or is deposited in bottom formations by chemical action or perhaps is made into shells by marine animals. Mining the land is like living on your savings; except for a few nonrenewables such as oil, mining the wealth of the sea will be like living on income. That is why men will be able to make large drafts on the ocean mineral bank without drawing down its reserves.

Mining the Sea

The *Aluminaut* is a three-man research submarine that normally moves through the water like a fish. In 1966, it donned wheels to roll across an undersea "highway" literally paved with mineral ore. Located off the southeastern United States, the pavement is a manganese-rich deposit laid down by the natural chemistry of the sea. Where the *Aluminaut* dove, it covers a relatively flat sea bed in depths up to 3000 feet. Arthur L. Markel, vice-president and general manager of Reynolds Submarine Service Corporation, which manages the *Aluminaut,* said the deposit "resembles a black-top road" and that the *Aluminaut* "rode along the deposits as though it were on a country road." Reynolds Metal Company geologists thought the deposit may be rich enough in manganese to be considered a good grade of ore.

This remarkable pavement typifies the mineral wealth of the seas. To begin with, it is formed by processes whose economic importance men only now are coming to appreciate. The deposit is precipitated by chemical action that occurs widely in the sea. Mining such ore is not depleting a fixed asset so much as it is working a self-renewing resource. This is true of many ocean minerals. Secondly, the pavement was found in an area beginning only then to be systematically explored. Estimates of the ocean's riches have been made largely on the basis of scattered findings. The need now is to find out specifically what the economically valuable resources are and where they lie. Thirdly, while the pavement would be a good ore on land, its real value depends on whether or not ways could be developed to recover it economically from the sea, and ocean engineering is just becoming equal to this task. Finally, the deposit represents a mineral in short world supply. The United States uses 1,719,000 tons of manganese oxide a year for making steel, plus another 123,000 tons for batteries and various chemical processes. It has to import virtually all of this. As world population rises and as today's underdeveloped countries build up their industries, men will have to turn to the sea to find enough manganese, as well as other minerals, to go around.

Thomas M. Ware, chairman of the International Minerals and Chemical Corporation outlines the challenge this way. "The oceans," he says, "are unavoidably intertwined with the role minerals play in the world. . . . If Africa were to develop the same kind of telephone system we have in the United States today, the copper demand [for wire] would exceed the world copper supply. This is a severe example, but one that emphasizes the mineral problem. . . . Seen in this perspective, the oceans take on new meaning. . . . Now we have to explore and explain [geologically] this area, which is roughly 2½ times that of the land mass, in one lifetime, whereas exploring the land took many lifetimes. The pressure for discovery is unprecedented. . . . We cannot afford to fail to recognize that the oceans represent a new frontier in a world where someone starves somewhere for each one that is adequately fed." This challenge is sharpened by the fact that international law has given many nations important new property rights to the mineral-rich shelves that border the continents.

When in June 1964, the United States ratified the 1958 Geneva Convention on the Continental Shelf, it gained more territory where its right of mineral exploitation is unquestioned than it did in the Louisiana Purchase (885,000 square miles) or the purchase of Alaska (586,000 square miles). The convention says in part that "The coastal state exercises over the continental shelf sovereign rights for the purpose of exploiting it and exploiting its natural resources." The treaty defines the continental shelf as "the sea bed and subsoil of the submarine areas adjacent to the coast but outside the territorial sea, to a depth of 200 meters (656 feet) or, beyond that limit, to where the depth of the superjacent waters admits of the exploitation of the natural resources. . . ." There are about 930,000 square miles within the 200-meter depth contour off the United States; that is about equal to 25 per cent of the United States dry-land area. The continental shelves of the world amount to about 10 million square miles, or roughly 20 per cent of the dry land of the continents.

Thus, at the stroke of a pen, many seaboard nations have acquired a potentially rich, undersea frontier; that they can claim even more undersea territory if they gain the capacity to work in the deeper water of the continental slopes should increase their incentive to develop it. It is already evident that gas and oil lie beyond the 200-meter limit, and probably the first of a variety of undersea-mineral riches to be exploited will be oil.

According to Frank N. Ikard, president of the American Petroleum Institute, "Important obstacles lie ahead as they do in opening any frontier. But within the petroleum industry, a development of prime importance is the search for offshore oil which has become world wide." As recently as 1960, only 8 per cent of the world's oil came from under the sea. Five years later, 15 per cent of the world supply was produced offshore. The undersea contribution is expected to reach 25 per cent over the next two to three decades. This is an encouraging prospect for a world whose oil demand is 2½ million barrels a day and still growing. Nobody knows how much the sea bed will ultimately contribute to world oil needs, but Lewis G. Weeks, former chief geologist for Jersey Standard, thinks the continental shelves and adjoining slopes hold at least 700 billion barrels of crude oil and natural-gas liquids plus 1.8 million billion cubic feet of natural gas itself. This is what Weeks thinks can be recovered directly. Another 300 billion barrels of liquids may be had by secondary recovery techniques.

This wealth is spread widely around the earth. Only seventeen countries were producing in 1966, but extensive exploration and drilling have been underway off the shores of another fifty nations. During the 1970s, many of these should be joining the ranks of oil producers. The North Sea area, for example, has turned out to be a major field for oil and gas. New fields have also been found off France and Italy. In the Persian Gulf, a field was found off Saudi Arabia which was the largest found up to 1967. Some 800,000 square miles off Australia seem very promising. So does a field found off Nigeria in 1963. The Soviet Union has discovered major new fields in the Caspian Sea. These examples show how explosively the offshore-oil industry is developing.

At the same time, the industry faces big problems in opening up many of these new fields. For one thing, oil wells must be sunk in depths too great for present offshore techniques to be used. A new technology is being developed for drilling and working in water hundreds of feet deep. Also, there is a lack of basic scientific knowledge. The geology of offshore areas needs to be mapped in detail to aid exploration. A greater knowledge of ocean currents and wave formation is needed to forecast working conditions many miles offshore. None of the problems are insoluble. They are of the kind that scientists and engineers now can lick if a determined effort is made to do so. Given a 7 per cent per year rise in world oil demand and given the vast offshore reserves, the oil companies are eager to do their part. In the United States, they look to the government to develop basic geological and oceanographic knowledge. But they are ready themselves to pioneer the new technology. Since 1945, they have invested some $3.5 billion in offshore operations. Ikard says that less than half of that investment has been recovered. Nevertheless, it is only the beginning of what is expected to be invested in the coming decades.

But oil is not the only mineral the sea has to offer. For one thing, there are vast deposits of a lowly but badly needed construction material—sand and gravel. In many areas, such as the heavily populated northeastern American seaboard, good-quality sand and gravel are becoming hard to find. Often the major cost

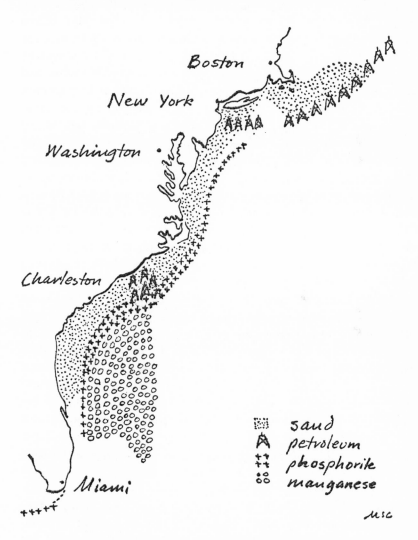

FIG. 50: Minerals found off the eastern coast of the United States (from U. S. Government sources).

of a load of gravel is for transportation. Yet large supplies are near at hand—on the continental shelf.

Dr. K. O. Emery of Woods Hole says that a blanket of sand and gravel covering almost the entire width of the continental shelf off the eastern United States was found from extensive sampling of the shelf during a joint-exploration project of Woods Hole and the U. S. Geological Survey. He also says that similar sand deposits have been found in the Gulf of Mexico, off the United States west coast, and off Brazil, China, Israel, and other countries and that such sands are often worth exploiting today.

Another prosaic yet potentially valuable offshore resource is calcium-containing sea shells, which provide calcium for making cement and for certain chemical-manufacturing processes. Over the past 25 years, 60 million tons of such shells have been mined off eastern Texas. They are gathered in a number of other areas as well. But, so far, this source of lime has scarcely been touched.

There is a glitter of more glamorous minerals too. The shallow shelves were once above water and contain many drowned river valleys and other extensions of land features. And they may have many of the minerals of these features too, especially the placer deposits. These are accumulations of relatively heavy minerals that have been winnowed out of lighter sand and mud by the action of running water and waves. Where there are placer deposits of minerals such as gold, tin, or diamonds on land, these are likely to continue onto the continental shelves. Diamonds are recovered from such deposits off the Orange River in South Africa now. Tin is dredged from extensions of river deposits in Southeast Asia. Gold and platinum deposits have been found off Alaska. Such placer deposits have only begun to be located.

Dr. John L. Mero, president of Ocean Resources, Inc. and a leading investigator of ocean minerals, says it is almost impossible to estimate the value of such deposits from present scanty data but that "we can expect it to be at least equal to the onshore potential, considering the enormous extent of the continental shelf in the areas where the offshore placers are being found."

Then there are the mineral resources unique to the ocean. Sea-shell mining at Faxa Bay, Iceland, illustrates one especially valuable aspect. The shells come from a rocky shoal where a variety of shelled animals lives. Loosened and crushed by winter waves, the shell fragments are swept into the bay by tidal currents at a far greater rate than the Icelanders mine them. They are a self-renewing mineral deposit, unlike the exhaustible deposits to which one is accustomed on land. Noting this, Mero explains that "this renewing feature is a common and highly significant feature of mineral deposits in the sea."

This is also true of the ocean's vast deposits of manganese, which are generally found as crusts on the sea bed or in the form of nodules. Shading from brown to black, these pebble masses and slabs were first discovered by the *Challenger* Expedition. They consist of manganese oxide precipitated from sea water, plus other materials, including small amounts of silicon, copper, nickel, and cobalt. Most of the deposits found so far are at the bottom of the deep sea. But some are in shallower water like the "pavement" of manganese-rich nodules off the southeastern United States along which the *Aluminaut* traveled. This pavement is part of a general deposit which seems due to special conditions created by the Gulf Stream. Mero says there are an estimated "1.5 trillion tons of manganese nodules on the Pacific Ocean floor alone and . . . they are forming in this ocean at an annual rate of about 10 million tons. . . . Even if only 10 per cent of the nodule deposits prove economic to mine . . . many elements are accumulating in the . . . nodules . . . faster than they are presently being consumed —in fact, three times faster in the case of cobalt, as fast in the case of nickel, and so on."

There is no doubt of the vastness of the supply. But is it worthwhile developing the deep-sea dredges, suction lifts, or other apparatus needed to mine the manganese deposits? Mero says flatly that "from all calculations thus far made, [the nodules] are indicated to be highly economic to mine at the present time." Emery, however, is skeptical: granting that some deposits are high in manganese and have worthwhile amounts of some other metals, he notes that they also have several per cent of silicon, an impurity which present manganese-extraction processes have trouble handling.

There is comparable expert disagreement over the value of sea-bottom deposits of a phosphorous-rich mineral called phosphorite. This occurs as nodules or as fine grains in sediments. They are generally found in shallower water than are the manganese nodules. Emery and others have found extensive deposits off Southern

California, and there are other deposits off the southeastern United States associated with the manganese pavement.

Again, Emery is skeptical as to the value of mining such deposits when there are ample phosphorous supplies on land. But Mero points out that there are some land areas not so well favored. Australia has to import phosphorus for its poor soil. It would be an enormous boon to Australia if promising regions of its continental shelf do hold phosphorite. Also, a large deposit of fine-grained phosphorite has been found in sediments 230 feet under water off western Mexico. The high-grade part of the deposit has an estimated 200 billion tons of mineral that could be recovered. That is 4000 years' reserve at the present rate of world consumption.

There is no doubt that vast reserves of minerals lie under the sea. Mero estimates that "deposits in the sea which are economically exploitable are of sufficient volume to provide the world with its total consumption of many industrially important minerals for thousands of years at present rates of consumption." There is also no doubt that, for the first time in mining history, the challenge of this wealth is being taken seriously. In its first report, the United States National Council on Marine Resources and Engineering Development noted in February, 1967, that "Almost every large [American] mining and aerospace firm has initiated feasibility studies related to the solid deposits of the continental shelf. . . ." These companies are proceeding cautiously. The offshore-mineral deposits are quite different from anything miners have handled before. There is the doubly difficult task of dealing with new types of ores and recovering them from beneath the sea. Yet the National Council observed that most of these companies are only "awaiting the identification of promising areas on the shelf and the development of improved sampling and recovery techniques before launching major development programs."

Meanwhile, the other area of ocean abundance—the vast amounts of minerals dissolved in sea water—also beckons. Salt, of course, has been taken from the sea for millenia. If you live in the United States, the chances are good that the metal in the magnesium stepladders in your local hardware store came from the sea. The United States derives most of its magnesium and almost all of its bromine from sea water. Other minerals may one day be taken as well.

There are some 166 million tons of dissolved solids in a cubic mile of sea water. Eighty-five per cent of them is common salt. There are also over 26 million tons of magnesium salts, 4 million tons of potassium sulphate, and a variety of other elements such as copper, zinc, tin, and iodine in small traces. Here, indeed, is a vast supply of minerals for the taking. This taking is complicated by the extreme dilution in which the minerals are usually found and compensated to some extent by the ease with which large quantities of water can be handled, an advantage no land mine can claim. With advances in chemical engineering, the dilution problem will undoubtedly be licked for a lengthening list of important minerals. Indeed, the National Physical Laboratory of the United Kingdom has developed a process of extracting uranium from sea water that it believes to be economically competitive with the recovery of that atomic-age fuel from low-grade land ores. Moreover, as desalinization becomes a widespread way of obtaining fresh water, the concentrated-waste brines from the desalting plants will be richer raw material from which to take minerals than is the water in the sea. To this prospect, Mero adds the possibility of finding bodies of water so rich in certain minerals that they can be considered a good grade of ore.

For centuries, the oceans have been barriers separating continents and peoples. Now they are being seen as mankind's last great reserve of minerals and food. This raises the question: who owns the mineral resources of the seas beyond the continental shelves? Who controls the harvesting of the food resources beyond territorial waters? Some international agreements, especially in regard to fishing, do spell out limited obligations to conserve the sea's bounty. But these are few and they deal only with fragments of the basic legal question. Mining companies, in particular, wonder what kind of claim they can stake beyond territorial waters. Can their government give them any kind of lease or license and guarantee exclusive rights to their claim? Should the United Nations or other international agency take over jurisdiction? Similar questions arise when one thinks in terms of possible future management of marine-food resources beyond the waters of any one nation. The ocean areas, where the only law has been the doctrine of freedom of the high seas, are fast becoming a common economic resource demanding international management.

ELEVEN

THE NEW OCEANOGRAPHY

The sea is challenging man as it never has before. It is challenging him to stop romancing about its "mystery," to stop dreaming idly about its untapped riches, and to start developing the last great frontier of our planet. Three trends converged during the 1960s to spark this intensified interest in the ocean. First, humanity's need for food and minerals is on so great a scale and grows so fast that it cannot be fully met unless men do turn to the sea. Secondly, international law has given nations tantalizing property rights on the continental shelf, as outlined in the previous chapter. Finally, marine science and engineering have developed so far that it is now possible to develop the ocean's food resources to banish protein hunger from the earth; it is now feasible to begin exploiting in a large way the ocean's mineral resources and to exercise the new national property rights to the continental shelf.

The science of the sea is thus entering a new phase of its century-long development, a phase marked by increased research activities throughout the world, enlarged capabilities for exploration, and especially by the emphasis being placed on international aspects of the science. Except for national rights on the shelves, the oceans belong to no one country; they are a great resource to be shared by all mankind. The new oceanography is focused to develop the basic knowledge needed to exploit this wealth and dedicated to defining the principles upon which wise international management of this community resource will be based.

Oceanographers have an impressive kit of new tools to help them do this. Satellites and arrays of instrumented buoys will enable them to make comprehensive studies over large areas, as indicated in Chapter Six. Computers help them to wring new knowledge from the mushrooming piles of data far more quickly than ocean scientists could process their measurements even as recently as the 1950s. And what may be most significant of all, oceanographers are breaking the barrier of the surface. Instead of just blindly groping with nets and trawls, corers and strings of instruments, they are increasingly going into the depths themselves. Deep-diving research submarines give them direct access to even the deepest sea floor. And, on the continental shelf, man is becoming a water creature. He is beginning to share this part of the water world with its established inhabitants.

Man Beneath the Sea

While astronauts are reaching for the moon, they have yet to be assigned any economically useful tasks. Aquanauts who are learning to live beneath the sea have already put in many hard days of industrial work. This is a telling distinction between the two great adventures in which men are moving into alien environments. Like Alice stepping through her looking glass, men who cross the interface between air and ocean enter a strange, sometimes baffling realm. Divers who go into the sea for only a few hours or less at a time scarcely get a taste of this; scenes in films or on TV showing them swimming through clear, often tropically warm water are especially deceptive. The environment of the aquanaut is more likely to be cold, dark, and unfriendly. It is as personally challenging as the airless, weightless environment of space. But, while astronauts are heading moonward under the banner "get there first," the aquanauts have a different motto. It reads, "Man is going beneath the sea to do useful and economically rewarding work."

The men who have rallied to this banner are as far removed from ordinary divers as orbiting astronauts are from the rocket-plane pilots who momentarily shoot above the atmosphere. As the term is used here, an aquanaut is someone who becomes adapted to the pressure of a given depth within the sea and then lives under that pressure for days or weeks at a time. The technical term for such an aquanaut is "saturated diver." He is "saturated" because his body tissues have absorbed their fill of the gases which he breathes.

For every foot you descend in the sea, the pressure increases 0.442 pounds per square inch. It is roughly 100 p.s.i. at 200 feet, a typical depth for working aquanauts at this writing. The fluids in the human body quickly adjust to this pressure so that the body is not crushed. But, in order to breathe, divers must have breathing gas at the same pressure as that of their environment. This is where the main challenge in diving lies and where the concept of saturated diving comes in.

Air is a mixture (by volume) of 78 per cent nitrogen and 21 per cent oxygen plus traces of several other gases. As the pressure of breathing air is increased for a diver, his body absorbs more and more of the nitrogen in a given period of time. This is of no great consequence if he stays under for a short time, but if he stays at a given depth long enough for significant absorption to occur, he can no longer return quickly to the atmospheric pressure at the surface. If he did so, the nitrogen would bubble out of his tissues like the effervescence of an uncapped bottle of champagne. This is known as "the bends" and can be fatal.

To prevent it, such a diver must return to normal pressure slowly enough for the excess nitrogen to pass out of his body through his lungs. Schedules for decompression have been worked out for various depths and breathing mixtures. The longer one stays at a given depth, the longer he has to decompress, up to the point where the body tissues are saturated with gas. After that, no matter how long he stays at that depth, he still has the same decompression time.

The difference between the aquanaut and the ordinary diver who works from the surface is that the aquanaut allows his body to saturate. He stays with his work until it is finished. This is an all-important difference revolutionizing the diving industry. A surface diver's job is calculated carefully to allow him enough time on his return trip to pause at various depths to decompress safely. An hour spent at 200 feet involves a four-hour ascent to the surface. In practice, working time at that depth is often much less than this. It can take several dives over several days to carry out jobs that would take only a few hours or less on land. An aquanaut, in contrast, works away unconcerned about decompression. He has a house in which he rests, eats, and sleeps. Its atmosphere is kept at the pressure of his working depth. He spends several hours at a time working. He decompresses only once—when the job is done. This practice has sharply cut the costs and raised the efficiency of diving operations and allows dives to depths never thought practical before. It should enable men to work freely in the water over the entire area of the continental shelves, whose depth is at most 600 to 1000 feet.

Aquanautics has developed rapidly during the 1960s. The concept of saturation diving was first suggested in 1957 by Captain George F. Bond, who started the United States Navy's Man-in-the-Sea program. However, the Navy was slow in following up Bond's animal experiments. Dr. Edwin Link, inventor of the Link aircraft-pilot trainer, and French oceanographer Jacques-Yves Cousteau, were first off the mark with manned experiments.

In 1962, Cousteau carried out Conshelf I, an experiment in which two men lived for seven days at a depth of thirty feet. The next year, he kept several men for a month at 34 feet and two men for seven days at 85 feet in the Conshelf II exercise. Then, in 1965, six men lived at 330 feet for three weeks in Conshelf III. This time, there were no surface vessels hovering overhead ready to give aid and send down supplies. Conshelf III was autonomous except for a power-and-communications cable that ran along the sea bed to land. This independence from the surface allowed the experiment to continue during a storm that would have ended it if the aquanauts had depended on the support of surface ships.

While Cousteau experimented with extended living in the sea, Link went after depth. In 1962, he kept Belgium-diver Robert Sténuit at 200 feet for twenty-six hours. Two years later, he sent Sténuit and Jon Lindberg to 432 feet for forty-nine hours. In 1965, Ocean Systems, Inc. took over the Link project and kept two men at the pressure of 650 feet in a test chamber for forty-eight hours.

In 1964, Bond kept several men at 192 feet for eleven days in Sealab I. In the mid-1960s, he began to get the support he needed; the nuclear submarine *Thresher* was lost and the American Navy's purse strings loosened. Efforts to locate the *Thresher* remains showed how badly the Navy needed a capability to carry out rescue and other work on all parts of the continental shelf and, to some extent, in depths beyond. This realization sparked the Deep Submergence Systems Project. In this, a variety of research and rescue submarines are under development. Bond's work has also been given a substantial boost. As he states it, he now is working toward the goal of putting "large numbers of people on the ocean bottom to do useful work for periods in excess of thirty days at depths of 600–800 feet." The first experiment in this new program was Sealab II in 1965, in which Commander Scott Carpenter, the world's only astronaut-aquanaut, led three separate teams on stays ranging from fifteen days to a month at 205 feet. At this writing, Bond is getting ready for Sealab III in which men are to live at 430 feet. This now is a fast-paced program, and Bond says he hopes to have a permanent base at a depth of 600 feet or greater which could, if desired, be manned on a year-round basis during the 1970s.

These experiments have abundantly proved that men can live and do useful work beneath the sea. During Conshelf III, divers worked on a dummy oil rig. Among other things, they installed a valve faster than this is usually done on land. It may have helped them to be able to swim up and down the rig rather than having to climb it. Also, some of the men of Sealab II floated an aircraft hull by filling it with buoyant plastic.

At the same time, the experiments have shown the tough challenge the aquanauts face. Except in relatively shallow areas, they cannot breathe air. Nitrogen at a pressure much above a few atmospheres has a narcotic effect. Also, it is a relatively heavy gas; as its density is increased under pressure, it is less effective in flushing the lungs. With each breath, it becomes harder for a man to get rid of carbon dioxide under these conditions. A lighter carrier gas is less dense and is much more easily breathed and thus is much more effective in bringing in oxygen and carrying away carbon dioxide. Oxygen alone cannot be used because under high pressure it is poisonous. So far, aquanauts have generally breathed mixtures of oxygen and helium. This avoids nitrogen narcosis and is relatively easy to breathe. But the helium distorts voices in a Donald Duck effect which has yet to be satisfactorily compensated by electronic equipment.

Then there is the sea itself. Bond describes the aquanauts' world as "black, cold, sometimes unfriendly." Cousteau says that, for man who is a warm-blooded creature, living under the ocean is "a fight, not a pleasure." Artificial light can make up for loss of sunshine, but it is no match for the suspended particles and stirred-up sediments that typify the waters in which aquanauts work. On top of this, cold is a constant drain on human energy. Water temperatures below 60° F. are the rule, and in places on the continental shelf they run in the forties or even the thirties. Good heated suits to cope fully with such a bone-chilling environment have not yet been developed.

Bond says he deliberately picked the "blackest, coldest (46°), most miserable water that I could locate" for Sealab II. It was at the edge of Scripps Canyon off La Jolla, California. Under such conditions, thoroughly chilled and able to see only a few feet ahead at best, an aquanaut can quickly become disoriented. He might start rising without being aware of it. Yet he lives under the injunction that he must not rise much above his general working level. He can make excursions to greater depths with no ill effects. But with his body saturated, he can't rise to substantially lower pressure without undergoing lengthy decompression. Also, except at moderate depths, he and his buddies are on their own. Surface divers can't help them.

An aquanaut's job is a physical and psychological trial. Cousteau summed up his impression of it with studied exaggeration when he compared working in 55° water to "standing naked at the North Pole." Bond gave his assessment in a word—"scary." Yet all of the aquanauts who have entered the water have shown that men can master such conditions. Bond says they even grow to like the adventure of it.

In spite of this "scary" challenge, the commercial virtues of using aquanauts have been clearly enough demonstrated for industry to begin to use them. A number of companies in ocean engineering or oil-production fields have versions of the on-site decompression chamber. This is a pressurized chamber in which divers can travel to and return from working depths. It enables them to spend more time on the job since they can decompress at leisure in their elevator. They can also use it as a refuge on the job. They may even have small pressure chambers at the surface where they can relax between work shifts or decompress as needed. However, such chambers are not long-duration homes. Westinghouse Electric Corporation put the first true-aquanaut teams into the field. Its system is called Cachalot (after the sperm whale, famed as a deep diver) and uses a pressurized elevator and a deck chamber. This chamber is spacious enough for a pair of divers to live comfortably in it for a week, remaining all the time under

the pressure of the depth of their job. Westinghouse has no aquanauts of its own but acts as a subcontractor, leasing the Cachalot
equipment to diving firms that want aquanaut facilities for a particular job. The first two jobs dramatically demonstrated the advantage an aquanaut has over a surface diver.

One of the jobs involved repairing trash gates at the Smith
Mountain Dam in Virginia. The water was fresh, but the working
conditions might have been ordered by Bond—39° water and near-
zero visibility some of the time at the working depth of 200 feet.
The second job was 30 miles offshore in the Gulf of Mexico
where two oil rigs toppled by a hurricane were cut up for salvage.
Working depths there ran to 235 feet. The job was done in less
than one season. Thomas F. Horton, manager for *Deepstar* (a
research submarine) and Life Support Systems in the Westinghouse Underseas Division, says it would have taken a small army
of men more than one season to do the oil-rig job using surface
divers, as practical working time for a diver at 200 feet can be as
little as twenty minutes. Likewise, he says, it would have taken
surface divers eight to ten months to do the Smith Mountain
Dam work which Cachalot aquanauts accomplished in two and a
half months.

Horton explains that "Our average time has run five to six
useful working hours per man per day. Also, diver efficiency has
gone up as the men gained confidence in the system and learned
how to do the work. We now are getting about 95 per cent of a
diver's work time in useful work at 200 feet rather than spending
most of it in decompression. The only lost time is thirty hours
decompression once a week when we change teams. Prolonged
saturation techniques are not useful for all situations. They're not
worth it, for example, for jobs that require half an hour at a time
in 100 feet of water. But they are what you want for situations
and depths that put divers in a saturation condition."

Part of the efficiency of Cachalot aquanauts is due to the fact
that they, unlike the Sealab and Conshelf pioneers, do keep
warm. To counter the 39°-water at Smith Mountain Dam, Westinghouse engineers rigged a hot-water heating system for the aquanauts' suits. These men do not breathe from tanks on their backs
but are tied to their elevator chamber by long, flexible tethers which
carry breathing gas from cylinders on the chamber and communications lines linked to the surface. They were modified to carry

hot water, pumped at proper pressure from the surface, as well. The water flows through tubes in the aquanauts' suits and recirculates to the surface. This does not solve the heating problem for divers who use backpacks, but it licks the cold for a commercial operation while portable heating units, perhaps powered by the heat of radioactive isotopes, are being developed. Eventually, homes for such commercial aquanauts will be put on the sea bed as they have been for the Sealabs and Conshelves. Horton acknowledges that this will further increase efficiency and free the men from dependence on surface craft. But right now, it costs five to ten times as much as the aquanaut home on deck. And in a commercial operation, cost counts.

The commercial aquanauts are already beginning to revolutionize the diving industry, according to Horton. The day of the diver as an undereducated, semiskilled worker in a risky occupation is going fast. Aquanautics, he says, is making diving much safer. At the same time, it demands men who are engineers with high-grade skills. Westinghouse engineers, like others in the industry, agree with the Cousteaus, Links, and Bonds that men can soon have the capability to work anywhere on the continental shelf. There will be many commercially useful, as well as scientific or military, jobs for them to do. Offshore-oil operations will greatly benefit from aquanauts' help in tending and opening new wells at depths below 200 feet. Many kinds of salvage will become possible, as the Sealab II team showed in floating a sunken aircraft. Indeed, whole new areas of marine engineering will probably develop as men come to feel more at home in the sea.

If this is to happen, a good deal of engineering effort has to be spent on the aquanauts themselves. They need better communications, heated suits, better lighting, and many practical items including a whole new tool kit. Bond points out that, in moving below 200 feet, we are moving into depths where the old tools are no longer very serviceable. New burning, cutting, welding, holding, and wrenching tools are needed. Horton says it is his personal opinion that "there's not a single [aquanaut's] problem in the sea that couldn't be solved in a few years, given the money," and most engineers in the business share his optimism. The entire American Government-supported oceanography program is being reviewed at this writing with an eye to invigorating it substantially. At the very least, it seems likely that Bond will be able to meet his goal of a year-round base at 600 feet or deeper with the kind of equipment his men will need to make good use of it. And that's just another way of saying that, within the next ten years, men will have the technical capacity to colonize any part of the continental shelf.

In doing this, men probably will not set up permanent communities comparable to cities on the land, at least not for a long time. Living in the sea is a battle, as Cousteau points out. But when it comes to scientific or commercial exploration, to military and industrial projects, the bases of men will be extended throughout the shelves. And what of the darker, deeper waters that lie beyond? Will man ever penetrate these as a free swimmer rather than as a prisoner in a submarine? Today, no one really knows.

As far as moving into waters as deep as 1000 to 1500 feet is concerned, those now engaged in aquanaut experiments have little doubt that this will soon be possible. It is just a matter of moderate extension of the present aquanaut range. There is nothing even to hint of any serious physiological obstacle to doing it; there is even a possibility of getting away from the problems of breathing mixtures, body saturation, and decompression altogether. Dutch physiologist Dr. Johannes A. Kylstra, now Assistant Professor of Medicine and Physiology at Duke University, has dispensed with gas entirely in animal experiments. He has kept mice alive for eighteen hours under water. Their lungs were flooded with liquid, yet they breathed. The oxygen content, salinity, and pressure of the water was carefully adjusted to meet their needs. Klystra says, "Once we make sure that we know exactly what oxygen pressure will be needed to sustain a water-breathing man, it may well be possible for future underwater explorers to breathe water just like a fish."

They might breathe some other oxygen-rich liquid too. Dr. Leland C. Clark, Jr. of the Medical College of Alabama and Dr. Frank Gollan of the University of Miami, have experimented with organic fluids such as silicon oils or fluorocarbon liquids, which have the advantage over water of being very good solvents for oxygen. Yet they are dangerous—the ones tried so far have damaged the lungs of animals.

The point of breathing liquid rather than gas is to eliminate the saturation problem. Once this is done, there is no known depth limit for aquanauts. Bond explains, "Assuming that one does this in man—and there is no reason to believe you can't do it—one might be able to prepare a man so that you could flood his lungs with a special solution which would be charged under pressure with pure oxygen. One might be able to give man a capability . . . of about two hours' stay on the ocean bottom, but this time to a depth of about 12,500 feet . . . with no decompression." Meanwhile, men are gaining firsthand acquaintance with such depths by visiting them in research submarines. The rapidly growing fleet of these craft is the second major development that is enabling oceanographers to break through the barrier of the surface.

Explorers of the Deep

The thrill of weightless flight through space will long be the privilege of a few highly trained astronauts. But the adventure of exploring the depths of the sea may well become the sport of average people. Already, millions have made themselves at home on the shallow sea bed with the help of scuba gear (Self-Contained Underwater Breathing Apparatus). Within the next few decades, the development of small, safe, and inexpensive submarines may make traveling over the deep-sea floor at least as widely available as are yachting and private flying today.

Dr. John P. Craven, chief scientist of the American Navy's Deep Submergence Systems Project, envisions "the quantity production of small, versatile submersibles in squadrons, even as aircraft are produced today. . . ." Dr. William B. McLean, technical director of the U. S. Naval Ordnance Test Station, foresees many people going down in the sea in glass bubbles. To a certain point, glass gains in strength with rising pressure. The deeper it goes in the sea, the stronger it becomes in resisting pressure. McLean thinks glass is a very promising material for ships that will explore the deepest ocean floor. And, as submarine materials go, it is cheap. Inexpensive equipment, McLean thinks, will bring the challenge of the deep-sea frontier to millions of people.

"I've been a skin diver for a long time," he says, "and . . . very interested in getting an easier mechanism for getting down, without putting on rubber suits, wearing tanks, and then being limited to depths of 150 to 200 feet. Once you can enclose a man so that he can see out easily and leave him at atmospheric pressure, he can go down as deep as he wants and come back very rapidly. And I think the real pay-off in this area would be to try to get a vehicle that can come within the budget of the private citizen or a small organization such as a university, rather than having to leave all of this exploration to the government or to very large companies."

The submersibles envisioned will be the direct descendants of the research and workboat submarines now operating or on order. Unlike the military submarines whose windowless hulls shut out all sense of the sea, these craft enable men to see and measure the marine environment and to do a variety of jobs within it. In all, there were over three dozen such craft operating or being built or designed at this writing in the United States. They are variously owned by the Navy, by research institutions, and by industrial concerns that are getting into the deep-sea field. Most of them are mesoscaphes, middle-depth ships. Their working depths range from a few thousand feet to the 15,000 feet of the *Aluminaut*— that's below the depths that military submarines can travel. But it is well above the 20,000-foot depth of the deep-ocean basins. The goal of the deep-diving submarine development now under-way in the United States is to build a variety of craft that will enable men to explore and do useful work throughout the sea down to this 20,000-foot level.

The ancestor of today's mesoscaphes is a true ultimate-depth ship, the famed bathyscaphe. This type of craft, which carries men to the deepest parts of the sea, uses a technique that first enabled men to reach the heights of the stratosphere—the tech-nique of the free balloon. With a floatful of gasoline to provide buoyancy, disposable ballast for controlling ascent and descent, and a pressure-resisting air-conditioned cabin for passengers, the bathyscaphe is very much the undersea analogue of the early stratospheric balloon. What is more, both types of vehicle were introduced by the same man, Professor Auguste Piccard, the late Swiss scientist-engineer.

The concept of the bathyscaphe began to form in Piccard's thought when he was a student at the Zurich Polytechnic School. He became intrigued with deep-sea exploration and wondered how a pressure-resistant cabin for human observers could safely be carried to great depths and returned. It never occurred to him to suspend the cabin from a surface ship by cable, as William Beebe and Otis Barton suspended their bathysphere. Instead, he envisioned the heavy cabin as being supported by a buoyant float.

For diving, this would be pulled down by the weight of ballast, which would be jettisoned when the pilot wanted to return to the surface. However, in those days, high-altitude ballooning was in vogue. Piccard had his first ride in such a pressure-resisting cabin suspended from a buoyant float in 1931 when he made his famous balloon ascents to a height of some ten miles to study cosmic rays.

The bathyscaphe did not remain long in the background. In the years before World War II, the Swiss inventor made engineering studies of his proposed submersible. They were supported by the Belgian research foundation, Fonds National Belge de la Recherche Scientifique. This was the same institution that funded the stratospheric balloon, which had been dubbed the *F.N.R.S.* in appreciation. War intervened, but toward the end of 1945, Piccard was again working on his dream ship with Belgian support. Under his direction, the world's first deep-diving submarine took shape, the bathyscaphe *F.N.R.S.2,* named in memory of the stratospheric balloon.

In 1948, with the help of the French Navy, the *F.N.R.S.2* was tested; it proved the feasibility of the bathyscaphe concept and

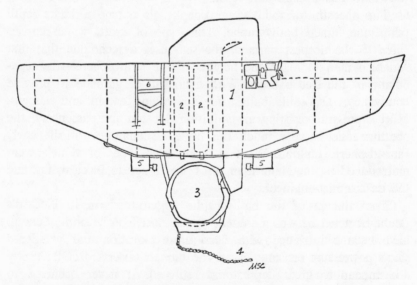

FIG. 51 : The bathyscaphe *F.N.R.S.3.* Entryway to cabin (1); shot silos (2); cabin (3); guide chain (4); ballast bunkers (5); fitting for disposable batteries (6).

pointed the way toward an improved design. The Belgian foundation retained Piccard as consultant and, again in co-operation with the French Navy, undertook to build a modified craft using the same cabin. This was the *F.N.R.S.3*, built, tested, and operated under direction of Commander Georges Houot and engineer Lieutenant Pierre Willm. Meanwhile, in the spring of 1952, a group of citizens of the Italian city of Trieste invited Piccard to head a bathyscaphe project in their city. He accepted. *F.N.R.S.3* was completed in 1953, and Piccard's *Trieste* was ready for testing that same year. They were the craft that set the first depth records; thus the world gained the first two ships that could carry men to abyssal depths. On February 15, 1954, Houot and Willm became the first men to reach the ocean bottom over 2000 fathoms down when they dived to 13,287 feet off Dakar. Then on January 23, 1960, the *Trieste* probed the deepest-known spot in the sea. The craft, which had been purchased by the U. S. Navy, carried Lieutenant Donald Walsh and Piccard's son Jacques to a depth of 35,800 feet, in the Marianas Trench.

These pioneering craft were simple in concept. But Piccard had to solve many practical problems to turn that concept into working hardware. First, he needed a stout cabin, far stronger than he had used to ascend to the high atmosphere. Pressures of many tons per square inch have to be withstood in the ocean's depths. The *F.N.R.S.2* cabin was a sphere 6 feet 7 inches in diameter, with a wall thickness of 3.54 inches, increasing to 5.91 inches around the portholes and hatch opening. It was made of steel cast in two hemispheres and joined together by a clamping device. The portholes were a special problem—they had to be both clear and pressure-resistant. Glass, at that time, failed in pressure tests. Plexiglass was tried in its place. It turned out to be an ideal material. Clear and strong, it was pliable enough to withstand the design pressure without cracking.

Given the cabin, Piccard had to support it in the sea. The Beebe-Barton bathysphere, hanging as it did from a cable, would have been a death trap if a cable break or prolonged failure of ship's power had occurred. Designed along the lines of a balloon, a bathyscaphe can bob back to the surface in case of malfunction. Piccard got the lifting power from a float divided into several compartments filled with gasoline. Other light and relatively incompressible materials, such as the metal lithium or tiny air-filled glass spheres imbedded in plastic, could be used. Gasoline was chosen because it was cheap, easy to handle, and readily available at the time. The float was built in such a way that the gasoline was always in communication with the outside sea water. As it sank, water entered the bottom, compressing the gasoline somewhat and ensuring that the pressure inside and outside the float were the same. The float itself could then be built of thin sheet metal, saving both money and weight.

The bathyscaphes were made to dive by loading them with a ballast arranged in such a way that it could be readily dropped. With one eye constantly on safety requirements, Piccard designed his ballast system so that, if anything went wrong, it would, in engineer's language, "fail-safe." He did this by holding the ballast with electromagnets. As long as the current flowed through the magnet circuits, the ballast was held fast. Should current fail for any reason, the ballast would immediately drop and, freed of its weight, the bathyscaphe would shoot to the surface. There were several types of ballast. The primary system consisted of steel or iron shot in cylindrical silos. These silos ended in narrow orifices. Magnetized by an electric current, the shot in the orifices was prevented from falling through. When the current was turned off, the shot poured out freely. This provided fine ballasting control. Other forms of ballast, the so-called "safety ballast," ensured that enough weight could be dropped in an emergency to enable the craft to return to the surface. They could be in the form of lead-filled bunkers, scrap iron, or even gravel-filled compartments, all held by electromagnets. Expendable items of heavy equipment, such as batteries, might also be held electromagnetically and serve as additional ballast.

In ways such as these, Piccard learned to turn his basic principles into working hardware as he worked out design problems of the early bathyscaphes. The principles are simply stated: first, make the craft self-buoyant so that it will return to the surface under all circumstances; second, hold down weight to achieve this buoyancy by keeping the heavy, pressure-resisting hull as small as possible (this means putting as much equipment outside it as possible); third, design a ballasting system so that there is always enough weight that can be dropped to enable the craft to surface (to this end, the ballast should be held by a mechanism that will fail-safe so the pilot can be sure of dropping excess

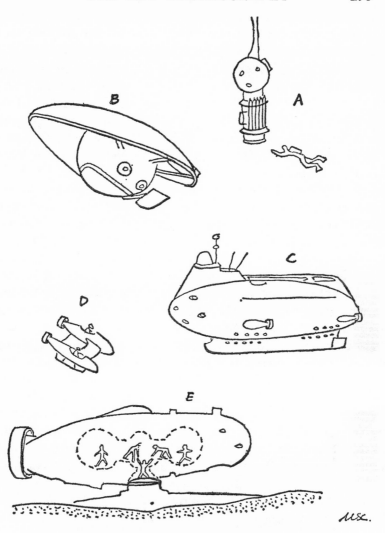

FIG. 52 : New research vehicles are helping oceanographers directly to explore the depths. A—submersible work chamber designed by Reading & Bates Offshore Drilling Company. B—Westinghouse Electric Corporation's *Deepstar*, which can dive to 4000 feet. C—Grumman Aircraft Engineering Corporation's *PX-15*, which is being developed in several versions capable of working down to 2000 feet. D—A double-hulled "wet" submersible for transporting divers. E—Deep Submergence Rescue Vehicle which is being developed by Lockheed Missiles & Space Company for the U. S. Navy. It will be equipped to rescue twenty-four men at once from a disabled submarine at depths down to 3500 feet.

Gulf Stream Drift. In early 1969, Piccard and several companions were preparing to use the craft to drift 1500 miles with the Gulf Stream along the North American coast. Indeed, by the time you read this, they may have already done so. They plan to remain at depths of 300 to 1200 feet throughout the journey. The craft has a chamber with an airlock so that divers can come and go. Grumman expects the *PX-15* design to be useful for other kinds of projects too. A sub could be fitted out to make detailed mineral studies of a sea-bottom site, which would include taking sediment samples. It could serve as a base for aquanauts in depths as great as 600 feet, supplying power for their work and transporting them to and from the job, and if it were equipped with manipulator arms, it could help in salvage operations down to its operating depth of about 2000 feet.

Designers of most of the research subs now operating, or on order, envision operations such as these down to moderate depths. They expect such craft to be operating to the 20,000-foot level of the main-ocean basins within the next decade. The biggest boost to development of these subs has come from the American Navy's Deep Submergence Systems Project (DSSP), which was born when the nuclear submarine *Thresher* was lost, and the Navy was suddenly made aware of its total inability to carry out any operations or rescue in depths greater than a few hundred feet.

Among other things, the program will develop a rescue submarine that can be transported by air and that can reach a disabled military sub in all depths where rescue is feasible. This means depths less than that at which the submarine hull would be crushed. Lockheed Missiles and Space Company has been given the prime contract to develop the prototype of this vehicle. The DSSP includes development of submarines that cruise down to 20,000 feet and pick up small objects. Probably the most advanced vehicle underwritten by the project is the *NR-1,* a nuclear-powered research submarine. Few details of its design have been released at this writing, but it is classed as a "deep-submergence craft," and will operate well below the depth limit of military nuclear subs. Craven has said that the *NR-1* "will have a near-bottom capability and will be built for the maximum practicable depth which can be safely assured with current technology." That may mean several thousand feet. With nuclear power, the sub presumably could stay at depth indefinitely, eliminating the need for a mother surface ship from which to make its dives. Also, with an aquanaut pressure chamber, it could land aquanauts on any continental shelf in the world without any sign of this on the surface. Craven observes, "Initiated without fanfare, this submersible may be the most significant innovation in the technology of the sea bottom. With the ability to free herself from surface support, the *NR-1* should be the pioneering prototype of the sea-bottom vehicles which have all the requisites to revolutionize our concept of the utilization of the sea."

The DSSP is putting substantial funds into development of American undersea capability. It expects to spend $300 million in the period 1966–1971. What is probably more important, it represents official recognition of the fact that much of the Navy's future lies beneath the sea. This means a continuing drive to extend ocean operations that will accelerate American exploitation of the undersea realm. Rechnitzer, who now is ocean-sciences director in the Ocean Systems Organization of North American Rockwell Corporation, explains that "the concept of deep submergence has enough justification in itself to move forward. It has good economic potential. However, the Navy's project will get it off the ground. The program has a charter broad enough to cover many things of interest to industry." He adds that industry can see enough economic potential in the sea to justify a good deal of effort without government prodding. But, he says, "There are some things, like deep-submergence craft that take a big joint effort to make them practical. Once you're over the hump, it begins to pay off."

For the deep-diving subs, the main hump is the lack of any material that has proved it can be used to build a craft for 20,000-foot pressures. Bathyscaphes use steel spheres for the crew chamber. But, to be mobile and safe, the new submarines have to dispense with floats such as the bathyscaphe gasoline tank. Their crew chambers should be self-buoyant so that men could come back in them without power in an emergency. Steel is too heavy for chambers of this kind. Titanium, aluminum, various ceramics, and fiberglass structures might do as far as weight is concerned, but they have yet to be made into chambers that have enough proven strength.

Then there are McLean's glass bubbles. In terms of weight versus strength, glass seems to have a lot of promise. A hollow glass sphere with a shell thick enough to stand up to the greatest pressure in the sea would have considerable buoyancy. Glass, as noted earlier, gets stronger under compression. The maximum resistance to pressure buckling for a glass spherical chamber that could be made today happens to come at the pressure corresponding roughly to 20,000 feet in the sea. The big question mark hangs over the ability of glass to maintain that strength throughout its service life.

Glass generally fails under tension, not compression. Even then, only when its surface has been scratched or marred is this material weak. Pressure can be transformed into tension when stresses are distributed through a structure such as a glass submersible. So Corning Glass Works, which makes spheres for McLean, has had samples put through some rough tests by the Benthos Company. Benthos engineers cut many gouges and scratches into the outer surface of spheres 8 inches in diameter. These withstood pressures of 15,000 p.s.i., equal to those 30,000 feet beneath the sea. However, when scratches were put *inside* the spheres, they failed at pressures equivalent to relatively shallow depths. Meanwhile, McLean's engineers have tested 16-inch spheres from Corning. The company itself is testing 44½-inch spheres, the forerunner of man-sized units. These tests have not yet shown that glass can stand up fully to the deep-ocean environment. Nevertheless, McLean remains confident that glass has a deep-sea future. Besides its cheapness and its potential strength, he notes that hydronauts will need the all-around vision a glass sphere provides. It is possible to become snagged in debris on the ocean floor. In that case, submarine pilots need to see all parts of their ship to work themselves free.

Also, the transparency of glass solves the problem of leading wires through the hull of the crew chamber. In the deep-diving craft, much of the ship is made so that sea water floods it freely. Most of the equipment is put in such flooded sections. This cuts down the volume that has to be protected from pressure. It also creates the need to get control signals from the crew to the equipment. Any penetrations of the chamber for wires add weak points to its structure. McLean envisions sending control signals by light beams through the glass wall of the crew chamber to photoreceptors in the outside hull. This would eliminate all penetrations of the crew's sphere. The men themselves would get in and out by opening the two halves of the sphere like a clam shell. This would be one of the strongest arrangements possible for a closed sphere.

Whatever materials finally are used for deep-diving craft over the next decade, the role of such craft should grow enormously. One of the most ambitious proposals for using them is embodied in the General Electric Company's speculative suggestion for a colony on the Mid-Atlantic Ridge within the next ten to fifteen years. GE calls it Project Bottom-Fix. In this, a station would be built somewhere along the ridge in water depths of about 12,000 feet. Men would live in a structure made of a series of interconnecting, pressure-resisting spheres. They would be ferried to and from this deep-sea encampment by some sort of deep submersible. They would use similar craft to explore and do work in the seas around them.

The project gives GE an opportunity to develop a wide range of important undersea equipment and operating techniques. For many of its concepts, it will seek government development contracts. The Advanced Development Council of GE's Aerospace and Defense Group is quite serious about reaching the goal; Otto Klima, Manager of Systems and Technologies in the Re-entry Systems Department admits that such a colony may seem far-fetched to many people today. "Many people," he says, "feel that probing the sea to depths of several miles involves insurmountable obstacles. These same people, however, quickly accepted men flying at 18,000 miles per hour in orbit for periods of several weeks. Yet a hard engineering evaluation of the obstacles in the deep-submergence undertakings shows them to be less difficult than those involved in space flight."

"Seeing" with Sound

Whether men do eventually inhabit the ridge, work on the continental shelves, or visit the deep in subs, they must find their way. They must "see" what they are doing. Light is not too helpful for it is quickly absorbed in the water. In moving into the sea, man, therefore, is a creature with blinders. Like the whales and dolphins, they must learn to "light" the sea with sound. Even in the clearest waters, light has a limited range. Sunlight is rapidly absorbed with increasing depth. The artificial lights of men shine out for only short distances. A range of 30 to 100 feet is typical. In many places, the water is so full of suspended matter that no light will enable you to see more than a few feet, or perhaps only a few inches, ahead. Sound is the natural mode of "seeing" for many ocean creatures. Passing easily through sea water, sound waves guide them in the murkiest depths.

Consider the dolphins. Dr. Kenneth Norris of the University of California, says that dolphin sonar has such fine resolution that one of these mammals can tell at five feet the difference between a ball with a 2½-inch diameter and a 2¼-inch ball. A dolphin can also tell the difference between a freshly killed mackerel and one that has been dead for a day, at a range of 500 feet. This rivals the performance of the famed acoustical "radar" of the bat. It gives human engineers an example of what they themselves will someday be able to do with sonar (sound ranging) when they have mastered sound in the sea. Attaining that mastery is one of the most demanding technical challenges posed by the ocean. Quite apart from developing necessary equipment, man must cope with the uncertainties of sound travel in sea water and with the ocean's own characteristic noisiness.

As light rays are bent when they pass from air to water, so the paths of sound waves are bent when they pass through regions of different density in the ocean. There water density depends on pressure (that is, on depth), on temperature, and to some extent on salinity as well. As lenses channel light, density differences in the sea deflect sound waves, focus them, and sometimes spread them out and dissipate them. These effects combine with reflections from boundaries between water masses of different density and from the ocean's top and bottom. If the sound waves are the probing beam of submarine-detecting sonar, these effects can create shadow zones in which the "enemy" submarine can hide.

These effects have also formed one of the most striking acoustical features of the ocean, the deep-sound channels which carry sound for thousands of miles. These are formed by the overall density pattern of the ocean, a pattern whose large-scale features undergo little change. The pattern is such that, throughout the ocean, there is a depth at which the speed of sound reaches a minimum. Sound travels faster both above and below this depth. Sound waves generated near this depth are bent to travel horizontally through the water as though confined in a sound-carrying channel.

In the North Atlantic, the deep-sound channel is at a depth of roughly 4200 feet. It lies at about 2100 feet in the Northeastern Pacific. The channel's sound-carrying capacity differs with season and location. But it is generally extensive. In experiments, the sound of explosives has been detected in the channel up to distances of 12,000 miles. This effect has been put to use in a SOFAR (Sound Fixing and Ranging) system for detecting the splashdown point of experimental missile nose cones. A bomb is released that explodes within the deep-sound channel. The sound is picked up by a network of hydrophones mounted on buoys. These, in turn, relay the sound to a monitoring ship. From the known location of the buoys and the times when the sound reached them, the splashdown point of the nose cone is computed.

Beyond the uncertainties of sound propagation in the sea, engineers have to deal with the natural noise of the ocean. Some of this is caused by wind and waves; some is reverberation, the echoing and scattering of a sonar beam by particles, bubbles, and animals; some of it is the noise of the animals themselves. Dr. N. B. Marshall of the British Museum of Natural History estimates, "There are 15,000 species of fish in the ocean and it is my growing conviction that together they make more noise than all the animals on land, man included." Part of the problem of using sound to probe the sea is to separate the snapping of shrimp or reverberating echoes from the signal one wants to detect. If men are to master underwater sound, they must learn to tell the difference between the sonar echo from a whale and from a submarine. They must differentiate between the enginelike throbbing of a whale's tail and the true engine noise of an underwater craft.

If we knew enough about the characteristic sounds of the sea and how they are made, equipment probably could be designed to make such discriminations. If we knew the temperature (density) structure of the ocean at any given time, as weathermen now know the temperatures in the air, then sonar operators could predict how their sound beams would travel. Again, equipment and data-processing techniques could be devised that would eliminate many of the uncertainties now making underwater detection of objects such as submarines very difficult. Attaining this kind of knowledge is one of the main goals of the American antisubmarine warfare (ASW) program. Since we are not concerned here with military aspects of the deep-sea frontier, it will suffice to note that the ASW program is a long way from this goal. Its director, Vice Admiral Charles B. Martell, says that the effective range of submarine-detecting sonar is at least ten times what it was in World War II. Yet he notes, "The ocean medium which conceals this underwater threat [enemy-submarine action] is a very unstable, uncertain, and complex environment. We are just scratching the surface of understanding its true nature."

In civilian research, it is sound that will map the ocean bottom to be explored and exploited. It will, in many cases, be the substitute for sight when men must work in murky water. Already, echo sounders are universally used to tell the depth of water beneath a ship. Sound probing using explosives or electro-mechanical noisemakers, has long been used to trace the layered structure of the undersea bed. Now, these techniques are being refined to give detailed pictures of the ocean bottom. By refining the frequency characteristics of sound and through improving data-handling techniques, engineers are building equipment that shows up different layers within the sediments on the sea bottom and within the rocks immediately beneath them. This kind of sound probing could be used to locate mineral deposits and generally to map out the detailed geology of an area.

One of the pioneers in this work, Dr. Harold Edgerton of the Massachusetts Institute of Technology, points out that, once the nature of sea-bed layers is determined by sampling, their extent can be quickly mapped by echo sounding. This, he says, can greatly speed up mineral prospecting and engineering surveys of specific sites. The amount of detail in such surveys depends both on the frequency of the sound and on the length of the sonar pulse. Lower sound frequencies penetrate farther into the sea bottom. The range of human hearing is roughly 20 to 20,000 cycles per second. Edgerton, working in the middle part of that range, has penetrated hundreds of feet into the bottom. The resolution, or smallest difference in depth of layers that can be detected, depends on the length of the sound pulse. Sonars operate by sending out a pulse and timing the arrival of its echo. From the known speed of sound in the water, the depth of the object or layer that returns the echo is determined. The shorter the train of sound waves in a pulse, the finer is the difference in depth between layers that can be distinguished. In the kind of surveys Edgerton has been making, there is a premium on short-pulse length. In tests in Boston Harbor, he has used sonar that transmits for only one to two ten-thousandths of a second per pulse. This has enabled him to measure the slight difference in the buried depths of the two tunnels under the harbor. The top of the new Callahan Tunnel is two feet deeper than the top of the old Sumner Tunnel at the spot surveyed. Such equipment is easily handled. It can be adapted to ocean-survey ships or built so that it can be used from a small open boat.

Besides such detailed bottom probing, sound is beginning to be used in an underwater version of aerial-photographic mapping. The depth-metering echo sounders of ships point directly downward and can be used for mapping. But it would be a tedious job making successive parallel runs to get a detailed picture of the bottom surface. The coverage of the echo-sounder beam is too narrow to do this efficiently. Sonars that look outward at a slant on both sides of a ship do a better job. These side-looking sonars, like the side-looking cameras of a mapping aircraft, cover a wide swath. The resolution they attain depends both on the equipment and the water depth. Towing the equipment below the ship, near the bottom, enhances resolution. By techniques such as this, it is now possible to map a strip of bottom as wide as half a mile on one pass with a resolution that picks out features as small as a few feet in length and width.

One of the latest mapping sonars has been designed for use with a precision-navigation system to pinpoint the areas it maps. This is FISH (Fully Instrumented Submersible Housing), developed by Scripps. Its side-looking sonars can map a path up to 1200 feet wide with a resolution of six feet. At the same time, upward and downward echo sounders tell how deep FISH is and how far it is off the bottom. With this aid, Scripps undersea mappers have towed the instrument as close as 100 feet off the bottom in water 15,000 feet deep. For navigation, three sonar-transponder beacons, located on the sea bed, send back reply-sound pulses to pulses sent out by FISH. Set five miles apart in a precisely located triangular array, these beacons enable Scripps mappers to locate the position of FISH to within 100 feet even when it is two to three miles below the ship.

Resolution as fine as a few feet is enough to improve vastly the detail shown by underwater maps, but it still does not give map makers a three-dimensional view. In aerial mapping, successive pictures overlap so that map makers get a stereo view and can determine height contours of the ground. While this is theoretically possible with sonar mapping, today's technology can't put that theory into practice. Reviewing the state of such technology, Joachim G. Stephan of the Battelle Memorial Institute says that it is similar to that of aerial photography forty years ago. He adds that, like aerial photography then, sonar mapping has a tremendous potential to aid in defining and exploiting natural resources, in this case of the ocean floor.

If men are to exploit fully what such maps may show, sonar will also have to help them work in waters where they cannot see. Today, when a diver works in murky water, he has to do his job by feel, under conditions in which his sense of touch is deadened by cold and the tensions of diving. When the crew of a research submarine can't see what they are trying to manipulate with their craft's mechanical arm, they have to give up the effort. Very high-frequency sonar probably could help in both cases. It could do under water what closed circuit television now does on land when men cannot directly view their work. The sonar picture would not be as sharp as a TV image. Yet it probably could be made to be as good as high-resolution radar.

Drs. G. V. Vogelis and J. C. Cook of Britain's Admiralty Research Laboratory have developed an early version of such a system. In this, sonar echoes are transformed into a visual display on a TV-like screen. In searching or approaching an object of interest, the sonar scans with a 30° beam. This can pick out objects as small as 18 inches across at 100 yards with an accuracy of 3 inches in measuring their range. To examine something more closely, an operator can switch to a 10° beam. This gives him three times better-ranging accuracy and resolution. This equipment gives a fairly detailed view of wrecks, shoals, or equipment such as fishing nets in action. An otter trawl, for example, shows up clearly in general outline, although the meshes of the net can't be seen. Equipment such as this can bring a submarine or a diver to within a short distance of his job. With further advance in the technology, short-range, high-frequency sonar should be developed that would enable men to "see" well enough to guide their hands or their craft's mechanical arm when they are close to their work. Nature has already shown that this sort of thing can be done in the skillful use creatures such as dolphins make of sound.

Now all man has to do is to catch up with a creature that, in this respect, is more advanced than he is.

This is yet another way in which the sea is challenging men to develop new skills and new capacities as they strive to understand, exploit, and to some extent become at home in the water world that covers over two thirds of our planet's surface. The fact that men recognize this as a meaningful challenge is yet another sign that we are entering into a new relationship with the sea.

The Last Frontier

When the Brown committee of the National Academy of Sciences reported on the needs of American oceanography in 1959, it issued a stark warning. With one eye on potential peaceful benefits and the other on military needs, it said that "action on a scale appreciably less than that recommended will jeopardize the position of oceanography in the United States relative to the position of the science in other nations, thereby accentuating serious military and political dangers and placing the nation at a disadvantage in the future use of the resources of the sea." It remarked that American marine scientists had to make do with a research fleet "inadequate for the job."

What a difference there was in the committee's supplement to that report issued in March 1967. Oceanography, the committee said, has "advanced on a broad front since the time of our first report." It explained, "The rapid growth . . . during the past eight years is abundantly evident. The Federal budget in oceanography has grown from $21 million in 1958 to $221 million in 1967. . . . Twenty new oceanographic ships . . . have been built and are now in operation. More are being built or planned. At least eight new laboratories have been established in the last six years. More than fifty universities and colleges now offer courses in oceanography. There is increased industrial interest."

Thus the trend is set toward vigorous growth of marine science and its applications, not only in the United States but in many parts of the world. The academy is not content with this. It sees need for an even stronger effort, for even more ships, laboratories, and other facilities. But these needs are widely acknowledged within the American Government and in industry. In January 1969, the Commission on Marine Science, Engineering and Resources, after two years' study, urged the United States to raise funding for civilian oceanography to around $2 billion by the late 1970s. It recommended creation of a new agency to take charge of environmental science, including oceanography and weather science. One way or another oceanography's needs seem likely to be met. The big problem now facing oceanographers and their countries is how to pursue their invigorated science and its uses in ways that respect the common interest of all mankind.

As men move beneath the sea as well as over its surface, as they begin to exploit its resources, they are truly opening up the last great frontier of our planet. Except for the continental shelves, this frontier is a common resource. It is not the preserve of any one nation or group of nations that happen to develop the ability to exploit more quickly than others. Men have scarcely begun to think seriously of how the ocean's resources beyond the shelves are to be distributed among humanity. Are they to be governed by new international law, perhaps even supervised by an international agency? At the close of the first International Oceanographic Congress in 1959, Columbus Iselin remarked that such considerations could overshadow all others in oceanography. After noting that oceanographers can foresee a number of ways in which the oceans will be exploited, especially in the realm of food production, he observed that it is high time . . . men began to think seriously how the potential vast resources of the ocean can be divided on an equitable basis. He added that, in his judgment, economic, social, and political problems involved in serious exploitation of the oceans seem "more formidable than the remaining unsolved scientific problems."

Iselin's assessment continues to challenge oceanographers and their governments. So far, very little has been done to meet this challenge. The need to tackle it grows in urgency with each year. Much of the increased governmental interest in oceanography may have its roots in international rivalries and the desire to make the most of the ocean's riches. But the questions raised by oceanographic research transcend national interest. Some are scientific. Others, as Iselin pointed out, will require the wisdom of statesmen to resolve. It is the special faith of the oceanographers with whom I have talked in the course of writing this book that the questions will be resolved and that the era of expanded exploration they have entered upon will bring great benefits to all mankind.

SUGGESTIONS
FOR FURTHER READING

GENERAL OCEANOGRAPHY

Founders of Oceanography and Their Work by Sir William A. Herdman. (London: Edwin Arnold & Co. 1923. 340 pp.)

A history of oceanography in terms of the lives of the foremost scientists in the field in the nineteenth to early twentieth century.

The Sea around Us by Rachel Carson. (New York: Oxford University Press. 1951. 230 pp.)

The famous best seller concerning many of the basic questions and theories about the oceans—a literary gem. Also published in a de luxe Golden Book special edition for young readers, magnificently illustrated and well simplified (New York: Simon & Schuster. 1958. 165 pp.)

The Edge of the Sea by Rachel Carson. (Boston: Houghton Mifflin Co. 1955. 276 pp.)

Natural history of the shore line, illustrated by the accurate and beautiful drawings of Bob Hines.

The Sea and Its Mysteries by John S. Colman. (New York: W. W. Norton & Co. 1950. London: G. Bell & Sons, Ltd. 1953. 285 pp.)

A short account of ocean science for the layman by a leading British oceanographer.

The Sea for Sam by W. Maxwell Reed and Wilfred S. Bronson. (New York: Harcourt, Brace and Company. 1960. 243 pp.)

A completely revised and updated edition of a classic book on all phases of ocean science for young teen-agers.

BIOLOGY

The Life in the Sea by Ralph Buchsbaum. Condon Lectures [July 1955], Oregon State System of Higher Education, Eugene, Oregon. 1958. 101 pp.

A paperback volume of lectures giving the essential points of natural history in the oceans.

Creatures of the Deep Sea by Klaus Guenther and Kurt Deckert. (New York: Charles Scribner's Sons. 1956. 222 pp.)

A detailed and readable account of the animals of the deep.

The Open Sea—Its Natural History: The World of Plankton by Sir Alister C. Hardy. (Boston: Houghton Mifflin Co. Riverside Press. 1956. 335 pp.)

The Open Sea—Its Natural History: Fish & Fisheries, Part II (Ibid. 1959. 322 pp.)

> The natural history of both fields by the renowned Oxford biologist. His water-color illustrations add greatly to the reader's enjoyment.

Larval Forms and Other Zoological Verses by Walter Garstang. (Oxford: Basil Blackwell. 1951. 85 pp.)

> Mnemonic verse setting forth Garstang's theory of evolution by the young of the species—larval stages—and other subjects.

The Search Beneath the Sea by J. L. B. Smith (New York: Henry Holt & Co. 1956. 260 pp.)

> The account of the discovery of the coelacanth and subsequent search for other live specimens.

GEOLOGY

The Earth Beneath the Sea by Francis P. Shepard. (Baltimore: The Johns Hopkins Press. 1959. 275 pp.)

> An up-to-date, readable account of marine geology by one of the pioneers in the field. Many lucid illustrations. See revised edition.

TIDES

Ebb and Flow: The Tides of Earth, Air, and Water by Albert Defant. (Ann Arbor, Michigan: The University of Michigan Press. 1958. 121 pp.)

> A concise semi-popular volume discussing theories and mechanisms of tides.

RESOURCES

The Sun, the Sea, and Tomorrow: Potential Sources of Food, Energy, and Minerals from the Sea by Frederick George Walton Smith. (New York: Charles Scribner's Sons. 1954. 210 pp.)

> A survey of food and mineral resources in the ocean.

EXPLORATION

The Galathea Deep Sea Expedition edited by Anton F. Bruun. (London: George Allen and Unwin Ltd. 1956. 296 pp. New York: The Macmillan Co. 1956.)

> A collection of articles by members of the Galathea cruise of 1950–52.

Exploring the Deep Pacific by Helen Raitt. (New York: W. W. Norton & Co. 1956. 272 pp.)

> A woman's (and layman's) view of an oceanographic voyage, with much pertinent information on theories, instruments, and data gathering at sea.

BATHYSCAPHES

Earth, Sky and Sea by Auguste Piccard. (New York: Oxford University Press. 1956. 192 pp.)

Piccard's account of the invention and operation of the bathyscaphe. Technical data on the bathyscaphes.

2,000 Fathoms Down by Lt. Cmdr. Georges S. Houot and Lt. Pierre Henri Willm. (New York: E. P. Dutton & Co. 1955. 192 pp.)

An account of the *F.N.R.S.2* and *F.N.R.S.3*. Technical data on the bathyscaphes.

INDEX

Page numbers in italic indicate illustrations

INDEX
317

Sea floor, 8, 9, 11–12, 13, 31, 38, 52, 54, 87–121, 141, 283, 303–4
effect on of wave patterns, 127–28
growth of, 67, *102*, 103–5, 121
mapping, 11–12, 38, 62, 76, 303–4
probing, *38*, 87–121
sediment layers, (*see* Sediment)
submarine research for, (*see* Submarines)
subsidence of, 106–7, 112–14, *113*, 116, 117, 119, 120, 121, 191
temperature of, 26, 75, 88, 93, 168
topography of, 61–86
Seafood industries, 248, 255
Sea grass, 198–203, 208
Sealab I, II, and III, 282–86
Sea level, *66*, 114, 119, 120, 190–91
Seamounts, 79, 105, 120, 121
Search Beneath the Sea, The, 243
Seas. *See* Oceans
Seas, landlocked, 79
Sea serpents, 32
Sea shells, 274–75
Sea urchins, 18, 198, 225
Seaweed, 199, 221, 224
Sediment, 8, 64, 66, 68, 71, 73, 81–86, 87–95, 98
average thickness, 85–86, 99, 120, 121
core sampling, 89–90, 93, 95, 302
echo sounding, 36–39, *38*
sound velocity identification, 97–98
temperature analysis, 92–95
Seismograph, 75, 141
Seismology (seismic measuring), *38*, 39, 87, 95, 97, 99, 120
Self Contained Underwater Breathing Apparatus (SCUBA), 40, 288
Seliger, Howard H., 239
Seychells, 79
Sharks, 31, 251
Shaw, Quincy, 27
Shellfish, 15, 198, 249, 267–68. 269
Shepard, Francis, 73–74, 117, 139–42
Shore, life zones of, 219–25, *220*
Shrimps, 159, 225
Silicates, 204
Silicon, 275, 287
Silt, force of, 71
Simpson, Sir George, 186
Siphonophores, 231
Skate, submarine, 80
Smith, J. L. B., 242, 243
Snails, 220, 221, 222, 223, 225. 241
Somali Current (monsoon), 166, 258
Sonar (sound ranging), 37, *38*, 80, 97–98, 299–304
Sonochemistry, 138
Sonoprobe, 37
Sorbonne, institute for marine studies, 32
Sound, low frequency, 37–38
ocean density effects on, 300–2
velocity of, sediment research, 38, 97–98
Sound Fixing and Ranging System (SOFAR), 301
Sound scattering layers, 230
South America, 65, 103
South Equatorial Current, 258
Southern Hemisphere, 170, 184
South Pole, migration of, 121, 188, 189
Soviet Novosibirskiye Ostrove, 81
Soviet Union, 252, 254, 272
Special Committee on Oceanographic Research (SCOR), 41
Spectrometer, 92
Spitzer, Lyman, Jr., 49, 50
Sponges, 207, 225
Spray, force of, 134, 138
Sproll, Walter P., 103
Squid, 208, 228, 239; giant, 31–32
Standard Oil Company, New Jersey, 272
Starfish, 15, 16, 198, 225, 264
Stars, 50, 53
Station Alpha (ice island), 81
Stations, oceanographic, 24
Stazione Zoologica (Naples), 33–34
Steenstrupia nutans, 196
Sténuit, Robert, 282

Stephan, Joachim G., 304
Stetson, Henry, 67–68
Stevenson, Thomas, 138
Stomiatoids, 233, *234*, 238
Stommel, Henry, 171, 172–73, 174, 176
Strontium, 204
Submarines, research and rescue, 40, 87, 96, 270, 282–83, 289–99, *295*
Suess, Edward, 100
Suess, Hans E., 94, 182
Sugahara, Isao, 207–8
Sun, 48, 49, 50, 153, 178–80
age of, 44
effect of on climate, 183, 185
evolution of, 58–59
radiation, 44, 58, 176, 179
tide-producing forces, 52, 143, *144*
Supercontinents, 100, 103
Surfboarding, 128–29
Surges, 148–49
Swallow, John B., 173, 174
Sweden, 191
Swedish deep-sea expedition. *See Albatross*
Swell, 124, 126
Symbiosis, beneficial, 108

Tahiti, 145–46
Television, underwater, 40
Temora longicornis, 209
Terror, ship, 16
Tertiary period, *46*, 93, 187
Thailand, 259
Thermocline, 167, 203, 204, 205, 228
Thomson, Frank, 20
Thomson, Sir Wyville, 16, 17, 20, 25–27, 33
Thorium, 44
Thorson, Gunnar, 264
Thresher, nuclear submarine, 282, 296
"Tidal establishment," 146
Tide gauge, 75, 150
Tides, 52, 123, 142–50, *144*
Tin, 274, 277
Tonga Trench, 78
Torry Research Station, 260
Trade Winds, 153–55, 164
Transactions of the American Philosophical Society, 10
Trenches, 9, 65, 78–79, 99, 100, *101*, 121, 207, 240
Trieste, bathyscaphe, 291, 293, 294
Tsientang River, 147
Tsunamis, 138, 139–42, 148, 149

Undertow, 130
United Kingdom White Fish Authority, 263
United Nations, 256, 277
Food and Agricultural Organization (FAO), 248
International Oceanographic Commission, 149
World Meterological Organization (WMO), 177
World Weather Watch (WWW), 177–93
U. S. Coast and Geodetic Survey, 28, 37
Department of Agriculture, 260, 261
Fish and Wildlife Service, 165
Food and Drug Administration, 260
Geological Survey, 53, 94, 117
National Council on Marine Resources and Engineering Development, 276
Weather Bureau, 190
U. S. Navy, Deep Submergence Systems Project, 282, 288, 296, 297
Depot of Charts and Instruments, 11
Electronics Laboratory, 70
Hydrographic Office, 12, 106
Man-in-the-Sea program, 40, 282
Ordnance Test Station, 288
University:
of Arizona, 59
of California, 43, 55, 300
of Chicago, 55, 94
of Leeds, 211
of Liverpool, 267
of Miami, 92, 232, 287
of Michigan, 217